EVERYTHING IS NEGOTIABLE!

Gavin Kennedy is Managing Director of
Negotiate Limited, an Edinburgh-based
international consultancy
(www.negotiate.co.uk)
and, since 1982, a Professor at
Edinburgh Business School.

For Patricia

Third edition

EVERYTHING IS NEGOTIABLE!

How to Get the Best Deal Every Time

Gavin Kennedy

ARROW
BUSINESS BOOKS

Published in the United Kingdom in 2000
by Random House Business Books

7 9 10 8 6

© Gavin Kennedy 1982, 1989, 1997

Gavin Kennedy has asserted his rights under the Copyright,
Designs and Patents Act, 1988 to be identified as the author
of his work

Arrow Books
The Random House Group Limited
20 Vauxhall Bridge Road, London, SW1V 2SA

Random House Australia (Pty) Limited
20 Alfred Street, Milsons Point, Sydney,
New South Wales 2061, Australia

Random House New Zealand Limited
18 Poland Road, Glenfield
Auckland 10, New Zealand

Random House (Pty) Limited
Endulini, 5a Jubilee Road, Parktown, 2193, South Africa

The Random House Group Limited Reg. No. 954009

Papers used by Random House are natural,
recyclable products made from wood grown in sustainable
forests. The manufacturing processes conform to the
environmental regulations of the country of origin

Companies, institutions and other organizations wishing to make bulk purchases of any
business books published by Random House should contact their local bookstore or
Random House direct:
Special Sales Director
Random House
20 Vauxhall Bridge Road
London SW1V 2SA
Tel: 020 7840 8470 Fax: 020 7828 6681

www.randomhouse.co.uk
businessbooks@randomhouse.co.uk

Phototypeset by Intype London Ltd
Printed and bound in Norway
by AIT Trondheim AS

ISBN 0 09 924382 2

Contents

Preface

I put down the success of the first two editions of *Everything is Negotiable!* to the way it talks the 'language of the deal' that practising negotiators speak the world over.

In the first edition (1982), I reported that the topics and issues discussed in the book were featured in my *Everything is Negotiable* seminar. They had been published in book form in response to the overwhelming demand from negotiators for the self-assessment tests that I had interspersed throughout the seminar (it being difficult to keep someone's attention over a six-hour stint just from talking to them).

In the second edition (1989), I removed two chapters and added in four new ones, mainly about negotiating as a foreigner in Japan, USA, the Middle-East and the Third World.

For this third edition, I have undertaken a much more ambitious revision, mainly to reflect the new materials and approach that make up my current *Everything is Negotiable Workout*. Seven chapters have been dropped and nine new ones have been brought in.

The format of *self-assessment tests* heading the chapters is the same, but instead of (arbitrary) scores for your choice of answers, I have introduced a new labelling approach that categorises your choices by reference to the alleged analogous behaviours of *Donkeys, Sheep, Foxes* and *Owls*.

I make no claims to having invented these analogies, though, to the best of my knowledge, this is their first application to negotiating behaviour – I first came across them in a report by Bob Lee (a fellow consultant) on somebody else's research into 'politics' in the workplace.

Their use in the text is purely educational, more as a foghorn message than the other kind. I believe that people learn best – and negotiators are prime examples – by memorable activities in an enjoyable and entertaining context. Each choice you make in the tests reinforces your understanding of the ascribed behaviour by identifying it with a Donkey, Sheep, Fox and Owl (see Appendix 1: The Negotiator's Grid).

In addition, four longer *Negotiating Scenarios* (in Chapters 4, 8, 13 and 19) are presented for a more challenging (but not too challenging) application of your negotiating skills to more complex situations than can be captured in the self-assessment tests. All four scenarios are taken from the *Everything is Negotiable Workout* series. About 3,000 negotiators have worked through them so far and their responses are most encouraging.

Having completed the book, I invite you to try the short '*Practice Examination*' in Appendix 2. This is a more demanding exercise than reading the text or trying the self-assessment questions and the scenarios. Take your time (about two hours) and attempt the questions after reading the scenario and reflecting on what you have read in the previous 26 chapters.

For those of you who would like your answers to be assessed, please respond as set out in Appendix 2.

With the purchase of this 3rd edition, you are also invited to send one of your negotiating problems to my *HELPMAIL* service and, provided you pay for the postage (mine included!), your first use of the Negotiate HELPMAIL service is absolutely FREE of charge!

But please, do not try to use the HELPMAIL service via the telephone – that's why we call it HELPMAIL. Over-eager beavers could clog up my phone lines and prevent me conducting Negotiate's business in a professional manner. Otherwise, I am happy to hear from you and to offer advice as a training exercise. For details, see Appendix 3.

I believe that adding value to a product is good business. The thousands of letters I have received over the past 14 years, since the first edition, testify to how popular this contact is and these innovations aim to extend that contact in a highly practical manner.

My challenge to all readers, therefore, is for you to beat all previous records in letting me know what you thought of *Everything is Negotiable!*, to make suggestions on how it might be improved, and for you to take up one of the new added value services.

Nothing I have ever written has been a solo effort. Without the inspiration of clients, whose negotiations provide much of the material from which I draw upon; the collaboration of colleagues, whose views, as ever, are expressed for the purest of motives; and the support of my family, whose patience has been legendary, not a line, not a word, not a '!', would have filled a single page, with what, I hope, is for you a worthwhile and profitable journey into some of the most exciting territory in the world – that of the professional negotiator.

Everything is Negotiable!, as ever, is dedicated – as I am – to Patricia.

Gavin Kennedy
Negotiate Limited
99 Caiyside
Edinburgh EH10 7MR
United Kingdom

Tel: [44] (0) 131 445 7571
Fax: [44] (0) 131 445 7572
email: gavin@negotiate.demon.co.uk
www.negotiate.co.uk

SELF-ASSESSMENT TEST 1
TRUE OR FALSE?

Read the following sentence and quickly decide whether you believe it is 'True' or 'False' by marking a box immediately and before turning the page.

'Faced with a difficult opponent, it is better to concede something of little value in order to create goodwill.'

True ☐   False ☐

CHAPTER 1

Of Owls, Foxes, Sheep and Donkeys

or why nineteen thousand negotiators can be wrong

The very first line of the recipe for rabbit stew enjoins you to: 'first catch a rabbit.'

There isn't much point you doing much else until you have caught an elusive rabbit (you certainly must not assume that you have got one).

Likewise, before you begin to improve your negotiating behaviour you must first benchmark yourself. Over the years I have used a simple one sentence test to sort out those negotiators with good intentions and fierce convictions from those ready to face reality and do something about it.

You should have taken the test by now – without cheating – because it will tell you more about how far you have yet to go to become a better negotiator than anything else you could do this early in your journey through *Everything is Negotiable!*

So if you haven't done so, go back to SA1 and take the test now!

You might pass it with flying colours (congratulations!) but don't think that a (lucky?) success absolves you from what follows. Oh, no! Catching the rabbit is only the first line in the menu – you still have much more to do before you get your dinner.

If you pass, you may go on to the rest of *Everything is Negotiable!* with some confidence; if you don't, you must definitely continue in search of more confidence.

First, a short plea in mitigation to my vegetarian readers: rabbit stew is a convenient analogy, not an issue of principle over which we need to fall out. If you like, the first line of the recipe for carrot soup, is to 'first gather some carrots'; a much easier task than catching rabbits and hence, a less dramatic way of making the point. (And please, no offence is intended to 'carrotarians'.)

In my self-assessment tests, your instant response counts most because when face-to-face in a negotiation your instant attitudinal responses to context and situations as they unfold rapidly are what drives your negotiating behaviours. You do not have time for a prolonged personal search for 'deeper' meanings.

Over the years, maybe 20,000 negotiators in all walks of life, in many countries, varying cultures and along the whole range of negotiating experience have taken this test. Overwhelmingly, the responses have been the same in the ratio of about 20:1.

Even people who have attended other people's negotiating skills programmes and then take my test conform to the same 20:1 ratio. (I usually suggest that they demand their money back!)

In my view, the statement is false.

Uproar often follows from some of those who mark it true, at least at the beginning of the *Everything is Negotiable Workout*. Few, in my experience, insist that the statement is true for long, once they realise the implications of the thoughts that guided them to their original conclusion. But, alas, there are always one or two a year who appear ready to go to the scaffold in defiance of my assertions.

And this is my first point: your negotiating behaviour is driven largely by your attitudes to the complexities of the situations in which you have to make rapid choices – sometimes under pressure – about which course of action you should take. If within your attitudes lie confusions about what is involved in negotiation practice, then you will behave in many negotiating situations less appropriately than you could if your attitudes had been subjected to the robust review of the kind outlined in *Everything is Negotiable!*

That is why SA1 is *the* litmus test of your negotiating awareness. Your choice of answer benchmarks your attitudes to the negotiation situation it describes. Your reaction to my analysis of your choice is also an indicator of your awareness of what negotiation is about.

For the record, let me take you through the confusion of attitudes you have revealed if, like the overwhelming majority, you marked SA1 as being 'True'.

● **'Faced with a difficult opponent'**
You should reflect on what images the words 'difficult opponent' generate in your mind. I am sure you have dealt with somebody whom even a Saint would describe as 'difficult' and several of whom you would never tire of kicking!

They could be behaving in a difficult manner (aggressive, abusive, irritating, shouting, swearing, etc) and/or they could be making things difficult for you to handle (interrupting, making extreme demands, rejecting outright whatever you propose, pressurising you, etc). Because the sentence adds 'opponent' to 'difficult', the picture is complete.

Incidentally, that is the last time I shall use the word 'opponent' in *Everything is Negotiable!*, preferring to think of those with whom we negotiate as potential partners, whose cooperation we need if we are to do better than fail to agree.

● **'it is better'**
'Better' is a comparative, hence you should be wary if you do not know what exactly it is alleged to be better than. In this context, it certainly is not better than the alternative.

● **'to concede'**
By the time you have completed *Everything is Negotiable!* you will know how sensitive all negotiators must become to the very notion of concessions and the habit of conceding. True, concessions are common enough in the language of negotiation

4

but the role in your subconscious of words like conceding is pernicious. These words sap a negotiator's focus and they pave the way to behaviour that is detrimental to what negotiation is about as a method for making decisions.

In short: never concede anything *without getting something in return*.

Never give an inch – trade it!

● 'something of little value'

To whom is your concession of little value? To you? To the other guy?

There is a significant difference in your answer. If it is of little value to you, it could be you are overly self-centred on a strategic matter. It is not how significant something is to you that is decisive – it is more important that you consider just how valuable it is to them.

What you concede may have far more significance to them than to you. If it has, then you most certainly must not throw it away. If they value it, you should ascertain what you can get back for it in exchange.

That is what a negotiation is about!

● 'in order to create goodwill'

An admirable intention, no doubt, but it is important that you challenge the assumption that if you concede anything to difficult people that this will create goodwill from them towards you. That is truly a monumental confusion.

Why does giving in create goodwill? Surely, giving in rewards their difficult behaviour and what you reward usually provokes more of whatever behaviour secures them their rewards.

That is one reason why some people behave in a difficult manner in the first place. Tantrum negotiating styles seek the concessionary behaviours you exhibit when you allow them to intimidate you, albeit in an admirable search for goodwill.

These five confusions lead you to an incorrect response – as a negotiator. And the confusions suggest that you are careless with your choice of behaviour when negotiating. By reading on you will clear up the sources of these and the other confusions that may afflict you, and, therefore, your choices of behaviour.

Let's divide the choices of negotiating behaviours into four kinds: those of Donkeys, Sheep, Foxes and Owls.

Each creature is representative of the set of characteristics of the choices you make when negotiating. All of the self-assessment tests in *Everything is Negotiable!* are graded into one of the four sets of characteristics and you can identify immediately the kind of choice you have made on each and every question you answer. You can also track your progress across the four sets of characteristics – where the names of the creatures become a symbol for the behaviour you have chosen.

Briefly, when faced with a negotiation situation and the necessity of making a choice as to what to do, the choices you make will conform to certain characteristics found in one of the four below:

- **Donkeys,** when you are blissfully unaware of what is possible. Commonly found when you also have a capacity for unthought-out, knee jerk and stubborn defiance when what you get (usually not a lot) is patently not good enough and when you have deep, though pragmatically flawed, 'principles'.

  Where ignorance predominates, 'stupid' negotiation choices assert themselves.

- **Sheep,** whenever you think that whatever you get is acceptable (*c'est la vie!*) and whenever you are too easily led into choices by other people – like lambs to the slaughter? You display some pragmatic flexibility but are a victim to the influences of others and have no sense of how to fight for your own interests, preferring to submit rather than annoy the other negotiator – or even disappoint them!

6

Like the proverbial goose, a 'boo' sends you scampering for cover.

- **Foxes,** when you really know what's going on and truly believe that you deserve what you negotiate. Many Foxes succeed only by sheer deviousness (we call it being 'sleekit' in Scotland) and you can be too clever by half when you misread the game for its own sake. There are few limits to your pragmatism and you are very good at exploiting the foibles of Sheep. People who make Donkey choices, of course, are no problem to Foxes.

  Devious is as devious does.

- **Owls,** when your negotiating choice shows you are wise to the longer term benefits of developing genuine relationships to get the negotiated results you truly deserve and when you show you are totally prepared for the threats and opportunities from the negotiating choices you must make. You earn respect for what you do and how you do it (and you certainly do not exploit Sheep, Foxes or Donkeys).

  All negotiators should beware: many Owls are closet Foxes!

On the limited information given above on the characteristics of negotiators where do you think you would be placed predominantly by an impartial stranger observing your negotiating choices of behaviour?

Tick a box in the matrix:

As a negotiator, presently I am most like the:

FOX	OWL
SHEEP	DONKEY

Throughout *Everything is Negotiable!* you will have many opportunities to refine your understanding of the full range of your behaviours and attitudes, so that on occasion you will find yourself switching between all four boxes. All the self-assessment tests label the choices you make but please do not fret if, following a choice you have made in one of the tests, your label is something with which you prefer not to be associated. As you go through the tests you could change your label several times – for better or worse and back again!

The self-assessment tests that head the chapters provide you with up to four choices, only one of which I recommend to competent negotiators as 'best in class' responses.

My choices, I freely admit, are not always acceptable to every reader. The self-assessment tests, and my labelling of the choices, have been tested in the *Negotiate Workshops* with many thousands of practicing negotiators and, judging from the lively discussions they provoke, I know they are bound to be controversial with a wider audience of readers.

In fact, that is their real purpose – to provoke lively debate. Nothing is more boring than a totally predictably 'safe' presentation that offends nobody because it challenges nothing. I prefer to create interesting learning experiences and I welcome dissent from which everybody can learn something, even if it is only to confirm their notions about negotiating.

My views are discussed more fully in each chapter, so that by the time you get to my comments on the answers at the end of a chapter, you have a chance to reconsider your own selections. But if you still don't agree, that is fine by me – after all, we negotiate to resolve differences and, if we cannot, we live with (or without) the consequences.

In this third edition, I have added to the original simple cameos several longer *negotiating scenarios*, so that you can apply your negotiating skills into more complex subject areas.

You see, in my experience, there is no such thing as so-called *advanced* negotiating skills. There is only the constant practical application of your core skills to ever more complex situations. Hence, this edition of *Everything is Negotiable!* provides new challenges for you. As you work through them, you can mark your progress as a competent negotiator.

You should also have some fun because whichever choices you make, they track your journey from Donkey, to Sheep, to Fox to Owl and probably to and fro between them!

Don't forget to mark the Negotiator's Grid in Appendix 1. As you read through you can track what kind of negotiator you are and what you have to do to negotiate differently.

Remember, it is not what you are at the beginning of your journey that is decisive, so much as what you are predominantly at the end of Chapter 26.

The entire philosophy of *Everything is Negotiable!* is about understanding the core skills of negotiation and applying them as often as practicable, so that you will become less of a Donkey, accepting what other people decide you should have, and more like an assertive Owl, securing what you want for yourself, without exploiting others.

COMMENTS ON SELF-ASSESSMENT TEST 1

The next thing you must do now is tick the appropriate column in the Negotiator's Grid in Appendix 1, corresponding to my comments below on your answer to SA1:

If you believed the statement was 'True' circle SA1:
- As a Donkey's choice, if you disagree with some or all of my explanation of the five confusions contained in the statement or you do not accept that your choice was wrong or any of my arguments.

- As a Sheep's choice, if you accept that you got it completely wrong and you are willing to accept and learn from my comments.

If you answered 'False' circle SA1:

- As a Fox's choice, if you made a lucky guess, chose 'False' for other reasons, misunderstood the statement and, most definitely, if you cheated in any way, including being tempted to do so now!
- As an Owl's choice if you anticipated something similar to my exposition of the five confusions in the statement or knew from practical experience how costly a mistake it is to follow the behaviour implied in the statement.

SELF-ASSESSMENT TEST 2

1 I have a lot of experience of negotiation. For you, is this:
 (a) True?
 (b) Not sure?
 (c) False?
2 A negotiator is only interested in winning.
 (a) Perhaps?
 (b) False?
 (c) True?
3 We can only negotiate if we agree on the facts.
 (a) True?
 (b) False?
 (c) Depends on what is meant by 'facts'?
4 If they won't accept my reasonable proposals I might as well walk out.
 (a) False?
 (b) True?
 (c) Maybe?

CHAPTER 2

In praise of cabbage

or, why you must revive long-forgotten negotiating skills

Your first negotiations occurred in the kitchen, not in the board room. You did not learn to negotiate at work. You learnt to negotiate at play and in the often ruthless pursuit of what you wanted from whomsoever had the wherewithal to satisfy your immediate desires.

Yes, you began negotiating as a kid in your nappies long before you got yourself into a business suit. What is a child's cry but an offer of a deal – 'If you feed me, or dry me, etc then I'll stop crying'?

Within a short while you got much cleverer at negotiating (there is a Fox in every child!). Your demands became more sophisticated and your selection of which adult to target with which demand reached degrees of subtlety that direct marketing professionals would give their all to achieve. All this, probably, before you were five years old.

You learned that the best time to approach somebody for something you wanted was just before the TV game or the TV show started. They would do much more for you at that moment, if it got rid of you, than they would *after* their favourite programme had started. But they would be likely to erupt negatively if their attention was disrupted by ill-timed demands.

You learned that grandparents are usually more indulgent

than parents when it came to satisfying your eminently reasonable demands – you quickly learned how steep to make them.

You could choose the right moment to get round one adult rather than the other. You also knew how to wheedle what you wanted out of one adult, when they were at 'war' with the other, particularly if you could hint with a smile or a cuddle that you were on their 'side' (it's that Fox in you again!).

COPING WITH THE WORLD'S WINNING NEGOTIATORS *(TO BE READ CLOSELY IF YOU CHOSE 'TRUE' IN SA1)*

Children think everything they want costs nothing and their parents are the only obstacle to them getting it. Hence, they make demands incessantly – and, as regularly, you give in.

All adults know how to bring up children; not their own mind you, those of other people! You never fail to meet an 'expert' who knows how to handle a difficult child in a supermarket, bus queue, beach party or doctor's waiting room, particularly when the noisy brat is someone else's. You seldom meet anybody who satisfactorily handles their own kids in a similar situation.

In the world of the child, you are a bottomless pit. All their needs are supplied 'free'; food, clothing, warmth, shelter, companionship, entertainment, love, support and access to a television and the internet. Those who are waited upon hand and foot are difficult taskmasters. At the slightest slip in service, they throw a tantrum. They also throw a tantrum when things are going fine, just in case you forget they are there. Children are only quiet when they are doing something they oughtn't.

The strength of children as negotiators lies in the asymmetry of values between them and you. They learn quickly what you want most, and they threaten to disturb or withdraw this in order to get what they want. If you want peace and quiet you will suffer noise and disturbance until their demands are met (a glass of milk, a sweet, an extra hour's play before bedtime, etc).

Adults wanting to watch television are distracted by their children until they give in; parents easily embarrassed in public are treated to a public temper tantrum that can only be bought off with ice cream, chocolate, toys or such like. In short, children know when to press their demands and are not restrained in their use or sanctions. It's intergenerational terrorism.

True, all parents fight back some of the time, and some fight back most of the time. They impose sanctions on the child, or threaten to do so: 'Any more of that and you'll go straight to bed / won't see Santa Claus / won't have your pals round.' Often the threatened sanction is unrealistic ('If you don't stop that, we'll send you home and we'll have a holiday without you'), but only the very young child is intimidated into line by such fantasies. By the time children are old enough to recognise unrealistic threats, they've escalated their demands and you are cowed into seeking the quiet life.

Of course, it did not always work out. Sometimes you were driven to tears of frustration when you could not get what you wanted, no matter what you had tried and how much you deserved to get it. In your sulky reflection on why the world was against you, you could conspire to be cleverer next time, to become devious and more determined to get what you deserved – the Fox in you was forming!

So were other countervailing forces. You could conclude that the best way to get what you wanted was to rely totally on what the adults around you were prepared to bestow and that whatever they did bestow was what you truly deserved. Can you hear the 'baa-baa' of the Sheep you were about to become?

Your frustration, however, could boil over into tantrums. Your indignation at not getting what you wanted – and when you wanted it, usually right NOW – could go one of two ways. Primarily, because adults have total control of the resources you coveted, you would grudgingly submit, albeit still utterly convinced that you were right and everybody else is wrong (hear the braying of the Donkey taking over?).

For a few, the tantrums became a weapon inflicted on selected people (often your younger siblings and those 'namby pamby' kids you knew at school) at chosen times. You were learning that enough people submit to pressure to make it a worthwhile way to get what you wanted but also that you had to be clever about whom you bullied and when. If you grew out of it, all well and good, perhaps. If you had a run of good fortune, because you found numerous submissives (the Sheep) on whom it worked, you were well on your way to becoming a Fox, albeit one with megalomaniac tendencies.

Consider an everyday negotiation between Annalise and Samantha, her three year old daughter.

Samantha was not eating the cabbage on her dinner plate because, she insisted, that she was 'full'. Now, Annalise quite rightly considered that cabbage was an essential part of Samantha's 'balanced diet' but did not want to open a discourse on 'the role of cabbage in nutrition' with a three year old.

So she resorted to negotiation, knowing that Samantha adored ice cream. She told Samantha that unless she ate all of her cabbage she would not get any ice cream.

Tears formed in Samantha's eyes, then determination shaped her brow. She refused to eat any cabbage but demanded to get at the ice cream. Annalise fruitlessly commented on Samantha claiming to be 'full' but not so full as to have no room for ice cream. Samantha ignored her inconsistency, probably thinking that it was perfectly possible to be too full for cabbage and not too full for ice cream!

Annalise tried a new proposal. 'Right,' she said, if you are a very good girl and eat four spoonfuls of cabbage, then you can have some ice cream.' Samantha shook her head and pushed her plate with the cabbage away.

Annalise thought it would be a good idea to get the ice cream out of the fridge in an effort to tempt Samantha if she ate her cabbage.

'OK,' she said, observing that Samantha was ignoring the cabbage and the ice cream, 'Let's make it two spoonfuls . . .?'

Nothing happened. Annalise pushed Samantha's plate with the cabbage back in front of her and said: 'One spoonful and then you can have as much ice cream as you can eat!'

Samantha then made a non-verbal reply. She covered her eyes with her hands steadfastly refusing to look at her plate.

'Damn it Samantha,' exclaimed Annalise, 'Just look at the cabbage and you can have some ice cream!'

Have you witnessed or been involved in such a negotiation, either in the role of an Annalise or that of a Samantha? With whom do you sympathise? More importantly which one of them 'won'?

Certainly, Samantha got what she wanted, ignorant of the despair she caused her mother about balanced diets. Samantha was ruthless in pursuit of her own interests. Annalise could have been ruthless too. She could have banned all ice cream, chocolate, fizzy drinks and all manner of other goodies from the house, hoping to keep Samantha ignorant of them in the interests of nutrition.

It would also have been fruitless for her to do so, because ask any school canteen server: who buys the most chocolate and fizzy drinks and such like? They will tell you that the biggest buyers are those kids whose parents forbid them to have them at home. What the kids think of their parents' 'betrayal' in their diet is anybody's guess (and we all know what they do when parents issue non-discussible edicts against smoking, drugs and sex).

KIDS v PARENTS: NO CONTEST!

Kids

- Know what they want
- Know how to get it (they have sussed out their parents before they can read)
- Are utterly ruthless about getting what they want
- Have no shame, no remorse and no feelings of guilt
- Have no 'milk of human kindness' if it gets in the way of what they want
- Believe parents have 'bottomless pits' for 'goodies'
- Have no long-term plans

Parents

- Inconsistently give in / don't give in to their children
- Give in to each other
- Have a sense of responsibility
- Are easily shamed
- Suffer constant remorse
- Feel guilty (are guilty!)
- Are fountains of human kindness
- Are not 'bottomless pits' for everything
- Think longer term

Result: Kids 'win' more negotiations than they lose.

That determination to go for what you want is common to you as a child but is usually lost by the time you are an adult. Something happens in between. The pendulum swings from one extreme to another. From winning your own way with ice cream, you end up swallowing far too much cabbage any time anybody gets in the way of you getting what you want. You go from one imbalance to another. They keep winning while you get used to losing.

Your negotiating character, however, has not formed completely by the time you reach your teens but its treadmarks are becoming evident. What is teenage courtship but a field experiment in serial negotiating?

The rituals shifted from when you were negotiating with a doting parent, who by definition suffered from an emotional weakness in your favour – they loved you to some (usually high) minimum degree – to when you negotiated with other teenagers, who had no such in-built predilections in your favour. They might come to 'love' you, and if they did, they might just as abruptly change their minds and go off and 'love' someone else, indeed, many other 'someone elses'.

The turmoil this created in you may just be a memory now, but think about it for a moment – imagine 'his' or 'her' face right now – and savour or suffer the joy or the embarrassment of it (curb that anger, please!).

Somewhere in those early teenage courtship negotiations, two things were happening to you.

First, you were losing the self-will of the negotiating child. You were losing that natural instinct to make high, near impossible, demands to achieve instant gratification from whatever transient appetites you had for whatever you wanted.

Second, you were learning to negotiate with yourself. Yes, that is where it started. You surveyed what you wanted, considered your poverty of choices and took whatever you could get. If you couldn't get the person you wanted in your dreams, you settled for the one(s) you could get in your greyer reality.

18

In short, you self-selected yourself into acts of compromising. (If you regretted that later, too bad, life moves on and, like last year's old toys, you might wonder what made you do it.)

Life is neither all ice cream nor all cabbage. One inevitably goes with the other. The art of the negotiator is to get a balance between them. What is perceived as cabbage by you is ice cream to the other negotiator, and vice versa. Your cabbage, what you offer to them, is their ice cream. Equally, their cabbage, what they offer to you, is your ice cream.

The art of the deal is find out what they want, and if you have it, you know you have a deal – if you want one.

Your aim is not to 'win' but to succeed. You cannot lose by succeeding and neither will they because the Owl in you drives you to ensure that they succeed too – they get some of what they want because you get some of what you want.

Everything is Negotiable! is about reviving some of the negotiating prowess you had as a child and channelling that, suitably sanitised, into adult practice.

COMMENTS ON SELF-ASSESSMENT TEST 2

1 a) Correct, assuming that you are more than a few days old. You have been negotiating all of your conscious life and your answer shows that you are aware of this. Mark yourself as an Owl.

   b) You are not totally unaware if you are aware enough but can't be sure, so this makes you a Sheep.

   c) No doubt you insist that the statement could have referred to your professional experience of negotiation and therefore it is false but it didn't, so it isn't. It refers to your experience of negotiation in general. You will not agree with this assessment which makes you an awkward person with which to discourse. Being pernickety without wisdom definitely makes you a Donkey.

2 a) Ah, we have uncovered a Fox! Smart enough to know that the sentence contains a verbal trap – what do we mean by 'winning'? – and cunning enough to avoid the trap, you choose, like all foxes, to keep your pragmatic options open for those occasions where 'winning' is the only prize to go for.

   b) Yes. If you are only interested in winning you may be missing deals that ought to be done. If you win and they lose, where does that take you next time? Far better – and wiser – to aim to succeed rather than to 'win'. Evidence of an Owl.

   c) You don't want to lose, so you must aim to win? Surely a limited view of your options? You are a Sheep, not yet smart enough to become a Fox, and well short of the wisdom of the Owl.

3 a) You are probably a personnel manager (or perhaps a lawyer?) handling grievance and discipline disputes. You are also a Donkey. It is precisely because there is a disagreement on the 'facts' and the substantive issues that you have a possibility of negotiating.

   b) Correct. Sure sign of an Owl.

   c) Why? True, there are your 'facts' and my 'facts' but we can still negotiate without agreeing on whatever we mean by the 'facts'. You are a borderline between a Fox and a Sheep, but in the interests of encouraging you with some 'cruelty', I designate this choice of answer as evidence of a Sheep!

4 a) False? Correct. A Fox.

   b) Incorrect. Nobody defines their own proposals as 'unreasonable' so your opinion of your own proposals is no safe guide to action. Anyway, 'walking out' is too serious a decision to be in the 'might as well' category. There are other options, including thoroughly understanding why they won't accept your proposals. However, you have probably walked out on me before you got to this sentence, so I'll shout Donkey at your disappearing back before you slam the door!

c) I know, you are going to tell me this is your tactic to 'soften 'em up'. (Weary sigh, on my part.) You're clearly not yet cunning enough to be a Fox, so you must be a Sheep. **Note:** if you must walk out, don't do so without stating a time for when you will return, otherwise your brilliant tactic of walking out will rebound on your credibility when you do return (which is how a Fox would plan it!).

Note: now mark your answers on the grid (page 356).

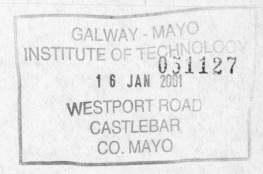

SELF-ASSESSMENT TEST 3

1 You want to sell your yacht and you know that you would be very fortunate to get as much as £150,000 for it. While you are considering placing the advertisement, a keen yachtsman approaches you and offers £165,000 in cash immediately for your boat. Do you:

   (a) Accept his offer without further ado?
   (b) Tell him to wait until the boat is advertised?
   (c) Haggle?

2 You are in the market for a yacht and have taken a fancy to the 'Isabella' which is advertised at £150,000. The most that you can raise is £143,000 from selling your own boat and borrowing from the bank. You meet the owner in the boathouse and casually tell him of your (strong) interest. You mention that you could raise £143,000. He agrees to sell you the 'Isabella' for that sum. Is this:

   (a) An offer you can't refuse?
   (b) A lousy situation?
   (c) An occasion to celebrate your bargain?

3 A young talented actress wants to get into the 'big time' and she meets a television producer who is desirous of securing her services for an important part in a detective film. He tells her that she cannot get top rates until she is 'known' but if she does this one 'cheap' and gets famous, she will see 'train loads of money' coming her way for her future work. Should she:

   (a) Tell the producer to 'offski'?
   (b) Agree, as she needs to start somewhere?
   (c) Demand top rates if she is to do a top job?

CHAPTER 3

The worst thing you can do to a negotiator

or how to avoid a 'bargain'

What is the *worst* thing you can do to a negotiator? At the Workout Clinics we invariably get answers like:

> 'Insult him.'
> 'Get her annoyed.'
> 'Go over her head to the boss.'
> 'Make him look stupid.'

All or any of these behaviours are to be avoided, perhaps. However, none of these responses is the *worst* thing you can do to a negotiator. The worst thing you can do is:

ACCEPT HIS FIRST OFFER!

Why is it so bad to accept a negotiator's first offer, especially if it is one of those offers which is 'too good to refuse'?

Junior sales staff are most given to thoughtlessly dancing to the 'offer-I-could-not-refuse' tune. Partly, it is the fault of their sales training that turns them into 'order-takers'. 'The order, any order, and nothing but the order' is drummed into them by trainers who have forgotten to beat the drum as loudly about the equally important business message of profitability. Graduates of these training programmes end up like computer-programmed football players who only know about scoring goals – including own goals! – because the programmer forgot to distinguish between them.

Partly also, junior sales staff make the cardinal mistake of first-offer-acceptance as a result of their lack of experience.

Euphoria is always generated when a difficult task is accomplished, and those readers who have been 'baptised' in cold-canvas selling will know how difficult it can be to get that first order from a prospective customer. It is the euphoria (or relief) that somebody wants to buy that leads junior sales staff to say 'Yes' to the first offer. They sign, grab it and run. This is why women often make the best negotiators – they learn at their mother's knee never to accept a man's first offer!

If this proclivity to first-offer-acceptance was confined to the inexperienced it would be a minor problem and self-correcting as time goes by. Sales staff gain experience – if they can't, or don't, they find another career – and experience will teach them never to always challenge a negotiator's first offer.

However, first-offer-acceptance is widespread among negotiators, some of whom have considerable experience. This presents you with the first challenge, and opportunity, to improve your negotiating performance, because you are bound to find yourself sometime in the near future, in a situation where first-offer-acceptance is a likely temptation, either for you, or for the other person.

Let me illustrate the traumas that first-offer-acceptance can cause to even the most experienced of negotiators. In the West of Scotland we have several famous yacht clubs. These clubs are patronized by a fair cross-section of the community, but, as with everything in life, there are various layers of affluence between the owners of the most expensive boats and those of the more modest.

The size and capacity of a boat helps in these circles to distinguish its owner's social position – such foibles are our ruin but few escape from them, which explains why somebody once described boating as a hole in the sea into which the owner pours money.

Some people buy boats for the pleasure of sailing, which in the West of Scotland tends to produce experts in handling boats in Force 8 gales, whereas in Bermuda or the Mediterranean it is about getting a sun tan. Indeed, at St Tropez, in France, people pay thousands of dollars to hire a boat for a few days and have absolutely no intention of leaving the harbour – the hirers of the most expensive boats sit on deck and sip champagne, and watch the crowds on the quayside watching them sitting on deck sipping champagne.

The owners of the boats are obviously meeting some deeply felt tribal need among their customers so are not ashamed to charge outrageously for meeting it.

Back in Scotland a modestly affluent small businessman (Angus McTavish) was looking for a bigger boat and took a fancy to the boat on sale in his club belonging to the Commodore (roughly equivalent to a Golf Club's 'Captain'). The Commodore wanted £153,000 for his boat. He too was looking for a bigger boat, being even more affluent than Angus.

WATCH THOSE FIRST OFFERS!

An impatient wholesale watch-seller, having experience of negotiating with his country clients, decided to short-circuit the higgling and haggling and get straight to a price near where he and the buyers settled last time.

He tried out this plan on his first call at a store right off the highway, up in the Catskills: 'Let's save ourselves a lot of time and sweat,' he told the owner, 'and cut out the ritual haggle between my high price and your low one.'

The buyer looked suspicious but said nothing. The seller took this for agreement with his proposal. 'OK,' he said,

'I'll give you my absolute best price – no kidding, no padding, and you tell me how many watches you want at that price. Then we can settle up and both go fishing this sunny afternoon.'

He opened with a good price, much lower than he normally started at and below that at which they had settled last time. The price was good enough to warm the buyer slightly.

'How many watches do you want at my absolute best price?', asked the watch-seller.

'None', replied the buyer. 'None?', queried the astonished seller. 'That price is better than last year's and it is my absolute best price. So how many do you want?'

'You must think we country folk are stupid or something,' replied the buyer. 'I learned long ago that any city slicker who tells you he is opening with his "absolute *best* price" still has some way to go before he reaches his absolute *bottom* price, and even when we get to that price, I might just tell you I don't want any watches at all!'

They haggled all that afternoon and long after the sun went down. In the end they settled below the seller's 'absolute best price' giving him a profit that wouldn't cover his gasoline for the sales trip.

This taught him how to make a negotiator happy: give him haggling room; and also that country folk never accept a city slicker's (or anybody else's) first offer.

The most that Angus could get together to purchase the Commodore's boat was circa £145,000. This was composed of the price he could get for his own smaller boat, plus a small loan from his bank.

It happened that Angus was in the club one afternoon and got into conversation with the Commodore. The subject of bigger boats came up and Angus expressed an interest in the

Commodore's. The Commodore said he would be delighted to sell his boat to Angus, him being 'such a good club member', etc.

Angus decided to go in near his top price and said; 'The absolute most I can offer you for your boat is £143,000 (he was holding back from his top price), but I don't suppose you'll take that for it?' He was stunned by the Commodore's reply: 'OK. I'll sell you the boat, Angus, for £143,000.'

They shook hands there and then and each went away to arrange the transaction (both are solicitors and in Scotland a verbal agreement is a legally binding contract).

Literally, within minutes Angus had doubts. In fact he felt somewhat sick about the whole business. Instead of rushing off to tell Mrs McTavish the good news that they had acquired the Commodore's boat (she being a keen sailor too) he wondered whether he had done the right thing.

What would Mrs McTavish say when she found that he had bought a £153,000 boat for only £143,000? She would ask how long the obviously prolonged negotiations took and what concessions had her husband made to get the boat at that price? If he told her it only took 15 seconds to clinch the deal, she would be sceptical, either about her husband's truthfulness ('was he paying much more than £143,000 and hiding the true price from her?'), or about the boat's seaworthiness.

Indeed, Angus himself could think of all sorts of blemishes in the Commodore's boat (he had sailed in it several times) and he began to worry about any blemishes he did not know about. Before the deal he was prepared to ignore these blemishes, even excuse them; after the deal they loomed before him. In fact the Commodore's acceptance of his first offer depressed him no end. Instead of a bargain, he wondered if he had a lemon.

We don't know how the Commodore felt as I got the sorry tale from Angus himself, but I guess that he was in no less of a torment than Angus once he thought about what he had done.

SEND US YOUR INVOICE!

Recently, I was approached by a multinational company with a view to my conducting a two-hour negotiating seminar for their senior managers.

The company president interviewed me before approving the arrangements for the seminar. He asked about the proposed contents and I showed a slide presentation on the worst thing you can do to a negotiator – accept his first offer! He expressed strong approval for the topic and desired it to be included as 'my people could do with that message'.

After various other details were agreed he said I could go ahead. He was about to close the meeting when I suggested we agree my fee for conducting the seminar.

'How much do you charge?' asked the company president.

'Normally, £1,800 a day,' I replied, expecting to have this challenged.

'Fine,' said the company president, 'Just send us your invoice!'

Exit one much demoralized negotiator, who to this day wonders what fee he should have shot for.

How would Mrs Commodore feel about her husband selling their £153,000 boat for £143,000 in a 15-second 'negotiation'? She would hardly be impressed with his business acumen (her mother's worst fears would be realised – behind every successful man stands a surprised mother-in-law!).

Angus would forever ponder: what price might the Commodore have gone down to as he had accepted £143,000 without blinking? Should Angus have opened at £141,000 or £140,000 or – why not? – £130,000? He would never know.

And not knowing worried him. In fact it worried him so much he derived little pleasure out of the entire transaction.

What had the Commodore done to Angus by accepting his first offer?

He had made Angus miserable.

Instead of a good bargain he had made it into a doubtful deal.

He had undermined Angus's self-confidence as a negotiator. He had also done the same to himself, if he thought about it. Instead of two guys happy with their deal, he had made it likely that neither would be happy with it.

By treating Angus's first offer with due respect as one negotiator to another, the Commodore could have made them both happier with the deal, even if Angus had to pay *more* than £143,000 for the boat.

How could the Commodore achieve the remarkable situation of an agreement on apparently worse money terms than the 15-second deal he arranged in the club?

Think what would have happened if the Commodore had haggled with Angus over his first offer of £143,000. How he haggles is not the point here (we look at haggling techniques later), only that he does so in some way.

Suppose after due time has elapsed, he gets Angus to raise his offer from £143,000 to his limit of £145,000 (or perhaps even higher by forcing Angus to see his bank manager). If they settle at a higher price than the first offer, will Angus be happier?

Yes!

He would rush home to Mrs McTavish to tell her what a brilliant negotiator he was. He had got them a £153,000 boat for '*only* £145,000; an absolute snip at the price'.

He would minimize the 'very minor' blemishes in the boat ('normal wear and tear; overall the boat is as sound as a battleship'), and he would promote the family image in owning such a 'magnificent' boat, – 'that's one in the eye for them next door and their holidays in St Tropez!'.

Altogether he would be feeling very very pleased with himself.

So, too, would the Commodore. He would have negotiated a better price than he was first offered. He would be £2,000 or more better off. His wife would be duly impressed, or at least less unimpressed as a result. He would have proven his ability as a negotiator.

All this would remain true even if *the final deal was at exactly the same price as the original one*.

How so?

If the Commodore had haggled and found he could not get the price up, but made an effort to bargain ('cash deposit now and the rest in two days, bare boat minus all moveables and less the radar', say) he would have made Angus *work* for the deal. And a deal somebody works for is a deal that they are happier with. I know. I've heard Angus on the subject.

It wasn't the money terms of the deal that were wrong. It was the way they were arrived at. And over 16 years later, they still wrankle because Angus continues to confide in me about the way he bought the 'Isabella' (like a lot of 'victims' he blames himself). As he still sails the 'Isabella', I suspect he has overcome some of his reservations.

EVEN SMART GUYS GET 'BARGAINS'

University professors generally believe themselves to be among the brightest people in the world and they often congratulate themselves on the 'bargains' they negotiate out of others.

A marketing professor at a European business school was asked to team up with an American professor and run a four-week top-level marketing course at a US mid-west university during the summer vacation.

He was asked to quote his fee for conducting the course. He sat and thought about it for a week and asked for £24,000. He justified this to himself on all kinds of grounds, including the joy he felt in 'showing the Americans that when they want the best, they have to pay for it'.

He was a trifle surprised, but nevertheless delighted, when the US university accepted his fee without a quibble, and he duly conducted the course in a euphoric mood at the bargain he had struck with them.

During the first week he got into conversation on the subject of fees with the other marketing professor (who came from Texas and whose constant refrain was: 'you get what you pay for').

He declared his own joy with his fee of £24,000 and how it had enabled him to bring his wife over for the course and for a holiday in New York afterwards.

However, he was mortified to discover that the Texan had obtained his 'normal' rate for top-level executive courses: £52,000 plus the family's expenses for accompanying him!

From this moment on the European professor's enthusiasm for the course sank to zero.

People like to get bargains.

Much of the retail trade plays on the desire for bargains in its promotion campaign and so-called 'sales'. 'Save 15 per cent by buying now', shouts the advertising. And it works. People who had no intention of buying the item, reduced by a notional 15 per cent, flock in to buy it. In effect they are not saving 15 per cent at all – they are *dis*saving 85 per cent!

But they are happy with the deal because they believe they

have paid less than they would have done if they had bought the item yesterday.

Negotiators expect to negotiate. They feel cheated if somebody does not recognize this. A first offer accepted without a haggle undermines their confidence in both the deal and themselves.

If the first offer is acceptable, what other offer might have been accepted if it had been tried first?

COMMENTS ON SELF-ASSESSMENT TEST 3

1 a) You are thinking only of the profit you might make and not about the problems you might create. These are the characteristics of a Sheep. Always challenge a first offer.

  b) How crazy can you get? His offer is already more than you were hoping for and to delay a decision by sending him out of your sight is foolhardy – he might see another boat on the way back to his car. This is the stubborn characteristic of a Donkey.

  c) Absolutely right! No matter how good the first offer, haggle: he might offer even more (the choice of a Fox) and, anyway, he will be happier with the boat if he thinks he squeezed the boat out of you at his price (the sure touch of an Owl if this is how you thought through the consequences of the problem).

2 a) Oh dear, you are an impetuous Sheep aren't you?

  b) Because he has accepted your first offer it must cast doubts in your mind about the *Isabella* and/or what you might have got it for if you had opened lower. If you have no irksome doubts, then you are a Sheep, otherwise you must be a Fox.

  c) How do you know it is a bargain? Sign of a Donkey.

3 a) Obviously a very determined and self confident young woman! But consider the risks that she blows it by trying to intimidate the producer. He might 'offski' and she might 'neverski'. However, if she thinks she can keep him in play while she batters him into a higher price through (c), then it could be a good move for a Fox.

   b) Terrible! He has pulled the 'sell cheap/get famous' ploy beloved by 'big' corporates the world over when dealing with Sheep.

   c) Has the tactical implications of (a) without its higher risks. She knows what she is worth. She can come down a little without losing out or relying on vague hopes and fantasies as in (b). If you sell yourself and your products cheap, then you will get exactly what you demonstrate they are worth! All Owls know this.

CHAPTER 4

So you wanna buy my business?

This is the first of the four Negotiating Scenarios in this book. They are my lively way to encourage you to learn in the 'safe' environment of your private reading. For your information, and to encourage you to try them, each Negotiation Scenario, plus the questions, has been tried by over 350 negotiators just like you. That's nearly 2,000 practising negotiators in all since 1991 and over 87 per cent of these respondents got them at least 50 per cent right.

You should read through the scenario a couple of times, perhaps making some notes or highlighting some of the data. Then think about how you would prepare for meeting with Sr Luigi and how you would put together an offer – remembering what you have covered so far in Chapters 1 to 3, and, perhaps, what your gut feelings tell you about the situation.

There is no point, however, in inventing 'facts' about the scenario to settle the case your way. If it is not stated in the scenario, it hasn't and won't happen. Simply stick to the storyline and prepare your responses from there.

So have some fun – and good luck.

NEGOTIATION SCENARIO 1: SO YOU WANNA BUY MY BUSINESS?

Sr Luigi owns a fast food pizza take-away shop, which last year had an audited turnover of £193,750, producing a net after tax profit of £36,750. The shop has been trading for several years, it is well located opposite a busy shopping mall and its nearest rival, a McDonalds, is over 800 metres away at the other end of the mall.

Luigi wants to sell the business as a going concern and has advertised it at a price of £175,000, inclusive of: stock worth on average £5,000; kitchen fittings worth, according to Luigi, £25,000 (they cost him £35,000 when new); restaurant fittings costing £19,000 three years ago; the freehold valuation of the shop premises; and the 'goodwill' of the business.

You own two pizza fast food shops elsewhere in town. You now want to expand your business by acquisition to save on the hassle of building up new outlets from scratch, providing that the price is right and the shop is in a good location. Your current shops are making good money and you believe that you have the right formula for success – strict financial controls plus pizzas that your customers like.

You have tried to buy other fast food shops but the deals fell through because their owners would not accept your 'best price'. You are also considering another shop elsewhere in town in addition to Luigi's, whose outlet appears to match exactly your requirements. One problem that you may have is that while your bank will put in some money, it is not enough to meet Luigi's price. Nor can you finance the purchase for more than 50 per cent cash and the balance spread over two, but preferably four, years.

Now try some questions to practise your negotiating skills on the problem and to explore, using your experience to date and drawing on your reservoir of common sense, how you might set about negotiating with Sr Luigi. You can work from your notes on a separate sheet of paper, or from brief notes and highlightings you have made in the text.

Remember, Foxes cheat without prompting, Sheep need to be prompted to cheat and Donkeys skip the exercise altogether. Owls decide on all of their answers *before* they compare them with my own comments.

QUESTIONS ON NEGOTIATION
SCENARIO 1

4.1 Assuming that Luigi's asking price of £175,000 is a relatively cheap price for a profitable pizza business in such a location, what must you not do, and why?

4.2 What are the main things that you must find out about Luigi's pizza business?

4.3 If you decide that you would not pay more than £170,000 cash for a new shop, what factors could you consider when deciding on what to offer Luigi to open the negotiations?

4.4 If you are prepared to go as high as £185,000 for the shop, but you can pay no more than 50 per cent in cash now, with the balance over four years, how should you lead Luigi towards this sort of proposal?

4.5 Assume that you are cautious of the profits claimed for Luigi's business, what sort of proposal could be constructed which would protect you from paying too much and yet still create a fair price for Luigi?

COMMENTS ON NEGOTIATION SCENARIO 1

4.1 Assuming that Luigi's asking price of £175,000 is a relatively cheap price for a profitable pizza business in such a location, what must you not do, and why?

Irrespective of whether you believe £175,000 to be 'a relatively cheap price', even perhaps a 'bargain', you must never forget that a negotiator always challenges the first offer. There are many other things you must not do, but challenging first offers is key evidence for at least the accolade, if not yet the substance, of Fox behaviour (you need to do much more to be an Owl).

Luigi's advertised price of £175,000 for the pizza business is his first offer (or his **entry**) price and he is bound to have a *last* offer (or **exit**) price that is lower than £175,000.

If you merely accept Luigi's entry price and do not even seek a price between this and his lower exit price, you are in danger of Luigi finding some excuse (and believe me this is not too difficult in practice) to move his first offer upwards if you appear to be keen to settle on £175,000.

Challenging a first offer, and expecting to be challenged, is an integral part of negotiating. Only Donkeys don't know that. Think of what you do to Mr Luigi if you accept his first offer without a challenge. In effect, you tell him that his asking price of £175,000 is so good that you can accept it at once. What does that do to Mr Luigi?

Certainly, when he thinks about it (taking only a few nanoseconds!) he will realise that he has priced his business too low, at least for you, and perhaps for others as well. If Luigi can, he surely will revise his price upwards, with you or somebody else (unless Luigi is also a Donkey). Failing that he would surely revise upwards the prices of those 'extras' you want that he might have been prepared to include in his original price, if only you had challenged him. It's known as the 'add-on' technique.

Some would-be negotiators assert that you will 'antagonize', 'upset', or 'cause a deadlock' if you challenged Mr Luigi's entry price! (Clearly, they are numbered among the 13 per cent who 'failed' the pilot testing of this scenario.)

Of course, no serious negotiator should behave in a manner likely to antagonise Luigi, or anybody else with whom they are negotiating. Nevertheless, Luigi would be a hyper-sensitive Donkey if he took exception to somebody asking him to justify his entry price of £175,000 (which is the minimum of what I mean when encouraging you to always 'challenge' a first offer).

4.2 What are the main things that you must find out about Luigi's pizza business?

Most negotiators do well on this question, including many of the 13 per cent who got Question 4.1 hopelessly wrong. The key here is to list the information that you need before making your first offer to Luigi.

Your information requirements include:

1 The physical state of the premises, inside and out, with a view to estimating their future maintenance and repair costs. How much has been spent recently by Luigi? What effect should a poor state of repair, inside and outside, have on your offer price?
2 What claims have been made on insurance which might prejudice your insurance premiums?
3 What is the inventory really worth? It is included in the asking price but it may not be worth anywhere near £5,000.

4 Similarly, what is the true state of the kitchen and shop fittings? Do they need to be replaced? Are they worth what Luigi claims for them?

5 What local planning considerations are there which would influence future sales revenue? Are there any plans pending, in or near the shopping mall, that include the opening of rival fast food shops?

6 What is happening in the shopping mall itself – is customer traffic changing upwards or downwards? Is it to be modernised, refurbished, superseded, etc? Could be a good idea to observe customer traffic over a week's shopping cycle.

7 What is the true financial record of the pizza shop? Are audited accounts available for each year and what do they show in the trends in revenue and net profit?

8 Why is Luigi selling a profitable business? Does he need cash urgently, is he retiring, or is there a surprise lurking in the background?

9 What can be gleaned from Luigi about the interest in buying his pizza shop from others over the past weeks? (Warning: Luigi is not likely to be too candid about this.)

10 What can be found out about the current customer visits to the shop, perhaps by some on the spot research?

4.3 If you decide that you would not pay more than £170,000 cash for Luigi's shop, what factors would you consider in your choice of your entry price in the negotiations?

The age old dilemma of negotiation – where to open, knowing that whatever price you choose inevitably will be challenged by Luigi (unless he is a Donkey).

You know that Luigi's entry price is £175,000 and you know that Luigi has another price, his exit price, which will be lower than £175,000. How much lower?

You do not know for certain (and probably never will) Luigi's exit price. However, you do know your own exit price of

£170,000. It follows that your entry price will be lower than £170,000, but how much lower?

It does not matter if you enter with a price below Luigi's, unknown to you, exit price. It is only an opening offer and it should be challenged by Luigi whatever price you open at. (If Luigi doesn't challenge it, you will know how Angus felt about the 'Isabella'!)

Generally, too low an entry price from you could cause Luigi to consider that you are not a serious buyer; too high an entry price (i.e. very close to your own exit price of £170,000) narrows the negotiation range and reduces your flexibility.

The best criteria for an entry price are that it should be credible, defensible and realistic. Experience teaches you how to achieve these qualities.

4.4 If you are prepared to go as high as £185,000 for the shop, but you can pay no more than 50 per cent in cash now with the balance over 4 years, how should you lead Luigi towards this sort of proposal?

The question suggests that you can put up £92,500 in cash which is well below Luigi's entry price of £175,000 and probably below Luigi's (but unknown to you) exit price. In order to make this proposal acceptable, you have to induce Luigi to accept delayed payment. For this Luigi is likely to require an improvement in the total price paid.

Now you do not want to jump in with an immediate proposal for delayed payment with an increased offer of £185,000. What you must do first is complete your challenge on Luigi's entry price of £175,000 (negotiations take time but this is time well spent).

You must establish the **negotiation range** for the deal. Assume that the negotiation range, all things considered, is between £165,000 (you) and £173,000 (Luigi). This is because you opened at, say, £160,000 and moved up to £165,000 and

Luigi opened at £175,000 and moved down to, say, £173,000, leaving a gap (the negotiation range) of £8,000.

In the course of the debate over the price issue, you are also seeking to determine Luigi's interests in the timing of the deal (e.g. why is Luigi selling?; what are his future plans?; for what purpose does Luigi want or need the money? etc).

Any signals from Luigi in response to your resistance to improving on your current offer price, could suggest that Luigi might be prepared to trade-off the price for payment term, by accepting some spread of your payments if you raised your offer price closer to his original demand. If Luigi hints at this sort of trade-off, you should first clarify Luigi's signal(s), and then ask him for tentative suggestions (otherwise known as proposals) on how this payment structure might work, and, of course, what sort of improved price Luigi is looking for.

Alternatively, you could indicate your willingness to make a better offer on price if Luigi permitted you to re-package the deal to include delayed payments. Luigi might (should) press you for more details on what you had in mind, or failing that you might offer them unilaterally.

In which case, the trade-off is a part payment (opening at £92,500 or 50 per cent of your top price, or, preferably less) with the balance (£92,500 downwards to £86,500) over as many years as you can get, with you using any price of the balance above £86,500 as the inducement to Luigi to extend the repayment period up to the full four years.

4.5 **Assume that you are cautious of the profits claimed for Luigi's business; what sort of proposal could be constructed that would protect you from paying too much and yet still create a fair price for Luigi?**

This question invites a proposal that addresses the future profits problem. A few negotiators remain concerned about not upsetting Luigi with implications of doubts about his profit claims!

This betrays a misunderstanding of the negotiator's role and deserves the description of being Sheepish.

You have a good reason to be cautious of Luigi's profit claims – it protects your interests to be cautious, hence the preparatory work recommended in Q.4.2. But Luigi's profit claims are only part of the problem because they refer to the past. You are buying a business in order to make profits in the future. Are past profits a safe guide to the future? Perhaps Luigi knows something that you do not (yet) about threats to future profitability?

What you need is a **contingency proposal**, i.e. a proposal which links payment now to future profits. Several are possible but they must be based on an understanding of the problem.

For example, relatively weak proposals, and possibly unworkable ones, include requiring Luigi to pay back some of the purchase price to you if profits are not achieved over some period of years.

The chances, however, of sustaining Luigi's commitment to repay you from money you have already paid him (which he may well have spent) are not good in the real world – Luigi could always claim you were inefficient or that the outlet's accounts are being manipulated by you.

Other proposals include some form of continuing equity deal with Luigi, through which you gradually buy out Luigi's share of your equity from the shop's future profits. This would meet to some extent objections from Luigi that he had no control of the business, because your desire to reduce his equity assures him your consequential requirement to pay him his money. Again this might be difficult to operate in the future, especially if there was clash of policy between Luigi and you over how the business should be run.

One possible proposal could be along the lines of:

'If Luigi accepts part payment in cash of £90,000 and the balance over 4 years, subject to net profit performance remaining at no less than 25%, then I will pay a total purchase price of £180,000 (with room to go to £185,000?). However, for every percentage point that profits fall below 25%, the yearly balance owed to Luigi would be reduced by (some percentage to be agreed) pro rata.'

Owls would anticipate Luigi's likely grievances that your contingent profit agreement was unfair to him because he was left vulnerable to your management of the pizza business; that he has no control over the government changing the tax regime which might affect the calculation, though perhaps not the reality, of net after-tax profits; that in future years there could be unforeseen changes in circumstances at the location; and that, crucially, because net profits can be manipulated, you have an incentive to produce low net profits to reduce your repayments.

SELF-ASSESSMENT TEST 5

1 You are in dispute with a supplier over items he has charged you for in his monthly account which, in your firm opinion, were delivered in a faulty condition. Do you:
   (a) Stall on payment of the total amount?
   (b) Stall only on the amount in dispute?
   (c) Offer to compromise on the disputed amount?

2 Your office is due for a rent review and you expect the landlord to demand an increase of 20 per cent. Do you:
   (a) Make a 'reasonable' offer of 10 per cent?
   (b) Demand a rent reduction?
   (c) Offer to go to arbitration?
   (d) Itemize all the defects that you want rectified?

3 You are managing a civil project for the Saudis, who have imposed a time-delay penalty-clause on you. A sub-contractor has missed a delivery of important machinery. Planned start-up times may not be met. Do you:
   (a) Check through the supply contract to discover their liability?
   (b) Ask the site agent to list all the failures associated with the defaulting contractor since the job began and fax their head office with your complaints?
   (c) Telephone their managing director and threaten to sue for any penalty costs imposed on you by the Saudis?
   (d) Arrange an immediate meeting with the contractor to put into operation an alternative delivery programme that your own engineers have drawn up?

CHAPTER 5

Why you can't negotiate a grievance

or how not to get your room changed

Have you ever been on the wrong end of somebody else's incompetence?

Of course you have.

People let you down. In fact, the only thing that is certain about some people is that they let you down, incessantly. The divorce courts are full of claims of broken promises, unrealized expectations and unfulfilled dreams.

And not just the divorce courts. Sit in any court for a few hours, and watch the litigious in pursuit of retribution for real or imaginary failings on the part of those they were happy to do business with, until the roof fell in.

The distribution of short straws is random enough for all of us to get one sooner or later, and not just in business. You can draw them at home, in a restaurant, hotel, or bar, at an airline check-in, theatre ticket office, passport control, shop counter, taxi rank, or even your local PTA.

Anywhere that Joe Citizen meets Fred Citizen there is a possibility that one or other, or both, will find cause (real or imaginary) to complain about something the other does, or does not do, that they expected them to do, or not do. (Throw in their in-laws and you can have a real bust up, especially after a breach in the Christmas 'ceasefire'.)

Don't just take my word for it!

How many hours is it since you last thought you had cause to complain about something or somebody, either in your professional business or elsewhere? If you answer more than eight you are either of divine origin or you've been asleep (and if you were asleep I bet you *dreamt* you had a complaint). Complaining is part of the social intercourse of human beings.

This chapter is not a plea for moderation in the habit of complaining – far from it, but unless King Canute's humiliation against the waves was in vain we have no call to struggle against the irresistible tide of human nature!

My purpose here is quite different. It is to improve the effectiveness of your complaining about the failings of others by giving *them* an alternative to merely telling *you* to get stuffed.

Not all negotiating relationships are sweetness and light. Some can get very acrimonious, and I am not just thinking of industrial or international relations. Commercial deals can fall apart when one of the parties believes the other is failing to meet its commitments in some way.

Not only are promises not kept, but deliveries are not always made on schedule, quality controls sometimes fail, performance can fall short of specification, and earnings may be less than expected, etc.

Agreeing on a deal is only part of the commercial relationship – keeping the deal implemented is the other part. In complex production systems, there are many opportunities for failings to occur and some way has to be found for resolving the conflicting interests that arise after contracts have been signed.

The problem with most people faced with a business (or domestic) grievance is that they have a remarkable facility for doing the one thing that is *least* important to them and their grievance, while at the same time, they display an astonishing incapacity to do the only thing that *is* important.

People, almost without exception, play their strongest suit in the pure mechanics of *complaining*. People, undoubtedly, are good at complaining, especially when their grievance is tinged with a perceived slight of some kind or when an element of unfairness is felt to be present.

But they are usually absolutely bereft of ideas about their most important interest, namely, getting their grievance *remedied* in some way. That's why I urge:

> DON'T JUST COMPLAIN,
> NEGOTIATE A REMEDY!

Remember, it is not the other person's failings that need sorting out – it's your *interests* that need attention.

DON'T RING THEM, CALL US INSTEAD!

A large property development company, operating in a rapidly changing market, relied heavily on information of its financial status. This was particularly critical during the first hour of business each day.

If their funds ran down overnight, they needed to know *before* they placed deals that day in case they were forced into borrowing short-term 'hot' money at high interest rates to bridge gaps of a few days. A firm of their nature going into the market for temporary funds more than a few times a year could start damaging speculation.

However, a problem developed when the accountants found it increasingly difficult to get through to the local bank on the telephones early in the morning. This caused friction between the bank tellers and the firm's accountants.

Relations got so bad that pressure appeared for the account to be moved to another bank on the grounds of the bank's 'incompetence', 'delay' and 'bad faith'.

A 'crisis' meeting was arranged with the bank, and the

accountants spent a weekend documenting the 'failings' of the bank over the past month, itemizing the alleged costs of telephone delays to the property company's finances.

Before the meeting, the managing director of the property company rejected the entire approach of his accountants and threw their thick report into the waste-paper basket.

Instead, he asked them what arrangement would suit their needs either with the current bank or a new one. In lieu of an answer, he suggested that they get the bank to ring them each morning at 9.05 on a special line instead of them fruitlessly ringing the bank. He also noted that this would save them the cost of the phone calls!

The bank willingly agreed to this proposal.

There is no doubt that had the accountants' report been discussed there would have been a bitter row and a break-down in the relationship.

I can illustrate how easy it is to fall into the lack-of-a-remedy trap, by recounting an incident from my own experience. (The best lessons are our own mistakes.) In October 1977 I arrived in Rome late one wet Sunday evening, having driven there by car from sunny Edinburgh (via a North Sea ferry, of course). I was very tired, to put it mildly.

I had been seconded to a United Nations agency for three months and they had reserved me a room in a small hotel on the Aventino. The room I was given had one major failing: it was damp. In fact it was very damp. It was like a sauna – only a cold one!

It was also late, I was tired and had nowhere else to stay that night, so I remained dressed, put on my overcoat and spent a very restless night on the damp bed.

By now you have the picture: *I had a grievance*.

In the frequent moments when the dampness woke me I

rehearsed the speech I intended to make to the hotel management next morning. My imaginary agenda began with a description of the lousy room I was in, the management's total lack of consideration of my health, let alone my comfort, and the extortionate price they were charging the United Nations for a cold sauna. My *pièce de résistance* was a sarcastic 'joke' about the ancient Roman proclivity for bathing being taken too far when it was brought into the bedrooms! My imaginary speech ended with an account of the exhausting extent of *my* car journey and finally what *I* thought of their Roman welcome to strangers.

Believe me, through the night the agenda was altered several times and the levels of authority I considered invoking escalated – a fax to the United Nations in New York, perhaps even a meeting of the Security Council (you can see how delirious I was as a result of the dampness).

I had no doubt that the force of my complaint, if not natural justice alone, would immediately provoke the management to apologize profusely and move me to a magnificent room, complete with marbled bathroom and private balcony.

Next morning, I marched to the reception desk ready with my complaints, and spoke to a young man – he had that Roman air of authority and also that charming Italian male's indifference to anybody other than young women.

So I told him about the dampness in the room, but copped out of the more outrageous of my prepared agenda – including my 'joke' about Roman baths.

What was his reaction? *He suggested I tried shutting the window*! What he did *not* do was offer me another room. I was flabbergasted, and withdrew a defeated and demoralized complainer.

But reflecting on this episode – as I did later that day from my dry room in *another* hotel – the excellent S. Anselmo, Aventino, Roma – I had nobody to blame but myself.

AS I HAD NOT ASKED FOR ANOTHER ROOM
WHY ON EARTH SHOULD HE OFFER ME ONE?

If my remedy was to be given another room – a perfectly reasonable proposal unless the hotel specialized in damp rooms – it was up to me to say so.

By not stating *my* remedy, I left the initiative of suggesting a remedy to the other guy – and one thing you can be certain about, if you leave the initiative to somebody else, it is likely that they will only consider their own interests in framing their remedy rather than yours. Hence, his suggestion that I shut the window.

This is all the more certain if, as is usual in situations where you feel aggrieved about something, you colourfully blame the other person for their failings.

Attack someone and they defend themselves.

Attack them ferociously and their defence is returned with interest.

Impugn their competence and stand back while they dissect yours.

Challenge their parentage and they will challenge that of your children.

Tempers are never calmed by being tested and the longer the row goes on the less the likelihood that you will get anything other than a sore throat – and perhaps even a thump on the nose for your trouble. Try the hopeless tack of making them responsible for the problem and they will deny responsibility.

In Italy, for instance, hotel receptionists, car hire people and airline check-ins have a devastating way of shrugging their shoulders and blowing hard through tight mouths when they want to deny either responsibility or concern for your plight. (Though, I must say in defence of Italian *waiters*, they are the very best in the world.)

The lesson is clear. Time spent preparing for a blazing row about your grievance is totally wasted – so is the nervous energy.

What of the alternative? To negotiate a remedy you have to have one. And thinking through what your remedy ought to be requires preparation – another reason for not wasting time thinking up articulate insults about the other person's incompetence. The case for you negotiating a remedy is fourfold:

1 You take the initiative in choosing the remedy and your remedy is more likely to start with your interests in mind than theirs.
2 The negotiation will be on your remedy and not stuck in an argument about the legitimacy of your grievance.
3 By proposing a remedy you provide helpful information to the other person – he does not have to guess what will assure him of your future business.
4 The other person may very well be relieved that you want so little and are not demanding, like an American attorney, grossly exaggerated recompense for your 'losses'.

Putting the discussion into a business context, suppose, say, you just complain to a supplier about a missed delivery of components. You can be fairly sure that their shipping department will justify, excuse, explain, blame or even apologize for the delay. They might just tell you to 'offski' – they have bad days too.

But, remember, if you have no remedy prepared you leave it to them to choose whether to do anything or nothing about deliveries in future. If you attack them they are unlikely to be motivated to do anything other than defend themselves.

It is not always within your power to withhold business from them – at least in the short run – and if you haven't clout like that you had better be careful that you don't provoke them into turning their system's 'gremlins' loose on your deliveries in the future.

The capacity for people in large organizations to quietly screw up their own systems in pursuit of private revenge on 'difficult' customers is known among the *cognoscenti* as the 'buggeration factor'.

Anybody who has ever suffered the 'run around' in business will recognize the seriousness of my caution.

But even if you have clout, you have no guarantee that pushing them will produce a remedy suitable to your interests. If pushed they might do something for you, but only the minimum possible. If, however, you state your (reasonable) remedy you could be half way to getting them to agree to it.

One way to avoid grievances is to anticipate them and, where possible, to design the remedies for them occuring before they arise. That way you define the remedies beforehand.

It is also easier to secure agreement on a remedy – and its limitations – before the parties are vulnerable to each other's failures, than it is during the emotional storms that accompany the consequences of these failures.

That is why Owls negotiating with Luigi (Scenario 1) will anticipate the grievances (using the 'what if' technique) that he might have about the nature of their proposals and they will seek ways in which they can ameliorate his concerns, if such ways exist.

They don't always.

Covering every contingency in a business contract is an Herculean task (much loved by grasping lawyers because, apart from the fees it generates, it reminds them nostalgically of half-forgotten legal moots at the law schools of their youth). But where there are key issues that one party demands the other attend to, you may have no choice but to adapt simple proposals into more complex ones.

For example, how do you meet Luigi's objections that he is left too vulnerable on how you conduct the business after he hands it over to you (for less than 50 per cent down and the rest paid over four long years)?

Foxes might take a judgement on the balance of power and, if favourable to them, might tell Luigi that he will have to take the risk that they will behave badly (which of course, they 'have absolutely no intention of doing') if he wants to sell his business to them today. After all, they would tell him firmly, Luigi's concern is the reverse of their own concern that his business may not be able to sustain the profits that he claims have determined his price for it.

Owls, on the other hand, would explore, for example, the implications of switching from net profit to the total turnover during the next four years as a possible determinant of the contingent price for Luigi's business.

This answers Luigi's fear that you might manipulate net profit, it being more difficult to manipulate turnover legally. This leaves you to take responsibility for generating your own profits out of the currently known turnover, provided Luigi guarantees (by legal warranty) that his current turnover is sustainable.

Neither you nor I know the perfect answer to this and other related questions but that is not my point.

Owls keep looking for answers, having identified the likely questions. They are interested in getting on with their business, based on their confidence that they can create a margin between costs and turnover – otherwise why buy Luigi's business?

Foxes might think about possible questions but prefer to find answers only if and when somebody asks them something. That way, any holes in their proposals might pass off unnoticed but they take the risk of future grievances arising from the unnoticed holes.

Sheep and Donkeys are unaware of the link between today's questions and future grievances, with Sheep panicked when they arise and Donkeys resorting to their lawyers.

The greatest source of grievances are vague or implied promises.

ON NOT BEING SERVED

On entering an Italian restaurant in Edinburgh last year, we were confronted with an Italian scale row between the leader of a party of six and the owner. The issue appeared to be the inability of the restaurant to sit the party at their booked table because the people already there had not finished their meal. The spokesman was adamant that his party be seated immediately (clearly an impossible demand unless the owner physically ejected the party at the table), and went on to lambast the restaurant for accepting his booking and then not having a table ready for when he and his guests arrived.

We were swept aside as he led his party out to the street to cries of 'I'll never return to this so-called restaurant again'. I stepped forward and the visibly angry owner turned to me, no doubt expecting a repeat run of 'what a way to run a restaurant'. He explained that my table was still occupied by the earlier diners and that it would be 15 minutes (which means 25 minutes at least) before we could be seated.

'I see,' I said. 'In that case, myself and my guests will avail ourselves of complimentary drinks at your bar until the table is free.' To which he replied: 'Fine, no problem. Rocco, serve Mr Kennedy's party with whatever they want, no charge.' Which is precisely what we did. More than halfway through a bottle of Chianti Classico we took our seats, much the merrier for the free drink. Also, the owner and Rocco danced around our table with Italian style attention all night, grateful no doubt that somebody loved them.

A reasonable solution is often acceptable to those embarrassed by a failure in their usually reasonable

> *service; embarrassing them by unreasonable abuse usually means no service at all and no compensation for their embarrassment at failing to serve you reasonably.*

So when something goes wrong you should think what (realistic) options you have, and you must concentrate entirely on the issue in dispute and not irrelevant side-issues. If the meal was rotten, make that the issue and not the way they took your coat (that's a separate issue). In the same way, if your spouse is late, that is the issue and not your mother-in-law or last year's missed anniversary.

Lastly, look for trade-offs that will meet your interests. Will a reduction of the bill make up for the lousy lasagne? How about a free video for the machine that needed repair within two days of purchase? Why not a free meal in the hotel where the room TV is not working, or a free taxi when reception forgot to call you for your train?

Recently, British Airways mislaid my luggage in Amsterdam and through overbooking shunted me into the Economy cabin from Business Class. I told the cabin crew that I was not best-pleased with British Airways at that moment but that a free brandy would go a long way to making me smile again. I was instantly given two brandies! (And they found my luggage too.)

COMMENTS ON SELF-ASSESSMENT TEST 5

1 a) The first thing you must do because it brings maximum leverage to the problem while you negotiate with them the remedy for your grievance. Donkeys worried about the 'ethics' of not paying a bill can relax – you are enjoined only to stall on your payment and not refuse to pay at all.

Most managers know this and select this action, showing that there is a little bit of a Fox in most of us.

b) Do this and you reduce your own leverage and the size of their problem. A regular Donkey's choice.

c) Never as a first option! Only Sheep give up all leverage – let the supplier offer to compromise.

2 a) You are in danger of implying a 15 per cent compromise rent increase before you know how strongly the landlord is pressing for his demand. Evidence of a Sheep at work.

b) A strong opening for an apprentice Fox – better left as a support for d).

c) Arbitration removes your veto from the decision about the rent. Much preferred by Donkeys.

d) Opening with the defects (and there are always defects in a property) to preface your case for your remedy – a lower or no rent increase or even a reduction if joined with b). At a minimum all defects must be put right first. Could reduce the pressure of the landlord's ambitions. Signs of a full fledged Fox.

3 a) It's a bit late to be checking liability and anyway this does not resolve your own liability with the Saudis. A Donkey move.

b) A waste of time and fax money as it does not move the machinery to your site. A fastidious Donkey move.

c) Threats won't get the machinery to the site. An emotional Donkey move.

d) Owls don't just state their grievances, they negotiate practical remedies! (They also avoid civil litigation.)

SELF-ASSESSMENT TEST 6

1 If they reject my proposal I should:
Select one:
(a) Amend it to take account of their valid objections only?
(b) Wait for them to propose their solution to the problem?
(c) Reject their invalid objections?
(d) Ask them for their suggestions?

2 I need not drop an issue if they say it is non-negotiable.
Is this:
(a) True?
(b) False?
(c) Sometimes false?

3 Deadlines are helpful in negotiation.
Is this:
(a) True?
(b) False?

CHAPTER 6

When even the Gods battle in vain

or why seven 'no's' are no way to get a 'yes'

I have met a lot of bright people in my time, many of whom generate nothing less than awe in me when I am in their presence. Intellectual giants stride the planet while we mere strivers after common sense can only keep out of their way in case they accidentally, or even deliberately, step on us.

In consultancy, the absolute worst situation for a negotiator is where the answer to a client's negotiating problem seems so blatantly obvious that it flashes at you in 10 metre high neon lights. Why don't they see it too?

Have you missed something so simple that to leap to the obvious solution would betray your own naivety? Struggling between keeping a straight face and blurting out the obvious is hard work, I can tell you.

Recently, I was briefed by some fund managers about a problem they had. Now, you must understand here that we were not dealing with a back street operation fantasizing about big deals while it couldn't pay its rent. This was the kind of player that regarded £2 million as loose change. In fact, the principals I was advising were the type who drew on £1 million a year bonuses – in a bad year.

Now, I hope you understand that I am not trying here to show how bright I am (Heaven forbid!). After all, I have made more than my share of negotiating mistakes – which is why I am confident about what you have to do to avoid them.

It is so easy to make simple mistakes no matter how well you might fare in an intelligence test. In short, if the best and the brightest make these mistakes and you can learn to avoid them, how much better could you do when you are up against the so-called 'smart' guys, especially those who can be abominably stupid when push comes to shove?

In this case, I sat in a padded captain's chair in the oak panelled meeting room, with a King's ransom in food and beverages set out on attractive trolleys which were parked around a highly polished and spacious mahogany table that looked like it cost a rain forest to put together.

The senior partner led the discussions, with occasional confirmatory intervention by his legally minded co-partner and other gentlemen whose roles were not mentioned.

The gist of the problem they faced was that a business deal they were involved in had gone wrong. They were shocked to discover a multi-billion escudos black hole in the accounts of a business they had bought in Portugal for a client, having received an 'all clear' from the advisors hired to conduct the 'due diligence' procedures for them.

Obviously, their advisors' diligence left a lot to be desired. In brief, they wanted the black hole filled with a large contribution from their former advisors.

On the merits of their case I have no comments – their lawyers were making the usual meal out of it.

On their conduct of their negotiations with their errant advisors, I have several critical comments, especially as these guys were in no way what in other contexts would be known as 'nine bob notes'. They were members of that elite of the elite – *la crème de la crème*.

And yet they had boobed, and badly.

The gist of their negotiating dilemma was how to deal with

their former advisors who had not made a single proposal in response to their own.

Apparently, they had merely ignored, though sometimes they vaguely rejected, whatever they had been offered as a settlement by the bank.

This left the bank with a problem: what should they do next? Well, what they had done, before I got there, was the worst thing possible.

When they made a proposal and it was ignored or vaguely rejected, they made another proposal, normally containing some concessionary variation in their former advisor's favour.

Oh, dear!

Now, be clear, this was not a misunderstanding or a misplayed tactic. They had not just made one proposal or even two or three. They had made no less than seven unilateral proposals, one after the other, over a period of just over a year. This was a tactical error in Spades.

So when the senior partner asked me bluntly, as he did after going over the circumstances for a couple of hours, what I would recommend that they should do next, I was forced to reply, as bluntly: 'I think a long period of silence from you would work wonders for your negotiating position.'

His body language said it all. Eyebrows raised, chin pulled in, sitting up straight, slightly leaning back in this seat, he looked back at me, as if he was incredulous at my response. 'Is that all?', he was saying without speaking, probably rehearsing whether he had to pay me my fee for so little.

But I had little doubt then and have had even less doubt since, that his negotiations had been undermined by his repetition seven times of the same fundamental mistake:

IMPROVING YOUR PROPOSAL BEFORE YOU HAVE RECEIVED A PROPOSAL FROM THEM IS, er, CRASS.

This seems such an obvious stance that even Bob, who can't spell his name backwards, knows of it.

Why is this such a basic mistake?

Consider the sequence of events. After discussions about the problem with the other party, you have a choice. Stick out for the full amount of the money that would fill in the black hole. This, surely, would be your opening preference? It compensates you fully for your losses.

If the other party, Messrs Slack, Casual and Indiligent, accept their liabilities and agree with you, then the dispute is over and we can all go home. Of course, they may not be so inclined. After all they have to find many billions of escudos out of their own coffers to satisfy your first offer of a settlement.

Your other choice is to sue them for your losses. But once anything gets anywhere near a court, Barrister Feign, QC, supported by his junior counsel, Ms Swerve, and her new 'devil', I M Gravitas, have an awesome way of finding leaks in absolutely 'water-tight' writs.

So to avoid that fate, and to cope with their disinclination to accept your first proposal, what should you do? This puts you on top of a very slippery slope.

If, in the spirit of being reasonable, you redraft your proposal to require something less than full recompense, you answer their silence with your movement. Immediately, you are trapped and down the snake you go, instead of up a ladder.

If they have no reason to move (indeed, they might totally reject that they have any liability) what do you do next?

Move again, and again, and three times more again? And where is that taking you, besides further away from billions of escudos to maybe only millions, and perhaps to hundreds of thousands?

Messrs Slack, Casual and Indiligent only have to wait on your next proposal, for surely one is certain to be on its way, even after the seventh!

They have no incentive to settle, no incentive to make their own proposal, and no incentive to do anything other than sit on their hands.

To prepare for an exchange of proposals and a fairly short run to a settlement, you would be better – providing you have a defensible case – to let the writ run its course. This imposes the costs of preparing their defence on them and when the lawyers' fees mount, as they inevitably will, their attention will turn to the costs and benefits of an out-of-court settlement.

The same lottery of justice that rattles your determination, rattles theirs too. As the courtroom doors loom in the diary, the urge to settle does too, no matter how good they believe Mr Feign, Barrister-at-Law, to be. Suppose he has an off-day, suppose your barrister plugs the leaks found by Swerve and Gravitas, suppose the judgement goes against them on some technicality, like a misplaced memo? How much less than several billion escudos will you accept to settle?

At this moment, you can make, and hopefully receive, settlement proposals and move to a negotiation, always being careful to exchange proposals in a strictly sequential order.

Joe Sludge, the pig farmer, can enlighten you about the deficiencies of buying pigs in a poke, which in this context means you do not amend your proposals without details of theirs.

Negotiations usually involve at least two solutions – yours and theirs – to the same problem. You know your solution but do you know theirs? If you don't, you should find it out before you go further, once you have presented your entry offer.

Remember, there are four bits of information present in all negotiations. You know two of them – where you will enter and where you intend to exit. You must find out the third – where they will enter. You can't know where they intend to exit but if you don't know where they will enter you will end up negotiating with yourself.

Not knowing their proposals is like being deaf at an auction – you keep bidding against yourself!

COMMENTS ON SELF-ASSESSMENT TEST 6

1 a) Seems reasonable to Sheep but will it progress the negotiations? Having raised objections to all or parts of your proposal, it is incumbent on them to suggest how they want them handled. Too obvious a willingness to accept specific 'valid' objections sets the wrong tone for dealing with the 'invalid' objections, given that their objections may be of mixed value to them and all equally valid as far as they are concerned.

   b) You could wait a long time, like a too cunning Fox. Much better for you to be more assertive: Tell them what you want them to do.

   c) What a Donkey would do!

   d) Correct. The Owl flushes out not just what they object to but also their aspirations for a settlement. Do not make another proposal, even an amended one until they have identified their version of the solution. You need two solutions on the table – one of yours and one of theirs – to safely negotiate a common solution.

2 a) Yes. Context will tell you what is absolutely non-negotiable for them – in effect their conditions for a settlement – and you can decide how to proceed. Remember, while you cannot negotiate principles, you can negotiate their application. You can also 'park' sensitive issues while you address the others and then return to the 'non-negotiables' on the basis of progress you might have made elsewhere. Owls know that a negotiating agenda is jointly

determined and they approach non-negotiables in that context.

b) No. Allow them to unilaterally declare this or that non-negotiable and you will soon be negotiating only on what issues they allow you to influence. A Sheep's response.

c) A very timid Sheep's response.

3 a) Yes. If the deadline is geniune, it concentrates minds on a settlement and raises the time-cost of disagreement. If it doesn't matter when you come to a settlement there is no point taking up time looking for one! Every Owl knows this.

b) No. Only a Donkey lets a deadline become unhelpful by revealing when they are on one or by getting themselves impaled by a 'senseless' deadline (i.e., one imposed for no good reason).

SELF-ASSESSMENT TEST 7

1 You run a courier business and one of your vehicles breaks its big-end just before a busy weekend. A friend has a spare van and agrees to loan it to you until your own vehicle is back on the road. He asks you to sign a receipt that reads: 'One vehicle, £500, one week's rental.' Do you:

   (a) Sign as asked?
   (b) Insist on a properly drawn up legal contract?
   (c) Tell him a receipt is not necessary between friends?
   (d) Ask for more details?

2 You have been approached by a Saudi Arabian company to handle the management contract of a large civil project. Do you:

   (a) See this as an opportunity to get into a lucrative Middle East business and therefore go in easy on your initial fee?
   (b) Assume that as the market is strong enough to take a high fee you can go in 'high'?
   (c) Prefer to 'wait and see' what fee is likely to be acceptable to the Saudi company?
   (d) Base your fee on what is profitable to you?

3 When they are clearly factually incorrect it is best not to interrupt them. Is this:

   (a) True?
   (b) False?
   (c) Sometimes true and other times false?

CHAPTER 7

The negotiator's most useful question

or how to avoid a one-truck contract

Experience is a great help in dealing with the routine – you know what to expect if you know your line of business and there are few, if any, surprises left. Experience in one field of negotiation can also help in another where you are totally ignorant of what is considered 'normal' and what is 'out of the question'.

But how can you make up for lack of experience other than by taking the time, which you may not have, to get it?

If you have to make a decision, perhaps with a lot of money (or something more important) riding on the outcome, and you have almost no experience to draw upon, you will need more than just luck to help you out.

Fortunately you can apply the principles of negotiating to give you the elbow room to make your decisions.

Now it is important here that you do not concern yourself with the actual amount of cash involved. That is of no relevance to anybody in a *new* market, though it is often the first rationalization made by newcomers for why they accepted the first offer.

If your money flow tends to be stuck in the tens and units range, try not to show that you are overly impressed when someone opens their offer with a number followed by several zeros – it weakens your negotiating position.

Likewise, don't fall into the opposite trap of being unable to negotiate seriously for what are bagatelles compared to your daily business quotas – more than one top negotiator, handling millions of dollars a deal, has confessed at a workshop how they tend to get done in the little deals worth a few hundred dollars or less.

If anybody offers you what appear to be '*big*' sums of money for what you value relatively lightly (or its converse, pennies for what you value greatly), remember:

THEY MAY NOT BE NUTS – *YOU* MAY JUST BE NAIVE!

Therefore, don't sign, grab it and run. The bargain price for a product in one market can be sheer robbery in another. And there is nothing worse for your ego than finding out later that you cheated yourself.

An offer you 'can't refuse' is one you ought to think carefully about. Consider: what is the price for a gallon of water for a thirsty tourist in the middle of Glasgow?

Not much, considering the amount of water that falls on Glasgow at most times of the year. Certainly you are unlikely to get mugged for water in Glasgow – though, I cannot discount the possibility of you being taken for a half-bottle of the local 'water of life'!

But what of the price for a gallon of water in the middle of the Arabian desert? Years ago, I was driving a Range Rover round up-country Oman selling diamonds to ex-patriate Brits working in oil exploration, and such was the dehydration that I drank a gallon of water every 20 miles – just to stop my mouth cracking like sandpaper.

And that was only part of the discomfort. I was under strict instructions from the Old Arabia Hands in Muscat not to drink alcohol even if I found an unlocked brewery; not to complain about having sand in every orifice of the body; and under no circumstance was I even to *think* of women – 'If you must look at a camel, make sure it's a male one' I was advised! I can tell you straight, if for any reason I had been cut short of water for any length of time in that climate I would have traded all my diamond samples for a glass of water, and probably thrown in the company's Range Rover as well.

So, a bargain can look different depending on from where you are looking at it. That is, you need a lot more information about the *appropriate* money worth, and implications, of the deal if you are to prepare a negotiating position quickly.

So many deals come undone that it is a wonder any get put together, but the time to concern yourself with the small print of a deal is *before* pen is put to paper, not afterwards in your lawyer's office. And bringing in the lawyers doesn't help too much – they tend to throw spanners in the works of any deal they are associated with and always deny any responsibility for the deals that get past them.

In new business fields – particularly in countries new in your itinerary – you will have to handle the negotiations yourself and hope that you survive long enough to acquire the experience that will protect you from the pitfalls that are obvious to the old hands.

You can start improving your performance in 'one-off' negotiations by first of all not trusting to luck to take care of your interests. Look after them yourself, instead. And to look after your interests you have to identify them.

Because hindsight is a cheap forecaster of the deals we should avoid, the bars and dinner parties of the world are full of smart guys willing to give you advice on what you should have done after you have already done something else. Foresight, a much scarcer commodity, is all the more valuable for that.

One type of deal we must avoid, though circumstances often conspire against us, is known as the 'one-truck' contract. These are lethal because everything that can go wrong probably will (Murphy's famous law) and anything you insure against only happens after you miss a premium (floor joke at Lloyds).

The time to avoid the disasters of ill-thought deals is when the deals are being negotiated and this can be illustrated by considering the following contract to hire a truck offered by a 'pal' in Muscat:

'One truck, $1000, one month's rental'

What is wrong with a clean and simple 'one-truck, etc.' contract like that? No complications, no red tape, and no hassle, just pay your cash and drive off. The basic problem with 'one-truck' contracts is that they leave almost everything to the mercies of Murphy's law.

And this is true for *both* parties to the deal.

Neither of you is protected in the slightest by the 'one-truck' contract you have negotiated: if you sue them you will either lose the case or waste your cash in a deadlock. Either way the only people laughing in the court are the lawyers, and their bank managers (and if you think your own country's lawyers are expensive, they are positively penurious compared to any foreign lot).

If you are the hirer, you have no assurance that you will get the truck your 'pal' showed you in the compound and not some wreck he keeps out of sight at the back of his lot. Of course, you may protest: 'I trust him, we went to the same school'. Indeed, he could be your best friend, etc.

Fair enough, but many a member of the down-and-out fraternity begins the story of their road to ruin with: 'I went into business with my closest friend and a loan from an awfully nice bank manager'. If you are the owner in a 'one-truck' contract you have no assurance that it will be returned in the condition that it left you.

When (if) it comes back it might have to be parked behind your lot because it is too dangerous to park in the compound. Then you will have to off-load it onto the first fool to walk into your office looking for a 'one-truck' deal!

There is more than enough room in a 'one-truck' contract for disagreement about the condition of the truck, when it is to

71

be returned, who is responsible for insuring it and who pays the parking tickets it collects while out of your sight.

How then do you avoid 'one-truck' contracts? Easy. The only thing you have to do is ask lots of questions that begin with two simple words, and to keep asking questions until you are perfectly satisfied that you have covered everything. The words to put in front of every question are:

WHAT IF?

Applying this to the hire of a Range Rover for an up-country mission in the bleak wastes of Oman, you could ask, or need to be ready to answer:

What if *the truck breaks down up country for a reason unconnected with my usage or unrelated to parts for which there are spares?*

Agree on warranty and responsibility for delivery of replacement parts or a new truck.

What if *the truck breaks down after being improperly driven?*

Insist on a 'no claims' for improper usage condition, and the return of the truck to your premises at the hirer's expense.

What if *it is stolen and I cannot complete my sales trip within the month?*

Agree an insurance premium that covers immediate replacement of the truck but avoid any acknowledgement of liability for his estimates of his loss of sales (no salesperson ever reckoned somebody else was responsible for them losing a *small* sale – they're worse than anglers with the 'fish that got away').

What if *your carelessness about parking causes it to be stolen?*

Have a waiver clause inserted that absolves you of liability

72

in these cases – try to get your brother as sole and final arbitrator of any decision about the extent of 'carelessness'.

What if *it is repossessed by one of your creditors and I cannot complete my sales trip?*

Get this covered by the insurance premium for immediate replacement and insist that this is paid for by the truck owner.

What if *your creditor damages it out of both our sights?*

Shove in another waiver claim but insist that the hirer gets a signed statement as to the truck's condition before he parts with it.

What if *you socially misbehave and the locals smash up the truck in revenge – or shoot at it if a camel is involved?*

Insert a high 'returnable' deposit condition that is withheld in these cases (again, try to get your brother nominated as arbitrator).

What if *you knock down a camel and the locals hold the truck in ransom?*

The 'returnable' deposit isn't.

What if *the truck is unlicensed for cross-border journeys and I accidently make one?*

Commit the hirer to usage within the territory and liable for all breaches of local emigration laws. Charge him a 'lieu of export deposit' and also *sell* him a map of the territory.

What if *we dispute the amount of damage or the extent of the seriousness of minor scratches?*

Clearly covered by the appointment of your brother in the arbitration clause.

What if *I find you are not the legal owner of the truck and it is repossessed by the authorities?*

Demand legal proof of ownership or, in the absence of the relevant documents, get a *large* discount off the hire charge and the insurance premium.

What if *you fail to return on time at the end of the rental period?*

Insert an excess-hire charge at a steeply rising *per diem* rate and, of course, loss of the 'returnable' deposit.

What if *you use the truck for some illegal purpose and it is impounded by the police?*

Require legal usage on pain of forfeit of the 'returnable' deposit.

(*And,* **What if** *we don't settle the 'what ifs' before it is time for me to return to Britain?*)

(Clearly the Hustle Close tactic. Tell him if he agrees to your terms he can have the truck now. Otherwise later.)

These **What ifs** are somewhat tongue-in-cheek but they have a serious message for all negotiators.

Look at the following summary of an Omani hire contract and compare it with the 'one-truck' contract above:

One 1998 model Range Rover, as new, 12,020 miles certified on the clock, with all parts in working order, serviced at 12,000 miles, complete with spare tires, fan belts, exhaust system, plugs, a new battery, a wheel, chain and tackle and 25 gallons of fuel. Delivery to your hotel by 6 a.m. Tuesday next. $1000 COD – cash only. Insurance for month's use and all legal penalties for traffic and other offences to be borne by hirer. Any defects in bodywork to be notified at delivery, otherwise as is. Rental fee covers one month's hire and unlimited mileage from Tuesday next to 2 November next only. At the end of the rental period the hirer must return vehicle by 6 a.m. fuelled and in sound condition to the company and pay (cash only) for any damage, defects or missing parts on return.

Now I freely concede that even this contract is not *legally* cast-iron but it is certainly better than the original 'one-truck' deal offered by a 'pal' in Muscat. You can see this by looking at your last car rental form. The big rental companies are experts at avoiding 'one-truck' deals – their rivals who didn't are no longer in business.

However, car-rental companies are not quite as cautious as the airlines who have exclusion clauses on their tickets (which by the act of buying you are deemed to agree to) such that even if a 747 knocks you down on the runway and reverses over you twice, you, or more likely your widow, will find that they are absolved from all liability by something called the 'Warsaw Convention'.

That is why people of a nervous disposition about their chances ought *never* to read the small print of their airline tickets – they could die of shock and still not have a claim on the airline!

In a large deal there could be numerous *what if* questions that need to be asked and answered if the parties are to protect their interests. In a *new* deal, or strange country, it is even more necessary to do your preparation with a list of what *ifs*.

Negotiators face a big problem when a previously prepared contract that suits the interests of the other party is presented to them – that's why it's previously prepared! – and do not know where to start opening it up for discussion.

WHAT IF THEY ARE COVERED AGAINST COCK-UPS?

In any 12-month period over 400 claims for faulty design, inaccurate calculation and inadequate checking of work are made against consultant engineers by their clients from all corners of the globe.

Insurers are convinced that the cause is 'weak supervision' or 'inadequacy of the site engineers'. The insurance association recommends that consultants refrain 'from accepting contractual responsibility that performance criteria would be met!'

It is also adamant that consultants must not disclose, even casually, that they have professional indemnity cover for their actions. The most common cause of this disclosure is for the consultant to include in his contract the limitations of his indemnity, which only encourages the litigious client to try to recoup something from a contract that does not meet his expectations.

Apparently they only sue those they know have some cover, irrespective of the justice of their claims.

It is a fact that many construction companies open a file for claims the instant they receive a contract and set to work to make claims even before they start work on site. Some companies are rumoured to have larger claims departments than they have estimating departments.

The asking of questions, and particularly the act of thinking them through *before* the negotiation, will suggest terms for negotiation. In every deal, there are dozens of *what ifs* and consideration of them is a useful way of creating negotiable variables for you to trade against the liabilities you are being asked to accept.

Of course, in some parts of the world in times of disorder a 'one-truck' contract is all that you can get. On these, thankfully few, occasions you may have no choice but to take it.

In the mêlée for the last plane from Kabul, you are not advised to negotiate a seat in the 'no smoking' section using *what if* type questions, nor to demand that the 'one-truck' liabilities be amended before you remove yourself from the tarmac and get on board.

However, you could still try to negotiate a deal on the price if you've run out of dollars and the pilot is being difficult. Ask him if he accepts payment by American Express – you never know, he just might have a 'pal' in Muscat who has an Amex account (too bad if he only accepts Diners Club) and you *might* be able to negotiate the surcharge!

COMMENTS ON SELF-ASSESSMENT TEST 7

1 a) A very risky (and Sheepish) decision on your part (and his).
   b) If you had time but you haven't (a Donkey choice).
   c) Oh dear! As a lamb will you last long enough to become a Sheep?
   d) Yes. Get more details. Owls ask *what if* questions.

2 a) 'Sell cheap, get famous' is no way to riches but Sheep don't know that.
   b) Assumptions are dangerous until tested, but Foxes are bold.
   c) Sheep are cautious.
   d) Correct but be ready to react when you find out how badly they want your services and, like Owls, always know the difference between high and low profits.

3 a) It is so seldom best to interrupt a negotiator, factually incorrect or otherwise, that Owls will always caution you against doing so. Foxes don't like this question – they prefer to be flexible.

   b) Ask yourself if you like being interrupted? I have never met anyone anywhere on a Workout who admits to liking being interrupted. Now ask yourself: 'Have I ever interrupted anybody?' I have never met anyone who claims a clean record of never interrupting anybody. Donkeys should think about that!

CHAPTER 8

It's their reliability, stupid!

This is the second of my Negotiating Scenarios in *Everything is Negotiable!*. As with the other scenarios, they are a lively way for you to learn in the 'safe' environment of your private reading.

Read through the scenario a couple of times, making notes in whatever way suits you. Then think about how you would prepare for your meeting with Zeugma and how you would put together an offer, remembering what you have covered so far in Chapters 1 to 7 and, as always, what your gut feelings tell you about the situation.

There is no point, however, in inventing 'facts' about the scenario to settle the case your way. If it is not stated in the scenario, it hasn't and won't happen. Simply stick to the storyline and prepare your responses from there.

So have some fun – and good luck.

NEGOTIATION SCENARIO 2: IT'S THEIR RELIABILITY, STUPID!

Lothian Public Health contracted out its payroll processing to Zeugma, a computer bureau, ten months ago. Zeugma won the contract in the face of stiff competition from external and in-house bids. The contract is for five years and it is worth £180,000 per year (£15,000 per month) in turnover to Zeugma.

Last month a machine malfunction resulted in a failure to process the payroll, also resulting in Lothian failing to pay its employees on time. Considerable disruption occurred when staff left their posts to hold meetings and greater trouble was only averted when emergency payments were made manually.

Lothian had several telephone conversations with Zeugma regarding their failure to process the payroll in accordance with their contract. During these conversations they were told of certain actions Lothian intended to take. These were also followed with a memo.

As a result of disruption in the hospitals, caused by staff seeking their wages from the pay offices in response to rumours that they would not be paid, several demands were made that Lothian alter its payroll arrangements.

Zeugma were told that they were being held liable for damages, if the hospitals' claims were established, and these were estimated to be £100,000. They were also told that they would be held responsible for this amount if the claimants pursued the issue and that Lothian reserved the right to seek additional claims in the event of future costs being awarded to the hospitals.

Lothian also announced that it was claiming £10,000 as the cost of an emergency processing of, and paying out, the payroll manually.

Most critically, Lothian announced that it was suspending forthwith Zeugma's present status as the 'preferred bidder' in the ongoing pre-tender discussions on the extension of computerisation to new areas of hospital administration.

[Assume, now, that you are a negotiator for Lothian

You acknowledge that Zeugma has made extensive efforts to sort out the problem and their service has been satisfactory up until this incident. Industrial relations in some of the hospitals are believed to be poor.

You have had discussions with Zeugma, as the preferred bidder, on the computerisation of accounting, costing, treatment scheduling and personnel records, thus potentially increasing their level of business by a factor of five ($5 \times £180,000 = £900,000$; 5 years $\times £900,000 = £4.5$ million). You understand that currently you represent 20 per cent of Zeugma's turnover.

Since you wrote to Zeugma, you have heard from the hospitals who were affected during the staff disruption, that they have either dropped their claims for damages or have sharply reduced them. Your present liability is around £17,000 and may reduce further as you talk to the hospitals. Zeugma does not yet know of these reductions in your liabilities for claims.

Your claim of £10,000 for paying out emergency funds refers to the labour cost of calculating, packaging and issuing the cash only, and was the figure quoted by Zeugma for this task in their original analysis of the total payroll processing costs. It does not include the full costs of the original manual payroll system; including records, tax administration, security and handling employee queries. For you it is a symbolic charge for your inconvenience rather than an attempt to receive total coverage of your costs.

You could change your bureau from Zeugma if they do not come some way towards meeting your aspirations for a settlement and if they fail to make proposals to prevent a repeat occurrence. There is a penalty charge of £53,000 if you cancel the contract.

Zeugma told you that they received incorrect data from

the pay office (the wrong tax week code) but have admitted that their operator failed to notice this at the time. They also suffered a major computer malfunction which did not allow the job to be redone in time and then their back-up computer crashed when they fed it the garbage data, causing further delays.

A meeting is to be held shortly with Zeugma.

Now try some questions to practise your negotiating skills on the problem and to explore, using your experience to date and drawing on your reservoir of common sense, how you might set about negotiating with Zeugma. You can work from your notes on a separate sheet of paper, or from brief notes and highlightings you have made in the text.

Remember, Foxes cheat without prompting, Sheep need to be prompted to cheat and Donkeys skip the exercise altogether. Owls make notes on all of their answers *before* they compare them with my own comments.

QUESTIONS ON
NEGOTIATION SCENARIO 2

8.1 What is the most important objective for the Health Authority in this situation and why?

8.2 What would be a major negotiating error for the Health Authority?

8.3 What are Zeugma's prime interests in this dispute?

8.4 What shape of deal should the Health Authority aim for?

8.5 What should Zeugma not raise in the negotiations and why?

COMMENTS ON NEGOTIATION
SCENARIO 2

8.1 What is the most important objective for you in this situation?

Your main interest is in ensuring that a failure to pay the staff does not happen again. You must concentrate your negotiating energy on securing from Zeugma evidence that their employees will not fail to be paid again throughout the remaining years of the contract.

Zeugma's failure last month to ensure that payments were made to the bank accounts of your employees is the cause of the dispute, but what happens in the future is the main issue for you. While not downplaying the significance of the consequences in financial claims for Zeugma's failure, you must face the future because compensation for a past event does not ensure proper performance in the future.

It is up to you and your fellow negotiators to secure adequate assurances from Zeugma about the future and to have detailed guarantees of what they intend to do to prevent another failure. Zeugma's claim that your payroll office supplied garbage data (the wrong tax week code) must be addressed by both of you but Zeugma must explain what they intend to do about their operator not noticing this. Is training required for both Lothian and Zeugma personnel and who pays for it?

Zeugma's guarantees of future performance are not, however, enough if they are not backed with some form of sanction and you should consider a stiff financial penalty for any recurrence of the incident. Zeugma can hardly resist accepting a penalty clause if they are to have credibility with their verbal guarantees. If they are so sure that it will not happen again, they have no defence against accepting a stiff penalty if it does happen. Any hesitation to offer or accept a guarantee would cause you to question the value of Zeugma's guarantees and their commitment to your interests.

8.2 What would be a major negotiating error for the Lothian?

Your biggest error would be to see this negotiation as being about compensation for last month's failure and not about the assurances needed for the future.

The letter you sent to Zeugma specifies £100,000 for the liabilities' claim and £10,000 as a symbolic manual payment. If you were to plan to concentrate on getting as much as you can in financial compensation, you will not only miss your real interests but you risk the dispute going to litigation through a deadlock.

Zeugma is bound to emphasize that the failure was not all their own fault – they got garbage data – and therefore they will argue that any compensation would need to be shared between them and you and not by them alone.

The sheer size of your claim, set against the value of the current contract to Zeugma, is bound to provoke their stiff resistance. They do not yet know that your claims have dropped to £17,000 and how you handle this as yet undisclosed fact is crucial to your tactics. If you fail to disclose this drop in your claims on Zeugma – or worse, actually try to increase it by saying that the claims, for instance, are now £200,000! – you will make the task of securing a settlement that much harder.

While some compensation is important, it is not among the high, or 'must get', category of your priorities. You can use the compensation issue to set the tone but you should not focus too much on compensation at the expense of making sure that a payroll failure does not happen again.

It might be better for you during discussions on compensation, to switch from claiming or sharing liabilities for the £100,000, to proposing a formula for sharing a percentage of any final liabilities. This device enables the good news of the drop to £17,000 to be introduced without rancour.

84

The issue of the £10,000 can be separated out as this is a symbolic claim on Zeugma, who might regard payment of it in full a necessary confidence building measure if they are to succeed in being restored as the preferred bidder for the new business.

8.3 What are Zeugma's prime interests in this dispute?

Zeugma's prime interests must be to regain preferred bidder status for the additional £4.5 million contract. This new business must be of great interest to Zeugma and it has a chance of winning it if it is the preferred bidder and less chance if it is not. (It has no chance if it does not reach agreement with you in this dispute.)

To regain preferred bidder status, Zeugma will have to address your prime interest, namely the guarantee that this computer payroll failure will not happen again. To do this it will have to satisfy you on the details of the steps it intends to take and will likely have to agree (if not to offer) a financial penalty in the event of a reoccurrence.

Zeugma should spot this as its client's main interest and in consequence should direct its negotiating efforts towards satisfying you on this issue.

Zeugma must also be interested in reducing or eliminating the compensation you have claimed because of the severe pressure that this will put on its finances, if they were to pay anything like the amount mentioned in your letter.

Paying you £100,000 would eliminate more than half of their annual revenue (£180,000) from the current contract and probably most of their unspecified profit from the five-year contract. Zeugma will likely seek to mitigate this figure, probably using a formula linking shared blame (garbage data and their operator not noticing it in time) to a shared liability.

On the £10,000, Zeugma is not on strong grounds here because it is the amount their proposal quoted for the manual payout process. Set against the £4.5 million new business value,

Zeugma would probably pay up (or offer a credit note) for this amount.

8.4 What shape of deal should you aim for?

You should aim for a package deal that meets your own interests and those of Zeugma's.

It will require that Zeugma satisfies you that its measures to prevent the failure again are sound and detailed. It will expect or impose an unconditional financial penalty in the event of a failure reoccurring in the future.

On reinstatement of Zeugma as a preferred bidder, this would be conditional on Zeugma meeting your reasonable requirements on non-reoccurrence of the failure and on the acceptance of a financial penalty clause. What happens in the actual bidding process would depend on the quality of Zeugma's bid and its subsequent behaviour in performing its payroll contract.

On compensation, you could probably expect to receive the £10,000 nominal claim for the manual payroll but would have to consider carefully your claim for £17,000 (perhaps less by the time the deal is negotiated). You could impose the whole amount on Zeugma or settle for a shared liability in view of the information about the garbage data (if satisfied that it is genuine).

8.5 What should Zeugma not raise in the negotiations and why?

The one thing that Zeugma should avoid raising is charges regarding the industrial relations problems at some of your hospitals. It is tempting for them to do so because they might mistakenly see it as a stick with which to beat you. If they do, they risk raising the temperature on an issue that is nothing to do with their own failure to perform the payroll contract.

There is one thing for sure, no matter what the state of any organisation's industrial relations, they are always made infinitely worse by not paying people their wages on time! Of course, poor industrial relations will lead to individuals using the payroll problem to criticise their local managements, but the disruptions occurred in all the hospitals and not just those where this problem exists.

If Zeugma wants to widen the argument and raise the tensions, the industrial relations issue is there for them to use but it is a 'red herring' in the context of the current negotiation. It not only jeopardises the settlement of this dispute, it also jeopardises the future business goals of Zeugma. Negotiation over fractious subjects are difficult enough without making them worse by diversions. Much the same applies to you if you concentrate on compensation at £100,000.

SELF-ASSESSMENT TEST 9

1 You are a manufacturer of optic fibre cabling and have been granted an interview, after many last-minute cancellations, with the boss of Europe's largest cable TV firm, who insists that you meet him at Terminal 4, Heathrow, a few minutes before he flies off to Australia. This is your big chance! While walking towards Passport Control, he opens with a demand for your 'best price' for a six months' contract to supply standard sygma optic cable repeaters. Do you:

   (a) Show him what you can do by quoting the lowest price you can in order to get your 'foot in the door'?
   (b) Go in slightly above your lowest price?
   (c) Go in high and leave yourself room to negotiate?
   (d) Wish him a pleasant flight?

2 The buyer for a large chemical company responds to your price for Naptha by telling you: 'The competition is very strong and you'll have to do better than that.' Do you:

   (a) Offer to cut your price in exchange for the order?
   (b) Ask him how much your price is above the others?
   (c) Suggest that he accepts the other offers?
   (d) Ask to see the other offers?
   (e) Ask him what he likes about your proposal?

3 You are negotiating with a CD-ROM publisher in New York who has offered to market your series on management education. They offer you an advance against royalties of £50,000 – £25,000 on signature of the contract and £25,000 on acceptance of the material. They reject your demand for £80,000 split similarly. Do you:

   (a) Accept their offer?
   (b) Tell them it is not good enough?
   (c) Offer them a repackaged proposal?
   (d) Walk out?

CHAPTER 9

The myth of goodwill-conceding

or how to teach wolves to chase sledges

It is paradoxical that the handling of concessions is probably the most difficult task facing the negotiator, despite the fact that the rule for above-average performance is fairly simple:

In negotiating, be more like Scrooge than St Francis of Assisi.

Why should you accept this somewhat uncharitable advice? Because in negotiating, generosity is *not* contagious. Would that it was.

Indeed, experience suggests that liberality in concession-making is the worst thing you can do if you want to get concessions from the other person. If you concede why should he do likewise? Surely, by remaining where he is, he might induce you to concede yet more?

In this chapter I discuss the 'goodwill' theory of concession-making, hopefully to eradicate it from your repertoire. Where does this goodwill-concession theory come from?

Its origins are obscure but I have traced it back as far as the unlikely named Bjorn McKenzie, who was a travelling salesman for a short while in the 1890s in the Hudson Bay area of Northern Canada.

Whether further research could throw new light on the origins of goodwill-conceding is, perhaps, less important than the fact that it appears now to have a widespread grip in all walks of

90

business. You have only to ask negotiators if they practise goodwill-conceding to realize just how prevalent it is.

Strange as it may seem, those people who wax lyrical about goodwill-conceding cannot understand criticism of it. This has led to some stormy sessions at the Negotiate Workshops. Two of the most common defences of goodwill-conceding take the form:

1 I concede a couple of little things early on, just to soften them up.
2 Somebody has to push the boat out or we'd never get the negotiations underway.

Both of these defences, in a triumph of delusion over experience, indicate utter confusion as to the tactics that produce better deals.

Naturally, at the workshops, when I put it so bluntly, I do so in order to ruffle the feathers of the afflicted negotiators and to get them thinking about the consequences of their beliefs.

Consider the first defence. What is the evidence for this?

I won't go so far as to say *all* research findings – in case I have missed some – but certainly all I have seen suggest the very opposite is the case:

GOODWILL CONCESSIONS BY ONE PARTY DO NOT 'SOFTEN UP' THE OTHER SIDE, THEY MAKE THEM TOUGHER!

True, the research I referred to is mainly conducted in the hallowed halls of Academe and therefore is vulnerable to being loudly dismissed to the sound of raspberries by 'practical' people.

I too have laughed loud and long at some of the research projects conducted in our universities: not so long ago, someone was researching the phenomenon of 'deviance' (ie, criminality) among *left-handed* immigrants into the Orkney Islands, and another, this time an anthropologist from the London School of Economics, was studying 'gossip in a Highland village'.

But these are totally atypical of the serious academic research into negotiating behaviour conducted all over the world during the past 50 years. Incidentally, much of this research is also largely confirmed by the practical experience of those negotiators who are free from the curse of goodwill-conceding. You have only to consider what the goodwill-believer is suggesting to see that they must be wrong.

The idea that concessions 'soften up' opponents suggests that negotiators are provoked by evidence of your generosity into being generous themselves.

Now why should your 'early' concessions have that effect?

Consider it from your opponent's view. In seeing you make a concession, she can interpret what you are doing in one of two ways: either *you are displaying goodwill*, or, *you are displaying your weakness*.

GOODWILL IS A PRECEDENT

A supplier of electrical switch gear was asked to quote a contractor for a job in the Middle East. They went in with their list price and ran into serious resistance from the contractor who flatly refused to pay the list price for anything.

An exasperated sales negotiator eventually pressed the question: 'Why are you so adamant about getting a reduction from our list prices?'

'Because you gave a subsidiary of ours a ten per cent discount off your prices last year,' replied the contractor.

'But that was a once-only introductory discount for a special job in anticipation of future work,' the negotiator replied.

'Well, this contract I am offering you is part of the "other work" and as far as I am concerned I want to be "introduced" to your below-list prices too!'

Even if she accepted the first interpretation, there is no compelling need for her to react with reciprocated goodwill and be generous in return. She still has the tempting option of taking a less compromising stance herself.

And if she makes the second interpretation of your conceding behaviour, she will be even more inclined to take a tougher stance.

Certainly, the likelihood of her reacting with goodwill must be very small, unless both of you are imbued with an overwhelming desire to be generous despite your perceptions of each other's relative strengths:

If both of you are compulsive 'goodwill' negotiators, may you always *only* negotiate with each other! But what happens if your next negotiation is with someone who is not a believer in goodwill-conceding, either by conviction, from practical experience, or on the evidence of academic research?

Your goodwill strategy then relies entirely on her being 'converted' to goodwill-conceding by your example.

How do you 'convert' her? Do you tell her that the purpose of your concession is to 'soften her up' (which will go down like a lead Zeppelin), or are you going to be less than candid (farewell St Francis!) about your motives and merely hope that her defences are down?

What is the most likely consequence of your attempt to 'soften her up'? You don't need a PhD in human nature to suppose that she is most likely to read your concession as a sign of weakness and act accordingly by getting tougher.

Turning to the second defence of goodwill-conceding ('to push the boat out' and 'get things underway'), you should note the sense of desperation in the tone of this line of defence. As a tactic it is as vulnerable to the same response as the other one: it is more likely to provoke a tougher stance in the other negotiator, rather than an outbreak of goodwill, because she will interpret your concession as a sign of your weakness. But there is a more fundamental criticism of it.

Presumably, if you are feeling a need to get the negotiation under way, so is the other person. If this is the case, why is a goodwill concession your *best* move?

Far from getting the negotiation under way, you only succeed in moving your own negotiating position towards the other person's. In effect you have moved onto the slippery slope to surrender. If you concede when I press you, my best bet is to keep pressing until I am convinced that you are not going to move any further.

Up in the Northern Tundra the people are smarter than your average goodwill-conceder. They know about the fallacies of conceding as a negotiating style. They learned it the hard way.

Indeed, drop into any little town inside the Arctic Circle, up in Northern Norway, or Canada, or Alaska, and announce over your beer that you are a devotee of goodwill-conceding and they will throw you out into the snow (even at 40 below).

Some trading posts have Local Ordnances against the practice of goodwill-conceding, and Sheriff Courts up there show no mercy to city folks brought before them charged with the offence. In fact, goodwill-conceding in the Tundra is positively anti-social.

Why?

Well years ago, when the first travelling salesmen went up there to sell them the benefits of civilization – refrigerators, suntan lotion and icecold beer – they were welcomed in the warm and generous spirit that snow people are renowned for the world over.

The salesmen went from outpost to outpost carrying their wares on sledges pulled by dogs. (I refer to sales*men* rather than sales*persons* because the disaster was entirely the fault of smart-assed males from down south, and in those days the only women in the Tundra were born there and were too sensible to ride around on sledges selling suntan lotion.)

The trouble was that some of these salesmen brought with them their 'civilized' vices, one of which was the filthy practice of goodwill-conceding.

At first, the locals didn't realize the poison that had been brought into their midst by their new friends and life carried on as normal. The trouble began when the locals taught the salesmen how to hunt for meat to eat on the long sledge journeys between outposts. The practice that led to disaster was slow to gather momentum, but once it got going drastic measures were needed to stop it.

It seems that Bjorn McKenzie, a cold-beer salesman, presumably of Swedish and Scottish extraction (the accounts vary and are probably mixed up anyway), found himself, one afternoon, being stalked by a wolf, some miles up the track. He had just shot a large elk and had struggled might and main to get it onto his jumbo-sized sledge. The piercing howl of the wolf made Bjorn jump, as it seemed to be very near.

Fear forced him quickly to evacuate his camp and he set off, as fast as the dogs could pull him, down the track to the nearest outpost. The wolf followed just out of rifle range. Bjorn increased the dogs' pace and the sledge lurched forward, groaning with the heavy weight of him, his cold-beer samples, and the dead elk.

As the wolf closed in – he swore he could hear it panting behind him – he searched desperately for a solution to his predicament.

It was then that Bjorn had a blinding flash: of course, the wolf was hungry and wanted some of his elk! 'What better way to get the sledge moving faster than to cut off some of the elk meat and throw it behind to the wolf?', Bjorn asked himself, and immediately congratulated his mother for having such a brilliant son.

The hungry wolf, Bjorn reasoned, would be satisfied and stop hounding him if he was given *some* meat to eat, and, meanwhile, Bjorn could give it the slip and reach the safety of the outpost.

Hence, Bjorn cut off a small slice of meat – a difficult task as the sledge was moving fairly fast at the time – and threw it behind him. He had plenty of meat left and he thought that a small slice would not matter much to himself but would likely help to lower the wolf's hostility towards him.

Everything went according to plan for the next two miles. The dogs strained away and the sledge fairly skidded along over the icy track. Bjorn was already composing the story of his brilliant escape for his pals at the outpost.

But suddenly he heard the howl of the wolf again.

And this time he thought he could hear two of them – perhaps three!

Bjorn's heart thumped away and it was all he could do to remain in a state one degree short of panic. Thinking quickly, he concluded that he had not given the wolf enough meat – he did not bother to ask himself where the other two had come from – and so, he cut off some more meat and threw it behind him.

This time he threw out three portions, just in case one wasn't enough, which still left Bjorn with lots more for himself. He swore later to his pals that he had only gone a few hundred yards when he heard the howl of wolves again. There must have been more than three behind him this time and he could see several more coming through the trees alongside the track, all racing like crazy for the sledge.

Bjorn whipped the dogs harder, and croaked out 'mush! mush!' (as they do in the movies), and also began to cut meat off the elk at a furious rate, throwing out great chunks of it in all directions.

And still the wolves came on.

Dozens of them.

From every direction they raced after the sledge. Yelping for more.

And more.

And yet more.

They howled in what Bjorn was convinced at the time sounded like derision when they got a chunk of his meat at their feet. Nothing, apparently, would satisfy the wolves and they appeared to have gone crazy (they were already wild, of course, but now they were furious too).

Bjorn started throwing meat to specific wolves, hoping that by pleasing them they would recognize a friend if it came to the final supper with him as the main dish.

Before long Bjorn was running out of elk but he didn't run out of wolves: now there were hundreds of them!

He threw the last of the elk to the wolves just as he reached the safety of the outpost.

It was a close-run thing.

Bjorn felt lucky to escape with his life. True, he had thrown away all of the elk, though he had intended only to throw a few small bits away. But he was alive and able to tell the locals and his fellow salesmen of his brilliant ploy to get the better of the wolves.

The locals had never heard the like of his tale in all the years they had run sledges in the Tundra. No wolves ever came near their sledges and certainly no packs of wolves ever bothered them in the slightest. They shook their heads and put it down to the city slicker's imagination.

In contrast, the salesmen, who had no experience of wolves or what they were really like, immediately made preparations to load up their sledges with elk steaks; they were not going to be caught in the Tundra without a defence against ravenous wolves!

And that was the source of the disaster.

For the next six months, Bjorn and the other salesmen raced

around the Tundra, plying their refrigerators, suntan lotion and cold beer, and throwing meat to any wolves that chased after them. They considered Bjorn's discovery of how to handle wolves the most brilliant idea that they had had since their companies had sent them to the Tundra to make their fortunes.

True, none of them had made a fortune yet, but neither were any of them eaten by a wolf.

They were absolutely shocked beyond belief when the local people ganged together and sent them packing down river at gunpoint. 'Haven't we brought you the prizes of civilization?', they asked as the locals herded them with menacing looks into makeshift canoes.

'Yes', the suntanned locals replied, as they distributed more cold beer from the outpost's refrigerators to the armed guards. 'But what about the wolves?', they demanded, much to the astonishment of Bjorn and his pals.

'Wolves? What about the wolves?', Bjorn asked. 'My fellow salesmen and I have done nothing to any wolves. In fact,' he added, 'we've been following my infallible system for keeping ravenous wolves at bay.'

At this, the locals almost lynched Bjorn there and then on the spot.

'You haven't kept the ravenous wolves at bay, you idiot,' shouted the locals. 'You've simply taught wolves that if they want food they should chase sledges!'

Now what happened to the good folk of the Tundra is a poignant lesson for the rest of us. They managed to eradicate the source of their trouble – wolves being taught to chase sledges to get fed – by deporting the salesmen who introduced the practice of goodwill-conceding into their territory. Eventually, as the wolves tired of chasing sledges, getting nothing but empty cold-beer cans thrown at them, they went back to getting fed nature's way and left the sledges alone.

Unfortunately, though Bjorn and his pals are long gone from this life, and the Tundra is free of the filthy practice of goodwill-conceding, no such remedial action was taken in the big cities of the world.

Negotiators still go around throwing out concessions to anybody who looks difficult, sometimes out of fear of not getting the negotiations started and sometimes in the hope that the other person will recognize a friend and be nice to them.

The disease is widespread and for those afflicted with it for more than a short time, it can become terminal – they get done so often by other (tougher) negotiators that they are fit only for a job in sales training, where they will teach tomorrow's bright young sales-persons Bjorn's infallible system for dealing with ravenous wolves.

COMMENTS ON SELF-ASSESSMENT TEST 9

1 a) He eats lambs like you for breakfast. His intimidation has obviously worked and he knows what you can do. And he'll be back for more!

  b) If you Sheepishly concede at your first (brief) meeting, what will he achieve at a longer meeting in a month's time?

  c) Much better, but still not your best move. You have out-Foxed his bullying tactics.

  d) Yes. Tell him to call you when he gets back and say that meanwhile you will talk with his technical people about what exactly it is that they need. They may let out that they need your optic repeaters more desperately than he wants you to know and he can worry about that all the way to Australia – and back! Owls know how to side-step intimidators!

2 a) You are bidding blind and he will still tell you your cut is not enough. Donkey fodder?

  b) He will bluff you on the difference if he is a Fox, tell you the truth if he is a Donkey and kid you that it is 'for him to know and you to find out' if he is an Owl. Which makes you a Sheep!

c) A risky call of his bluff if he ain't bluffing and even riskier if he is. A Fox, too clever by half?

d) A Fox too clever by three-quarters!

e) Ask him what he likes about your proposal? A positive Owl's move that could lead to a discussion of any differences between your offer and the others. Price is not necessarily the defining variable in variable bidding decisions.

3 a) Not if it is their first! And not unless you are a Sheep.

b) Yes, but what do you expect them to do next? Bid blind against your dissatisfaction? Lost the courage to tell them of your aspirations? Must be a Sheep.

c) Better. Suggest you get £30,000 on signature and £50,000 on acceptance. If they attack the £50,000 you could be on course for a £70,000 advance. Foxey!

d) You are a Donkey!

SELF-ASSESSMENT TEST 10

1 You want to buy a business that has an asking price of £192,000. Which opening offer would you consider making to the owner:
   (a) £190,000?
   (b) £192,000?
   (c) £182,000?
   (d) £194,000?

2 You have decided to replace your DTP system with a more powerful model and have been quoted a list price of £5,000 by a supplier. What size of discount do you expect?
   (a) 5%
   (b) None
   (c) 15%
   (d) 20%

3 You see a used Jaguar car for sale and have seen similar makes and models advertised recently for £5,000. You make a once-only cash offer to the amount of £2,250. Do you expect the owner to:
   (a) Haggle but take it?
   (b) Haggle but refuse it?
   (c) Refuse to consider it?

4 You are a fax machine sales representative and make an invited sales call at the local home for unmarried mothers. The social worker in charge indicates that she wants to purchase one of your machines which has a list price of £2,200. However, her budget from the Council fixes an absolute ceiling of £1,755. Do you:
   (a) Regretfully decline to do business?
   (b) Use your pricing discretion and make a sale?
   (c) Suggest that she considers a cheaper model?

CHAPTER 10

In praise of Mother Hubbard

or how to make them cut their prices

Jack lives in California. He was a Professor of Economics and became an Attorney-at-Law, thus combining the worst of both professions. As an economist he made fanciful assumptions to derive dismal conclusions, while as a trial lawyer he makes tenuous assumptions to argue fanciful conclusions. As a hobby, he collects old model (circa 1960s) Jaguar cars. Every couple of years he decamps from Berkeley to visit his wife's family in Edinburgh. While in Scotland he tries to buy old Jaguar cars, or bits of them, for export to the United States.

Apparently old Jaguars, or their parts, feature in the lifestyles of some of the affluent folk in California, who, having everything, also want the best, when, that is, they are not after the weirdest.

On his return to Berkeley, Jack lovingly refurbishes his own collection of 'vintage' cars with the worn-out parts from the assorted stock he brings back with him.

Occasionally, out of neighbourly compassion – rather then vulgar avarice – he sells a car (or just some bits of one) from his personal collection to desperate Jaguar fanatics (who 'crowd his space' when news gets round that he's back) providing that his beloved Jaguars go to a 'good home'.

I have been able to watch him negotiating the purchase of a Jaguar, mainly from his habit of requiring me to pull over and stop if he sees a Jaguar of early vintage parked on the road. (This habit of Jack's makes no concessions to where we are heading or what time we are supposed to be there.)

Jack loves every minute of a negotiation. If you're there to listen to him on his way back from a deal, he relives the moves with you (and if you're not, I'm sure he recounts them aloud to himself!). And when he gets back to his wife, his enjoyment is by no means diminished, for he tells her in detail how he got the deal.

I have never seen anybody so wrapped up in his negotiations and so good tempered about them.

If a deal doesn't come off, it joins the list of amusing anecdotes he has on buying used cars. Jack insists that a deal that failed did so almost always because he didn't use his cardinal rule for negotiating:

SHOCK 'EM WITH YOUR OPENING OFFER

Jack swears that this principle has served him well over the years.

How does it work? Simple. When you open make sure it is very low (if you're buying), or very high (if you're selling). Jack doesn't believe in opening with an entry price close to where he might be prepared to settle. He likes to leave himself lots of negotiating room.

If you do choose to open close to your expected settlement price, Jack argues, you might indeed settle at it (in which case you are no better off), or you might have to go above/below it considerably (in which case you could be worse off).

Opening is a risky business and if you open modestly you give the other person false ideas about how much room there is for you to move. If he believes you have a lot of room to move he must follow his best interests and haggle hard, perhaps forcing you to move a lot. As he does not know what your 'best' exit price (for him) is, he need not accept your protestations nor treat them other than as a bluff.

Whichever way you look at it, a deal on terms considerably

worse than your intended terms is not a good way to do business. You might be able to convince yourself that you are 'happy' with the deal 'in the circumstances', and the contribution of such delusions to your self-esteem ought not to be discounted, but if by your opening behaviour you can avoid the need for rationalizing your defeats, it seems sensible for you to do so.

This has all the more relevance when you observe that, by using his shock opening tactics, Jack finds that he settles many of his deals a long way short (on the better side) of his 'best' price.

Why is this so?

Because his shock entry price compels the other person to reconsider his expectations about the current value of his property.

Jack loses some deals because his offer is too far away from the other person's 'basement' price, but Jack claims that on average he will get most of his deals closer to his entry price than to his 'rooftop' best price.

And even if he has to go up close to his top price, he is no worse off than if he had opened close to it in the first place, except that by opening low, Jack increases the distance he will have to travel if the other person's expectations are for a price *above* Jack's (undisclosed) exit price.

OUT OF THE MOUTHS OF CHILDREN

A used-car dealer in Aberdeen had a 1962 Jaguar for sale, priced £1,850. Jack saw it in the lot and went in to have a look. The owner handled the negotiations personally and, after discussion, Jack said he would give him £1,250 for it.

The negotiations stalled but they kept talking about this and that for a while. Clearly, the dealer knew he wasn't going to get £1,850 but didn't know how serious Jack was.

While they were talking another Jaguar car pulled into the lot, driven by the owner's son. Jack eyed the car and they moved over to look at it. It was slightly newer than the other model and it was in much better bodily condition. Obviously it had been looked after.

The son said the car wasn't for sale as it was his. The owner contradicted him by saying that the car belonged to his company and if he wanted to sell it he would. Jack smelled a sale here. He offered £1,000 for it.

The dealer haggled a little and then asked how Jack intended to pay.

'Cash', was the reply.

Jack had enough cash (mainly in US dollars but, since the oil boom, they know about dollars in Aberdeen).

The deal was struck at £1,100 and the son was told to get his things out of the car, which he did with a face as long as a transatlantic cable. Jack drove off quickly.

Afterwards I asked Jack why he had gone in lower for the obviously better car. He said he originally intended to get the other car back into contention but the old man was so determined to show his son who was boss of the business that he accepted a deal close to Jack's low opening offer. 'This was a slight pity as the other car had genuine leather seats in it which are worth a small fortune back home.' However, the car he had bought was worth at least double what he paid for it in Scotland, let alone its value in the States.

In other words, getting a high price out of Jack is hard work. Not surprisingly, he values what the other guy has to work hard for, far more than something that comes easy – *even if he settles at a lower price than he expected.*

The art of making somebody happy by disappointing him with a price lower than he was originally looking for is not a mystery: it lies in your ability to make him negotiate every cent of the way.

Negotiators are always unhappy if you agree too easily with their entry prices, so make them happy by haggling!

Why does the shock opening tactic work for Jack?

First, consider the position at the start of a negotiation. When you are considering negotiating for something – be it cash, a Jaguar car, a million tons of Albanian cement, a Norwegian container ship, or a straw hat in a Mexican tourist shop – you have in mind a target price, i.e. what you expect to pay for whatever you are buying, or get for whatever you are selling, assuming that you know something about your business. Call this your *expectation*.

How expectations form in your mind *before* the negotiation is less relevant for this discussion than the fact that they change during the negotiation.

If you arrive at the negotiation with predetermined views as to the appropriate settlement, it does not follow that you will stick to them irrespective of events; they may be changed, for instance, by what you come to believe about your prospects of achieving your expectations once the negotiation is under way.

Alternatively, if your views as to what is attainable are formed during the negotiation (you having no predetermined views before you find out what is in the other person's mind), these views can also be reshaped by subsequent events in the negotiation, or, more correctly, can be changed by your interpretations of those events.

In these cases, you have the choice of reducing your expectations or seeking a deal elsewhere. It could also be the case that you have the choice of sticking to your expectations or revising them upwards if the negotiations reveal encouraging aspects of their intentions or perceptions.

Expectations in negotiation are entirely *subjective*. They do not have a life of their own independent of how you (and the other person) read the situation once you are in contact with each other.

It is Jack's belief that the most decisive moment in the negotiation to influence expectations is at the opening contact, when neither of you is too sure of what can be achieved. Hence, his belief that it pays to go in hard with a tough opening stance. This move has the immediate effect of undermining the original confidence of the other guy in any high expectations he has formed, or, if he has not yet formed his views, it severely limits the price he can realistically hope for from Jack.

In Jack's view, the greater the shock of the entry price the more effective the tactic.

If you are buying, go in low – really low – *if your opening is credible in some way*, and you will undermine even the toughest negotiator's confidence in his starting position. The same is true for going in high – really high – if you are selling.

Now neither I nor Jack claim that this move will *automatically* assure you of a successful deal. Audacity is essential but it is not enough. The main target of the shocking opening move is the other guy's beliefs about his position – you are trying to structure his expectations of the likely outcome of the negotiation.

To the extent that you reduce his expectations – even by a little amount – it has to be good for you as a negotiator. If he arrives thinking he is going to buy your business for £11 million and you open with a demand for £22 million, he is bound to have some problems with your opening: do you really mean what you say, is *your* price realistic, is *his* price realistic, has *he* done his sums correctly, are *you* in as weak a bargaining position as *his* accountants reported, and so on?

He may not roll over and play dead but it will certainly stop him in his tracks while he thinks it over.

You walk into a store to get a discount of 15 per cent and

the clerk tells you that the company only makes seven per cent gross.

What do you do?

If you even half believe him you know you have no chance of getting 15 per cent. So either you lower your expectation or try another store.

You decide to get your company products advertised on television and allocate a budget of £70,000 to the project. At your first meeting with the producer he tells you it costs £20,000 a minute to shoot 20 minutes of film which will be cut down to a 40-second commercial. Anything cheaper would get you a wooden Oscar.

What do you do?

Either you increase your budget or you forget about TV.

You pitch for a 20 per cent share of the gross income and your partners show that they only make ten per cent and then only if they sell 1,000 sets a month.

What do you do?

A SHOCKING TENDER

A city council called for tenders to demolish an old abattoir and clear the site. Several demolition firms submitted tenders prices ranging from £10,000 to £25,000. One company sent in a £1 tender. This was accepted (after checking it was not an unfortunate typing error).

Why did they only want £1 to do such a large job?

Because their survey showed them that there were about 500 tons of iron girders and iron piping in the building plus a hundred tons of other metals, with a scrap value in excess of £70,000.

Give up dreams of a Hollywood lifestyle or get new partners?

You ask a lady to accompany you to a convention in Acapulco and she tells you she might consider a dinner date in a month's time.

What do you do? Lower your sights or try dating her sister?

These cameos illustrate the impact that a shocking opening can have on the negotiators. Their sights must be lowered in the negotiation whatever else they do (such as try their luck elsewhere).

Moving someone from an opening that is a long way from your original expectations is like climbing the Eiger in the buff. If you aim for the stars and the other person intends to start with the trees, you have a long way to go to get him airborne.

It is a fact of negotiating life that the majority of us will not persist with what we come to *believe* are unrealistic demands. We will sooner back off than persist.

Generalizing from Jack's insight into negotiating behaviour, we can see that the best opening is the *toughest* opening. All else weakens your influence on the eventual outcome. The tough opening has, however, to be *credible* in some way. The shock opening tactic is of little use (in the sense of getting a good deal) if you believe that *any* crazy price will do. There is no point trying to buy the Empire State Building with an opening bid of $200 – though if you wait long enough the City might one day pay you to demolish it.

The difference between a shock opening and a silly one is not easy to define because the boundary between a negotiating move that pays off and one that doesn't is not always obvious. The only important difference between one and the other is that the shock opening is *credible* and the silly one is not.

A SHOCKING TYPING ERROR

A union official submitted a written pay claim for his distillery members and a week later met the management to negotiate the new contract.

He was surprised to be given details of company sales and costs. He also listened to a long presentation from the management on the financial prospects of the next year.

Perplexed by this unusual behaviour, the official scanned the papers across the table. On top of them he could see his written claim, and he read it upside down.

He spotted the cause of the problem. His secretary had typed the figures incorrectly: instead of a claim for a 12 per cent wage rise (with an expectation of settling at about seven per cent) she had typed 21 per cent. No wonder the company was making such an extraordinary fuss!

He said nothing and waited to hear what they would offer after their heart-rending presentation of how poor the company was at present. They opened with an offer of 12 per cent and eventually they settled at 15 per cent: eight per cent more than he expected to settle at before the meeting. This taught him about the modesty of his previous claims.

If you can defend credibly your opening you can make what, in some circumstances, would plainly be a silly opening into a winning one. Credible reasons for an opening position give it a lot of mileage. And remember the reasons you give for your opening only have to be credible to the person listening, not a panel of neutral judges.

Jack, for instance, has one disadvantage when he opens his mouth to negotiate in Scotland – he sounds just like what he is: an American, and, as every canny Scot knows, Americans abroad (unless they are in the Navy) have more money than sense.

Jack would be stretching credulity if he was to plead poverty as a reason for his low offer. So naturally he doesn't bother. However, he does have a credible line: he has to ship the vehicle all the way to California and this, he tells the sellers, 'doubles' his costs.

He always adds that his deal is a cash deal, the mention of which is often a strong incentive to settle where a used-car negotiation is concerned. Also, the fact that Jack is taking the car to California – thus removing him from the vicinity where the seller lives and therefore from comebacks if the car is not all it is cracked up to be by the seller's pitch – does not escape the seller.

These circumstances make Jack's negotiating position fairly strong.

Of course, the real issue that ought to concern the sellers is not what the car is worth to them in Scotland, or what it costs Jack to ship it home, but what the car is worth to Jack *in* California when he gets it there. By all accounts, the value of Jaguars in Berkeley exceeds by a long way the price Jack pays for them in Scotland.

In general, if your shocking or tough opening is credible it has a good chance of forming the basis of the negotiation, so open with the toughest credible opening you can think of.

One way to gain confidence in using the tough opening is to use the Mother Hubbard (of the 'cupboard is bare' fame) line. In this tactic you must convince the seller of two interconnected points:

1 That you genuinely want to buy the seller's product.
2 That you do not have the resources to reach the seller's opening price.

In effect you tell the seller that the cupboard is bare.

111

How close you pitch Mother Hubbard to the seller's opening price is a matter of judgment. Perhaps it will be best if you try it out first on prices close to theirs and gradually widen the gap in subsequent negotiations as you get more confident in its use.

You must decide just how bare you are going to make your cupboard and which stance is credible in the circumstances.

The seller is bound to ask you (if he has bitten the bait): 'How much can you afford to pay?' At this point you must be wary of being sidetracked into a 'deposit with a loan' deal or some such way of undermining your play (including the 'running two budgets together' move). You must establish that the *total* amount you have available for the purchase is *all* that will ever be available.

Let me illustrate the use of the Mother Hubbard by a barrister friend, Nelson, in London. We were having lunch in the Groucho Club in Dean Street, Soho when he asked my advice about a computer that his partners had charged him with purchasing. At the time I was working as a sales consultant to a computer company and was familiar with the market.

My friend's problem was that he knew which machine he wanted but was £2,400 short of the total price the computer sales negotiator had quoted him. There was also the important question of doing well in this negotiation as he had only just joined the practice at Lincoln's Inn as a partner and as their first black barrister he wanted to do well.

I suggested that he raise more cash but he explained he could not do this as he was already running two office-equipment budgets together by making the purchase at the end of one financial year and the beginning of the other.

So I suggested he use the Mother Hubbard, and was 'persuaded' to explain it in detail for the price of the lunch and a bottle of Chianti Classico. After lunch, Nelson returned to his office to meet with the computer negotiator (incidently, they were rivals of my client so I was delighted to put them under the squeeze).

Being imaginative (and slightly inebriated, for the Chianti was followed by several sambuccos) he contrived a very convincing 'script' and used it at the negotiation.

Nelson started (correctly) by making the computer seller go over the machine's virtues once again and he also booked a demonstration of the machine for his partners in the office later that week.

The seller really got to work on what he now considered to be a 'prospect' (sales jargon for someone likely to buy) and (correctly) he kept plugging away at the deal. However, he also disclosed (incorrectly) that he was anxious to get the machine into a legal practice as a basis for making sales to other partnerships among the Inns.

Nelson did not pretend to have the gift of those sales at his disposal but he hinted vaguely (correctly) that if the machine was as good as it was claimed, it was bound to have some effect on sales in the profession.

A week later, after the office demonstration, the Mother Hubbard was sprung.

The seller was told that the partners had approved the purchase of *a* computer in principle, but they had imposed a budget ceiling on the acquisition of £11,500.

'Not a penny more to be spent,' Nelson reported, and to underline this point he read the decision out from the minutes of the weekly partnership meeting. He placed the minutes across the desk in full view of the seller.

This was a correct (almost inspired) move on Nelson's part. Why?

Because, since Moses brought the tablets down from the mountain, the written word has an authority over the mere spoken word. People appear to accept almost anything as true if it is written rather than spoken, which is why sellers have their prices printed in lists to give them an altogether undeserved authority!

Regretfully, Nelson told the seller that as his machine was

113

priced at £11,500, to which was added a £500 training charge and an annual maintenance fee of £1,900 giving a gross price of £13,900, the partners had instructed him to look elsewhere for a more realistically-priced machine.

He regretted this move as he thought the machine on offer would meet their needs and he pointed out that the partners were less keen on modernizing than he was, but wanted to see some more demonstrations of other machines in the coming week.

The seller was visibly put out by this news (though it was a mistake to display his emotions) and, predictably, he tried several lines of attack on the ceiling price of £11,500. He offered (incorrectly) several concessions in the form of additional software free of charge, a reduced training package and an extended payment period.

His mistake was that none of these tackled the central problem of the £11,500 budget ceiling, though Nelson (correctly) made a note of the concessions for later use.

But on the gross price of £11,500 Nelson would not budge. As his shocking opening was credible – the written minutes 'proved' it – his regret was genuine. He accepted that searching for a cheaper machine was a 'drag' but he would have to do this as the price of £13,900 was way above his budget.

The seller was boxed in and he knew that if he wanted to make this sale he would have to come down in price. But £2,400 was some drop and he needed a good reason for arranging anything like that. As he didn't have a good reason to hand he agreed to get back to Nelson after he had 'consulted his head office'.

It would have been better for him to have said he would get back 'after he had thought it over' rather than disclose his lack of authority in the negotiation. Also, it was a risky decision to leave his 'prospect' in case the competition came in while he was away and introduced Nelson to a 'cheaper' machine (in

114

computers there is always a cheaper machine available or on its way).

'AT THAT PRICE I'D RATHER SCRAP IT'

Getting mechanical things repaired can cost a small fortune. This is especially true of cars, boat engines and light aircraft.

Harry Smith had engine trouble with his small weekend boat. He took it to the repair yard and asked them to diagnose the trouble. A week later the yard rang Harry and told him that he needed a new engine as the shaft had gone on his old one and it would not last another 20 hours. A new engine would cost him £900, and naturally the yard was willing to fit one for another £150.

There was no way that Harry was prepared to fork out £1,050 for a new engine on a boat he used only occasionally.

He tried a version of the Mother Hubbard.

He told the yard that he had decided to sell the boat for 'whatever it would bring' (probably about £800 in its current condition) and that he would 'collect it next Tuesday'.

On Monday, Harry turned up at the yard to collect his boat, implying that he had found a customer. He told the manager that with the money he got from selling the boat he would buy a dinghy. The money he saved by not buying an engine would go towards his holidays.

The manager was not keen to see a lost engine sale but could also see that Harry was determined to sell his boat. He asked Harry how much he was able to pay to replace his engine. Harry (springing the Mother Hubbard) told him that he was only prepared to stay with power boating if it cost him no more than £350, but that he was quite happy to go back to dinghy sailing as engines 'cost money to fit, to maintain and to fuel'.

The manager went for the £350 ceiling.

If Harry was interested, he could have a reconditioned engine from stock for £400 – 'a customer had left it three years ago and had not been heard of since' – plus £85 for fitting, if he could take the old engine off his hands for spare parts.

Harry agreed (eventually) after getting a warranty on the 'new' engine and a free fitting, all for £390.

Three days later, Nelson received a call saying that the computer company would make a 'special offer' of a machine at £10,500.

And there was more. The seller announced that his company would 'show their faith in their computer by postponing for 12 months the annual maintenance fee of £1,900'.

This 'never to be repeated' offer gave a gross purchase price of £11,000 'which is £500 inside your budget' (confirming the credibility of Nelson's Mother Hubbard).

The offer was conditional on the partners being willing to allow the computer company to quote them as clients to other partnerships but 'for obvious reasons' the special price they had been given was to remain 'confidential'.

I congratulated Nelson on his success and remarked that his deal might have been improved if he had tried to press them on the training charge of £500 – a wholly ludicrous proposition, in my view, that requires the customer to pay a computer firm for training its people how to use their machines. It is regarded as a 'give away' by many computer negotiators but you have to press them.

However, Nelson's first attempt at the Mother Hubbard saved

his partnership £2,400 – less the cost of lunch, Chianti and sambucco at the Groucho Club!

Some years later, I met Neville, the computer salesman who was on the receiving end of Nelson's Mother Hubbard. He introduced himself during a break at an *Everything is Negotiable Workout* I was conducting for negotiators at Heathrow airport's Sheraton Skyline Hotel.

He remembered Nelson, of course, and spoke with genuine affection of him as that 'six-foot-six good-looking fast-talking b****', who was his 'first real customer'. He was most grateful for what Nelson had taught him, as, at the time, he was relatively new to selling computers.

'Sure,' he insisted, 'I was taken in by his spiel and serve me right too, but you have to understand that I was so determined to get that sale that I would have gone down further in price if necessary.' (Proving that the Mother Hubbard is worth a try if you are on a tight budget and want to impress your boss.)

Neville explained that he had fallen out with his then boss, who thought selling was about randomly chasing people who happened to reply to direct mail adds. Neville had different ideas, he told me.

He decided to focus all of his sales efforts on a single business sector and had chosen legal firms by noticing that there was an awful lot of them in *Yellow Pages* and that scores of them were located around London's Chancery Lane within easy walking distance of each other. Once you understand the dynamics of a specific sector, Neville said, your first sale leads onto others, 'like falling off a log' (he didn't explain his simile).

He had chosen the Chambers where Nelson worked as his first target because they were next door to where he had been interviewed as a defence witness in a murder trial (he didn't go into details!).

He had used Nelson as a reference point for other legal firms. He was sacked by his boss ('a w****r with no patience,' was

117

how Neville crudely described him) soon after in a dispute about early results.

This caused Neville to take 'his' focused selling technique (standard sales practice in serious selling organisations but Neville was clearly chuffed with what he had in fact only 'rediscovered') to another and bigger computer company, where he 'was making over £120,000 a year in sales commissions, thank you very much'.

So you see – your drive to better your own negotiating position can work wonders for those with whom you deal (assuming they are not complete Donkeys).

Literally, you can change somebody's life by teaching them how to do their own business better and do yourself a favour too!

COMMENTS ON SELF-ASSESSMENT TEST 10

1 a) This is so close to her asking price that she must conclude she has a chance of getting an unusually timid Fox closer to £192,000. Are you a Sheep in a Fox's clothing?
  b) You are not trying very hard are you? Obviously you are a confirmed, if not incorrigible, Sheep.
  c) A classic Fox's opening indeed (Jack would be proud of you!). You risk not getting the business but if you do you're going to getter it cheaper than the Sheep.
  d) You have been hustled or have more money than sense and know something about the business that I don't. You must have got this information from another Donkey.

2 a) A modest expectation for a Fox.
  b) Oh dear! Definitely a Sheep.
  c) Good. Definitely a Fox.
  d) Jack is delirious with you! Could you be an Owl?

3 a) You're an optimistic Fox.

b) You're a pessmistic Fox.
c) You're a brave Sheep for having a go (were you put up to this uncharacteristic behaviour by a friendly Fox?) but you are a congenitally pessmistic Sheep for having no faith in the Fox.

4 a) A Donkey's close-out move. Try (c) first.
b) She's done the Mother Hubbard on a Sheep (i.e. you!).
c) Correct. What every Fox would try.

SELF-ASSESSMENT TEST 11

1 You want to sell your car privately to finance a new-car purchase. You think it is worth £5,500 and you know of its (to you) minor defects. Do you advertise it:
   (a) At £5,500 ONO?
   (b) £5,700?
   (c) At £6,000 ONO?
   (d) Without a price?
   (e) At £5,500?

2 You are quoting for the installation of a new kitchen in a house. Do you:
   (a) Give a detailed cost breakdown of every item in the quotation?
   (b) Give a rough breakdown of the costing?
   (c) Avoid giving a cost breakdown, only the total figure?

3 You have a old but serviceable trailer that doesn't fit your new car and decide to sell it via a small add in the local free-sheet. You think it is worth £500, given its good condition and the likely market with car owners who want a reliable trailer. What do you say about price in your advertisement?
   (a) £510?
   (b) £525?
   (c) £500 ONO?
   (d) Make me an offer?
   (e) First offer of £500 secures?
   (f) Nothing?

CHAPTER 11

Why ONO is a NO NO

or how not to get a better price

The used-household-goods market is small beer compared to the world of multinational business but it has some potent lessons for negotiation. This chapter is about some of them.

In Britain, kids sell old toys and conkers to each other (in America, I understand, they sell flick knives and horror comics) and all children, everywhere, soon learn to trade with their pals. Their parents are no different. Alongside the official markets of everyday business and commerce, there is a flourishing, almost underground, market for household goods.

In poor countries too, the ordinary people engage in trade, whatever the official laws say to the contrary. Walk down any main street in a poor country and somebody is bound furtively to offer to buy something from you – even your clothes!

However, I don't want to give the impression that private deals are confined to those living in poor countries. In Washington DC, I was once caught off balance in Kramer's bookstore by the clerk offering to buy the red striped shirt I was wearing for $20 cash. I admired his taste almost as much as I regretted his timing, as I was on my way to lunch at the International Monetary Fund two blocks along, and the thought of appearing there shirtless ruined the deal.

In fact, everybody at some time or another has sold something – a used car, some furniture, a box of old books or such like.

The deal could have been made with a friend, a neighbour, a member of the family, or a complete stranger. They hear of our intentions of selling by word of mouth or from an advertisement of some kind.

For example, many people in Britain sell their cars by placing a notice in a window with a contact telephone number. Often they include the price they are looking for:

For Sale
This Car
£5,200

As often, almost by the compulsion of convention, they also include the message:

ONO

meaning 'or nearest offer'.

Why do they add ONO after their price?

Answers vary.

Some say it stops a potential customer being put off by the price: if they believe the price is negotiable they are more likely to ask to see the car, etc. Others say they do it because they do not want to lose the chance of a sale even if they must drop their price a little. Still others do it because they have seen other people's ads use ONO in them and they presume that it is part of the 'rules' for used goods selling.

In my view writing ONO is a mistake.

In fact, I believe that ONO is a 'NO NO'.

Why?

Ask yourself what a buyer thinks when he sees ONO? It tells him that you are willing to accept *less* than £5,200 *before even hearing what he has got to say.*

This weakens your position. Instead of the buyer thinking he has to compete against others for the right to buy at a price *above* £5,200, he starts off knowing that the seller is worried about the possibility that he will not get a sale.

And who does that help?

The potential buyer of course!

It is generally true that in writing ONO you almost always weaken your bargaining position by disclosing your keenness to sell. You open the negotiations at an implied price below your opening £5,200, without having found out anything about the extent of the buyer's keenness to buy.

IS IT NEGOTIABLE?

A consultant had just completed a ten-minute presentation on how he thought he could solve the client's distribution problems, for a fee of £35,000.

The company president leaned over the table and asked: 'Is that fee negotiable?'

The consultant knew that if he answered 'yes' he would be pushed downwards on the fee and if he answered 'no' he might box himself into a corner on a price objection.

He thought for a second and replied: 'I am always prepared to listen to any constructive suggestions that will improve the acceptability of my proposals.'

The client noted his response and said nothing.

A week later he received the go-ahead to commence the project and nothing more was said about his fee.

That way you start off with a handicap – like opening at love-40 in tennis. For all you know, the buyer, because of a family commitment, may desperately need to purchase a car that very day – yours may be the fifth car she has looked at – and she has run out of time. This could make £5,200, or even more, for it a bargain for her (and for you!).

In negotiating you don't know what is in the other person's

mind or the extent of the pressures upon her – and you certainly don't know anything about this before you meet her. Once you are in contact with her you *might* get a clearer picture of her real position by what she says, but by using ONO, you forego that opportunity to find out her real position. Meanwhile, she knows something about your position as soon as she reads your sale notice, i.e. before she has met you. There is an asymmetry in bargaining information – in her favour!

If she knows something about your attitude to the asking price, namely, that you have so little confidence in it that you are willing to accept less before the negotiating begins, and you do not know anything about her attitude, namely, whether she thinks £5,200 a good or a lousy price, it follows that to the extent that bargaining strength may be determined by relative keenness to trade, the eventual price must be more to the buyer's advantage than to yours.

I believe that the use of ONO-type messages is a mistake on the seller's part, *and* that a failure to take advantage of them on the buyer's part is a mistake of equal seriousness. Experience shows that buyers often ignore the ONO invitation to make a 'near offer' and actually pay the asking price! In other words, buyers do not always get the message implied by ONO, and they let the seller off the hook he put himself on in the first place. Unfortunately, we cannot rely on our errors always being rectified by the errors of others, useful as they are as an excuse for our behaviour!

Why buyers fail to take advantage of the seller's ONO-type invitation could be a source of employment for an out-of-work sociologist or student of abnormal behaviour; it ought not to be the kind of mistake you make in future.

If you see something for sale with an ONO price tag, you must assume immediately that the *maximum* price he is expecting is certainly *less* than the asking ONO price. And you also know that his rock-bottom price will be lower still because the *minimum* price he will accept will be *lower* than his maximum expectation. You don't know what he will take until you try him out with some low (and I mean *low*) opening offers. Follow Jack's rule!

You might be the fifth potential buyer he has seen and he may be desperate not to lose you like he lost the others. Sooner or later, time runs out in every deal, and time might have run out for him.

The fact that he has used an ONO price indicates an amateur approach to selling, and you need not be shy about taking advantage of this. Indeed, you do him and the wider community a great service by teaching him how to conduct his business. The extra discount on the price in your reward and the gratuitous experience is his.

Could there be a fairer way of educating the ONO seller?

If you ask people (as I do at the Negotiate Workshops) why they include ONO in their advertisements (not just for cars) they often rationalize it by claiming that their prime aim is to sell the used item because:

I needed the space and it was in the way.
I needed the money for a trade-in deal.
I just wanted rid of it and any price was a bonus.

In other words they felt under pressure of some kind to make the sale – the money was a secondary consideration as long as it was 'around the asking price'. But remember, being under pressure to make a deal is not unique to you. Nor should you assume that the other person is not under even greater pressure. To do so is to make concessions before the negotiations begin, and, in making opening concessions without receiving anything in return, you are in danger of sliding down the slippery slope to surrender.

Self-induced delusions that the other person has all the power (commonly heard from trade union negotiators about the management, and from the management about the union, and from buyers about sellers and *vice versa*) can be a costly mistake.

126

The price you set for your surplus household items is often purely arbitrary – the price you would *like* to get, rather than the price you know for certain it will fetch.

Fortunately, you will soon learn if the market thinks your price is totally unrealistic. The notion that the world will beat a path to your door to negotiate a deal for a pile of old junk dies rapidly with every outbreak of seller's naivety in the suburbs.

It is not altogether different in business, despite treatises written by economists to show that price setting is a science rather than a hunch.

You are unlikely to know what the market value of used personal property is at any one moment, and, anyway, you are likely to be prejudiced about its value.

You might think the old table is worth a small fortune just because your granny got it as a wedding present – the market may see it as more fit for firewood – but good luck to you – at least you are not under-selling yourself.

I once raced across Edinburgh to see what was described in the advertisement as an 'antique desk', priced at £70. (At that price I should have known better.)

The desk in question was Clerical (i.e. the very bottom grade Civil Service, circa 1950). It had been bought by its redundant owner out of his own office when the Government had a clearance sale. For some reason he thought it antique because he had sat at it for 20 years.

You know what you paid for your household property, perhaps but you cannot know what other people are prepared to pay for it now until you attempt to sell it.

Not knowing what the price should be, you are tempted to use an ONO price tag as an encouragement to potential buyers to come and look at the item. But it is also an invitation to them to correct your assessment of what it is worth and, having taken the trouble to oblige you on the former, they are more than likely to help you with the latter.

Naturally, getting someone to your front door to look at your

127

car, or old washing machine, or box of books, is an essential first step to selling them. If nobody calls to see what you are selling, then certainly nobody is going to buy them. Hence, the temptation to set a price low enough to attract customers but high enough to make it worthwhile for your trouble.

Choosing the 'right' price is a difficult task – how 'high' is high and how 'low' is low? But having set a price, why choose to qualify it with ONO? By doing so, you undermine your decision on the price.

You know that anybody taking the trouble to see your goods is half way to buying them – searching around the second-hand market for a sofa can be a time-consuming business.

After a while the buyer is inclined to lower his sights if the price for something, not quite what he is looking for, appears to look like a 'bargain'.

You can define a 'bargain' any way you want to. You can compare the price for the used machine with its new list price; you can compare it with what you expected to pay, or with the price a friend paid the week before. The range is limitless – which is why we can rationalize our 'bargains' at least to our own satisfaction.

The buyer's strength is that he knows that the cost of newspaper advertising for low-priced household items can be a relatively high proportion of the selling price, particularly if the advertisements have to be repeated several times before a sale is made.

You must consider the consequences of a prospective customer hesitating over buying your car. This automatically produces prospects of additional costs (such as advertising *and* waiting) to attract alternative buyers.

If you are tempted to avoid these costs, you can only do so by being prepared to reduce the asking price from £5,200 to something near it. Hence, the mistaken reason for ONO: you want to make it clear that a 'near offer' will be accepted.

My point is that you ought to bear in mind that the buyer

also faces search costs and that she can only avoid these if she settles with you on your offer. The pressure on her to settle is just as relentless as the pressure on you, but she has no way of knowing what pressure you are under unless you tell her or indicate it to her in some way, e.g. appearing very anxious to close the deal.

THERE'S A RIGHT TIME AND A WRONG TIME

Graham is a farmer and he knows about the importance of the seasons. He also knows that there is a right and a wrong time to buy or sell almost anything.

He argues that most people forget the elementary rule of business: if you want to sell, avoid a buyer's market (and *vice versa*).

How do you avoid a market when the advantage is with the other person? For one thing, Graham argues, you can deliberately choose not to enter a negotiation when a moment's thought should warn you off.

He gives the following advice for timing negotiations:

The best time to buy a boat (Graham has three) is at the end of the season when the owner faces harbour fees for the winter if he doesn't sell; conversely, the best time to sell is at the start of the season when the buyer is itching to sail his new boat.

The best time to buy a house (Graham has three) is when the owner has to sell it irrespective of the season, hence enter the market in the winter if you're buying, avoid it if you are selling.

The best time to get cash, use of the car, and a late night at a party is when father is about to watch the big match on TV or mother is talking avidly to a girl friend.

The worst time to negotiate about anything is when you are in a hurry, you're tired, you've just been fighting, you're sexually aroused, you've something important on your mind, you're bored stiff, or you want to be somewhere else.

The best time to buy Christmas presents is right after Christmas in the New Year sales. Buy your Christmas cards in the Spring, Mother's Day cards near Father's Day, winter coats in the summer, summer clothes in the winter (especially if it is snowing), vegetables near closing time, food in the market or the cash-and-carry, booze at the brewery, travel at off-peak times, rent hotel rooms at the weekend, and property during a war.

If a reduction in your asking price is necessary to clinch the deal it is up to you to decide how far to move downwards, if at all (but make sure that any such moves are small and infrequent).

But what is not necessary at all is for you to signal at the *start* that the price is negotiable. If she wants to haggle, she will. You are no worse off by leaving that opening move to her. Indeed, you are better off because if you leave it to her to start haggling with you, she has to overcome any inhibitions she has about haggling in order to do so.

And lots of people find it very difficult to open up a haggle. They cannot bring themselves to do so without a great deal of stress and effort. They are inclined either to accept the deal as it stands or back off. If they accept the deal because of their shyness about haggling then you are home free.

If they need encouragement to negotiate you might have to provide that *but only in the negotiation*.

Ask questions, such as what they like about the item, is it what they were looking for, in what way does it suit their needs, etc.? The answer will reveal their inhibitions about price. If you

130

can coax out of them an offer you can decide how you want to handle it – offer them a 'deal' or go to deadlock.

This is by far a much stronger line to follow than ONO.

COMMENTS ON SELF-ASSESSMENT TEST 11

1 a) ONO is a NO NO! You are telling the buyer that your price of £5,500 will be reduced and that you are a Donkey.

   b) A stronger Fox-like move as it gives you room to come down if you need to and it is in touch with your target price.

   c) Out of touch with your target and weakened by ONO. Another example of a Fox being a trifle too clever.

   d) Might be OK if a Sheep turns up. More likely to be a Fox looking for a 'bargain', leaving you as Sheep vulnerable. ('You want *how much* for a car with all these defects?')

   e) Not so good – whatever you get will be below what you think the car is worth. Unless she is a Donkey too, she will assume that you are looking for less than £5,500 and as a Donkey you will have to accommodate her assumption.

2 a) Never *offer*, like a Sheep, to give detailed breakdowns (always ask for them!) as they encourage buyers to squeeze your prices.

   b) Ditto – do not even *offer* rough ones.

   c) Correct. A total figure helps Foxes to repackage. Wait until they ask for a breakdown before supplying one.

3 a) You can expect the buyer to offer less than your asking price, so you could get your target if they are not too ambitious and they move no further than £10. A timid Fox?

   b) Better because £25 is a bigger margin than only £10. A bolder Fox.

c) No. This only encourages her to pay less than £500 even without her seeing the trailer and realising what a Donkey you are!

d) Could be a Sheep's hostage to fortune if he opens at £450, forcing you to do all the work to get the price up into the region of £500 plus.

e) Better than (c) but not much. Suppose she offers £499: will you take it? If yes, how far down will your exit price be? You are a Sheep, not a very clever Fox.

f) If anybody turns up I bet you would be too euphoric to mention your £500 price. You're not even a clever Sheep.

SELF-ASSESSMENT TEST 12

1 You are the key accounts negotiator for a soft-drinks firm and have just been told by the chief buyer of the country's largest hypermarket chain that you must cut your prices by a penny a case or they will drop your brand. They sell a million dozen cans of your Cola Pop a year. Do you:

(a) Smile and say 'no'?

(b) Agree?

(c) Suggest a compromise?

2 Your next negotiation is with the rival hypermarket chain whose chief buyer expresses his delight at seeing you so fortuitously as your main rival has stopped deliveries because of a strike. He asks if you can fill the gap with an emergency order of 50,000 dozen cans of Cola Pop, delivery immediate. Do you:

(a) Smile and say 'yes'?

(b) Say yes, but tell him there will be a 5 per cent charge because of the additional costs of emergency delivery?

(c) Smile and say it isn't possible at such short notice?

(d) Tell him it's his 'lucky day' because not only can you deliver what he needs but you can also give him the bulk purchase discount that is being offered this month?

3 You have been working only three weeks in a new job as a shipping agent in Baltimore and had planned to get married on Friday 18 August (which you did not disclose at the job interview). Your 'intended' has demanded a proper honeymoon vacation of at least a week in Miami. It's now 16 August and you ask your boss for leave both for the wedding day and for the honeymoon. She is visibly put out by the request and asks stiffly how long you were 'thinking of being absent'. Do you say:

(a) The wedding day only?

(b) Two weeks?

(c) Three days?

CHAPTER 12

The Law of the Yukon

or how to toughen your resolve

Toughness in negotiating, in my view, does not attract enough serious attention from practitioners. As with the great classics of literature, which are more often quoted than read and of which most people only know their film versions, toughness in negotiating is more often spoken of than practised. It acquires its misleading public image from film stereotypes of guys and gals acting screenwriters' versions of being tough.

This chapter makes the case for toughness in your resolve and not the so-called toughness in negotiating which is often just intimidatory bad manners. I shall return to phoney toughness and how to deal with it later.

Toughness is not a simple subject.

Toughness, in the common parlance, is seen as an attribute of a negotiator's personality. Allegedly it is something you either have or you haven't got. As one 'tough' sales trainer in Australia put it to me: 'You can't make eagles out of ducks!'

Consider Joe, a key account manager for a firm of soft-drink manufacturers. He negotiates with major food store chains and has the authority to close his deals on whatever he judges to be the 'best price'.

He sells cans of fizzy drink in quantities of up to a million dozen at a time. His company is in heavy competition with others and he is under constant pressure from the buyers he deals with to shave a penny off here and penny off there. He is constantly told that his rivals are making these concessions and that if he doesn't match them his products will disappear from prime shelf positions.

Watching him negotiate under these conditions is an education in professionalism. He never betrays the slightest reaction to bad news of any kind, or to threats, or to shock-horror tales about what his clients have done or might do about his product lines.

He speaks very softly and manages to combine a nodding head at what he hears from the buyer with a smile as he says a clear 'no' to the latest outrageous proposal.

Obviously, for the buyers their tactics of squeezing until the pips squeak must work against the majority of sellers they see.

They don't hold their jobs at the top of the buying tree by failing to get it right more often than they get it wrong. It's just that with Joe they get it wrong when they try the squeeze on him.

Joe knows that once he starts competing with his rivals to shave his prices he will be as ordinary as they are, and, perhaps more seriously, he and they will start a slide downwards to the extinction of some of them.

Fortunately, Joe's company believes in sustaining a high-profile advertising presence in the media and is not dependent on the goodwill of particular food-store buyers. In this way it maintains public demand for its products and where there is demand there has to be supply. If one chain does not stock these goods others will – moreover, the local store managers don't like losing sales of popular products that Head Office refuses to stock to their rivals who are not so inhibited, and they are easily encouraged to put pressure on Head Office to ensure them of supplies.

Joe does not act as if he is at the mercy of the buyers. He may be alone in the buyer's office for a negotiation but he does not forget that he represents a large operation and that his products have a loyal support among the customers in the buyer's stores.

When buyers try to hussle him into thinking that pennies off his price are absolutely critical (after all that's their job isn't it?) he does not forget that the customer who buys a can of fizzy pop for thirsty kids to drink is not aiming to save a fraction of a penny per can (assuming the store passes on the discount instead of banking it as a profit, which is more likely in the retail grocery business). The truth is that kids like his company's fizzy drink enough to badger their parents into buying it.

While Joe's perception of the realities of why customers purchase his company's fizzy drink gives him enough confidence not to crumble at the bark of aggressive buyers, it is in no way sufficient to permit him to dictate terms. However, it is just enough not to lead him into the negotiations entirely naked.

Hence, Joe adopts an assertive position on his prices, and his concessions are miserly. If a buyer wants a penny off a case he is going to have to give Joe something in return to get it. Joe has established his style over the years and most of his buyers know he doesn't frighten easily – not that this stops them trying every now and again.

What do you do when the buyer hits you with 'you'll have to do better than that!'?

Do you cave in or do you refuse to panic?

The answer is to some extent a matter of personal concern to you alone – or it may depend your career progress, your material affluence and, indeed, your personal happiness. It is also of interest to your company because a lot of other people in the organization – whose welfare is every bit as important to them as your welfare is to you – depend on the negotiating abilities of you people in the front seats.

No matter what else those back at the office think of you as a person, you can bet your last pay cheque that they prefer you to get big orders for the company's products rather than small ones and they also prefer you to be unintimidated by aggressive buyers.

Every penny off the case you give away too easily is money taken away from their next pay increase – perhaps, even, from what is available to keep them on the payroll. Nobody profits from a company that makes losses and every step you take down in price is a step nearer to bankruptcy.

It is no comfort to argue that a penny cut by you is trivial. Despatch may concede a penny on vehicle repairs, the works may concede a penny, or more, on the wages, accounts a penny on bad debts, and administration a penny on carbon paper. And so it goes on.

Nobody thinks their behaviour counts because on its own it doesn't. But taken together, this habit of cutting and running could put your company out of business.

Of course, if the negotiators were dividable into only two camps – the 'tough' and the 'soft' – there would be no contest between them.

Research shows that toughness (when defined as someone who makes tough demands and sticks to them) usually 'wins' against someone who is soft (ie, someone who is frightened of the proverbial goose) whenever these types confront each other in negotiation (or, more accurately, whenever they confront each other in 'negotiating' experiments).

Well, what is the experimental evidence on toughness in response to a so-called tough demand from the other negotiator? Surprisingly it is extremely consistent.

Briefly, it pays! And certainly, responding softly to a tough opening is no way to do yourself any favours.

You would be less than real if you associated a tough stance from a negotiator as indicative of her generosity. You would be an eternal optimist if you concluded that you are going to get what you want from her on terms favourable to yourself.

Interestingly, many of the experiments showed that negotiators who had opened with a high demand (equated in the experiments with toughness) and who met with a tough response, counter-responded with a softening of their original stance. This, it was claimed, showed that toughness can generate softness in the other negotiator.

This is the substance of the case for acting tough – it provokes softness – and if you face a tough negotiator you are recommended by the researchers to act even tougher until you provoke the desired level of softness in him.

You can see, I hope, why critics of the 'act tough/provoke softness' school of negotiating shake their heads over its inbuilt recipe for deadlock. How tough do you have to get to be immune from collapsing into deadlock? And, as importantly, are the agreements gained by this process the best that a negotiator – even the tough guys and gals – can hope for?

The experiments showed that if you take a tough stance (ie, make high demands like Jack with his Jaguar cars) the other guy is more likely to soften his stance. And the converse is probably more obvious: if you open with an unexpectedly soft demand, it is more likely that she will revise her expectations of the outcome upwards rather than downwards.

This, of course, is precisely the basic flaw in goodwill-conceding. If you are soft and make unilateral concessions, he responds by demanding more from you. You cannot satisfy a wolf's appetite by feeding it, because it will keep coming back for more, once it discovers where it can get fed.

How much more likely is it that a deal will fold because you take a tougher stance? As nobody knows before the event the precise likelihood of a deal folding for a given degree of toughness, nobody can answer that question with confidence. (If you think you can predict this likelihood accurately there is a Nobel Prize – and $800,000 – waiting for you!)

That the likelihood of deadlock is higher for tough stances than for soft stances is indisputable. You will certainly get fewer deals, but the empirical issue for you is whether the gain from fewer deals at higher prices is greater than the gains from more deals at lower prices? Five negotiations at £12,000 is better than seven deals at £7,000, and if the number of hits is better than 5 out of 7, the arithmetic is even more favourable.

Now in this chapter I am not concerned with the experimental evidence, nor with the anecdotal, and I have no wish to encourage you to act so-called tough (or soft, for that matter). I am not referring to the content of your demands, nor the manner (or lack of them) in which you make your demands known to the other negotiator.

I am solely concentrating here on something much more important, namely, your **resolve** when negotiating. So many negotiators confuse content for resolve that the entire subject of 'toughness versus softness' in negotiating has become imbued with monumental confusion and is a source of frightful errors.

Being so-called tough as a negotiator is another one of those myths in the same league as the myths of goodwill conceding.

Go back to Joe for a moment. He is not your archetypal 'tough guy', all bluster and loud. He speaks quite quietly and is never ruffled by pressure, even the outrageous pressure some buyers try on him from time to time.

When Gloria Nearsight, Chief Buyer for the UK's most competitive food retailer, treats Joe to one of her legendary tantrums and threatens to de-list his Cola Pop if he doesn't cut a penny off a case, he doesn't collapse into a trembling wreck, nor does he reply in kind (he is not even tempted to do so!). He just smiles and says 'No'.

You see, Joe's toughness is not about aggressive stances or contests of intimidatory toughness with Gloria and her ilk, of which there are plenty around in chainstore buying. His toughness is of the only worthwhile and long-lasting kind – he is tough in his *resolve*. He doesn't give in easily. He doesn't lose heart. He doesn't wilt under intimidatory pressure (he is always prepared to listen carefully to the buyer's arguments and give them full consideration).

He is not an intimidator. Joe is steely in character. He knows what he is about, he knows how some buyers like to play the game. So Joe lets them get on with their tough acts without comment.

And then he smiles and says 'No'.

THE SHIFTING CHINESE MIDDLE

A European firm, world-renowned in the oil industry, was asked by the Chinese to enter into negotiations to supply its services to the small but growing domestic Chinese offshore oil industry.

The Chinese, who are anxious to develop their oil resources and are using Western technology to do so, went hard at the prices quoted by the European firm.

First, they got a price quotation for the company supplying its services for three years, then they demanded, inclusive in the quoted price, a lot of extras.

Among these extras were some very expensive add-ons, such as free training for Chinese nationals, free manuals for operating the specialized equipment, masses of spares and stores, and domestic charges for accommodating the company's technical staff. This last was a trifle ambitious on the part of the Chinese who insisted that the foreign staff be charged at the same *per diem* rate for subsistence that they were charged for their staff visiting Europe where prices and living standards are, of course, much higher.

The European negotiators fought hard to avoid pricing themselves into unprofitability and regularly complained that when they made a concession the result was not a reciprocal move on the part of the Chinese. Far from it. The Chinese regarded 'split the difference' moves as invitations to put pressure on the Europeans to move even closer to the Chinese opening position.

The remedy was in the Europeans' hands: pad their prices before they opened negotiations; never make a single concession without getting something back from the Chinese; avoid any 'fair play' illusions about 'split the difference' gambits; totally resist the 'add-on' ploys; and, lastly, sit it out, for the Chinese need oil technology far more than oil technologists need to work in China.

REMEMBER, THEY HAVE A CHOICE!

The gambling boom in the United States led New Jersey to attempt to cream off some of the glittering prizes flowing to Las Vegas. They invited casino operators to set up shop in the State.

Some of the locals thought this a heaven-sent opportunity to cash in on the bonanza.

One house-owner went too far.

His little two-storey brick house occupied part of the site that the Penthouse group wanted to build their casino on. He asked them for $2.5 million dollars for his house and refused all entreaties to budge his price.

Negotiators always have a choice of saying 'no' and this is what happened here.

The casino group gave up negotiating and built their casino right up to the house property boundary. The casino rises seven storeys above the house on three sides, completely blocking the 'view' except at the roadside.

Whatever the house was worth to the owner before the negotiations ($70,000?), it is now worth much less, except perhaps as a curiosity!

The adoption of a soft stance in the face of intimidation is wrong because it starts a process of creeping limpness in the people who operate it. First, they convince themselves that by being softer (read cheaper) they get business that would otherwise go to the competition. Then, as the habit of softness gets a grip on them, their outlook and their behaviour, they develop a cringe, and even palpitations, every time they see signs of the other person dithering on the brink of deadlock.

Naturally, unintentionally they convey this attitude to the other person and she soon learns – as if programmed – to exploit their incipient fears of not getting a deal. She lays it on and before long all their deals are at or below the 'bottom line' of profitability of their company.

TRAGEDY AT MAKOLA

Ghana's economy went through a bad time and a collapse in economic confidence led to a military coup. The military had good intentions but remained economically illiterate. Faced with serious food shortages and rapidly rising prices they chose the age-old method of intervention.

This never works. They sought popularity by blaming the shortages on black-market stock-piling; they took stern measures against smuggling; they instituted price controls and finally they turned the mob on the market traders at Makola (Accra).

The mob destroyed the market by fire, violently dispersed the market 'mammies', and still went home hungry.

By intimidating the only people who could be mobilized to get food into Ghana – not by exhortation but by self-interest – the Government perpetuated the shortages. If it had told the market mammies that they could keep all their profits from trade, if they had repealed all laws against smuggling, and if they had abandoned price controls – in other words the exact opposite of what they did – they would soon be ruling a fitter, fatter Ghana.

Why? Because it is a law of human nature that if it is worth somebody's while to put themselves out they will always do so, and if by doing so they bring in food to a starving country they will do more for the people than any other grouping. Next door to Ghana, the Ivory Coast had none of Ghana's draconian laws about food prices. It is also suffered none of Ghana's self-inflicted ailments and shortages.

If a buyer goes soft the response borders on the paranormal; hordes of tough sellers gravitate to the buyer's office carrying hard deals by the bundle. You see, the word soon gets round. Why?

What you are you don't begat: you create your opposite type.

How does toughness manifest itself in the negotiating crucible where the 'beam me up Scotty' option is not available?

Tough negotiators have high resolve. If they meet a tough opponent they either face it out or end up at deadlock. They don't give in to toughness by losing their resolve.

Tough negotiators are less concerned with deadlock than soft negotiators. Their main concern is with the deal being close to their expectations, rather than with *a* deal for the sake of it.

If you are worried about the order, your opponent will sense it like a dog always knows who it is safe to bark at and who it is prudent to slink away from.

If you can't walk away from a deal that is struck on unsatisfactory terms, you are psychologically half-way to rationalizing any terms you can get.

As I have said, in negotiating you must act more like Scrooge and less like St Francis of Assisi. In other spheres of human contact perhaps the exact opposite should apply. But negotiating is unique – it is a remarkable fact that negotiators who can stand up to intimidation end up enriching a far wider set of people than themselves. Those who aim for the trees never get off the ground, and drag more than themselves down with them.

Years ago, when I was a boy, my grandfather entertained me with stories about his days as a goldminer in Canada before the First World War. He told plain unsophisticated stories, for his was a hard labouring life.

There was a proud fatalism about the North American miners in those days and he often recited a few lines of verse that captured their spirit. They are an apt inclusion in this chapter:

> *This is the law of the Yukon:*
> *that the strong shall thrive.*
> *For surely the weak shall perish*
> *and only the fit survive.*

Remember the *Law of the Yukon* as you prepare for a negotiation, because it can call for great toughness of spirit to hold out for your target while looking into the cold, steely eyes of an opponent who thinks he has got your measure.

COMMENTS ON SELF-ASSESSMENT TEST 12

1 a) Definitely your best first move. A million dozen cans suggests a lot of happy customers the chain would not want to disappoint. An Owl would know this.
  b) Not unless you want price pressure every call and are a fully paid-up Donkey.
  c) Sign of Sheepishness. Make her work for her price cuts.

2 a) No. Are you an order taker or a negotiator? Your certainly are a Sheep.

b) Much better. A very plausible opening move of an Owl.

c) Surely not? Anything is possible at the right price, except to Donkeys.

d) You are obviously an out-of-work Kamikaze pilot (and deserve to be an unemployed Sheep). If you avoid taking advantage – even mildly – of a buyer's self-proclaimed predicament, courtesy of your rivals, you'll never survive when your rivals are back in business and he doesn't need you or your discounts!

3 a) No. An abject surrender which you will spend the rest of your married life Sheepishly trying to justify to your partner.

b) Good. Start high and work down if you have to. Your boss will respect your courageous assertiveness – eventually. A move for very clever Foxes.

c) Weak. She'll squeeze a Sheep like you to a weekend in Newark.

CHAPTER 13

Look before you leap?

This is the third of my Negotiating Scenarios for you to practise some of the lessons of *Everything is Negotiable!* As with the other scenarios, they are a lively way for you to learn in the 'safe' environment of your private reading.

Read through the scenario a couple of times, making notes in whatever way suits you. Then think about what you would advise Door Step Deliveries as it prepared for meetings with Daily Milk and Fresh Farm to negotiate supply contracts. How would you put together a negotiating strategy, remembering what you have covered so far in Chapters 1 to 12, and, perhaps, as always, what your gut feelings tell you about the situation.

There is no point, as always, in inventing 'facts' about the scenario to settle the case your way. If it is not stated in the scenario, it hasn't and won't happen. Simply stick to the storyline and prepare your responses from there.

So have some fun – and good luck.

NEGOTIATION SCENARIO 3:
LOOK BEFORE YOU LEAP?

The Daily Milk Company owns several dairy farms and bottles cows' milk which it supplies to Door Step Deliveries Limited, a milk distributor with numerous customers living in the eastern suburbs of Bristol. It also supplies milk to Walker Brothers, Door Step's rival distributor.

Farm Fresh Milk Limited, has decided to enter the milk supply business in Bristol, using supplies of milk direct from its own farms and has approached Door Step Deliveries with an offer to supply bottled milk at 3 pence per litre cheaper than Daily Milk's current price. Farm Fresh already supplies small quantities of milk direct to customers in several villages east of Bristol.

Door Step Deliveries is considering Fresh Farm's offer of cheaper milk because it is concerned that Fresh Farm might decide to deliver milk in direct competition with Door Step if it does not sign up with Fresh Farm.

However, Fresh Farm is sited 21 miles north of Bristol's suburbs and presently would be unable to supply customers direct, unless it built a refrigerated bottling plant closer to Bristol.

Daily Milk's exclusive supply contract with Door Step Deliveries terminates in one month and it wishes to renew the 3-year contract with them, on a price to be agreed basis.

The Daily Milk Company runs local depots in Bristol from which Door Step Deliveries draws its supplies. These depots are open from 4am, enabling Door Step to deliver bottled milk to individual customers and local stores before 7am. Its drivers can return to re-stock milk if demand exceeds supply, something they could not do if they had to drive 21 miles to Fresh Farm's plant.

The difference in price between Daily Milk's and Farm Fresh's milk is worth up to £3,000 per month in additional gross revenue to Door Step.

Now try some questions to practise your negotiating skills on the problem and to explore, using your experience to date and drawing on your reservoir of common sense, how you might set about negotiating with Daily Milk and Farm Fresh. You can work from your notes on a separate sheet of paper, or from brief notes and highlightings you have made in the text.

Remember, Foxes cheat without prompting, Sheep need to be prompted to cheat and Donkeys skip the exercise altogether. Owls make notes on all of their answers *before* they compare them with my own comments.

QUESTIONS ON NEGOTIATION SCENARIO 3

13.1 Where is Door Step Deliveries vulnerable if it switches suppliers?

13.2 What negotiating stance should Door Step Deliveries adopt with Daily Milk Co?

13.3 What negotiating stance should Door Step Deliveries adopt with Fresh Farm?

13.4 How might Daily Milk try protect its interests in a renewal of the supply agreement with Door Step Deliveries?

13.5 If Daily Milk Co moves on price to match Fresh Farm, how might it justify to Door Step Deliveries its past higher pricing policy?

COMMENTS ON NEGOTIATION
SCENARIO 3

13.1 Where is Door Step Deliveries vulnerable if it switches suppliers?

Vulnerabilities in negotiation are potential threats to commercial viability. There are constant competitive pressures on a business and the negotiators must search for and address vulnerabilities before adopting a negotiation policy, just in case the policy does not cover the vulnerabilities, or makes them worse.

Door Step Deliveries is already concerned that if it does not contract with Farm Fresh it will face direct competition in the suburbs of Bristol from a Farm Fresh initiative to deliver its own milk directly.

Door Step Deliveries should also be concerned that its rival, Walker Brothers, does a deal with Daily Milk on similar terms if Door Step Deliveries accepts the Farm Fresh offer. The price advantage from Farm Fresh could be removed and Walker Brothers would be able to target customers of Door Step Deliveries on favourable terms, including the location of three Daily Milk depots inside the city, as against travelling 21 miles for its milk supplies from Farm Fresh.

There is also the added likelihood that Daily Milk will not sit back and see its market share collapse if Door Step Deliveries and other distributors (including Walker Brothers) desert it for Farm Fresh. Daily Milk, too, could decide to enter the direct distribution of its milk in Bristol, using its local depots to do so.

Once Farm Fresh removes Door Step Deliveries from their relationship with Daily Milk it will gain accurate information on the quantities of milk that can be supplied to customers in the suburbs of Bristol, thus enabling it to assess the commercial viability of entering the distribution market itself while taking into consideration the investment required to open a refrigerated bottling plant in the area. In addition, if Farm Fresh also acquires the supply contracts for Walker Brothers in Bristol, its ability to enter the market will be increased.

Farm Fresh already has a 3 pence per litre price advantage over Daily Milk's price and presumably it could take that price down further to compete with existing distributors if it chose to do so. Hence, switching suppliers still leaves Door Step Deliveries vulnerable to Farm Fresh's intentions, including the possibility that, having eliminated Daily Milk as a supplier, it could raise its prices to the distributors, while undercutting them with its own direct distribution prices.

Door Step Deliveries is put into a quandary by these possibilities from a changing situation. However, a vulnerability is no cause for panic. Identifying the vulnerabilities is a first step to developing a strategy for dealing with them. Just because Door Step is vulnerable does not mean that there are no costs and benefits for both Daily Milk and Farm Fresh, and for Walker Brothers, the rival distributor, who face similar vulnerabilities to Door Step, whatever Door Step decides to do.

13.2 What negotiating stance should Door Step Deliveries adopt with Daily Milk?

The price per litre of milk is going to be an issue between them. If Door Step Deliveries can achieve 3 pence per litre off its current price from Daily Milk and gain £3,000 a month in revenue, it could use some of that margin to gain a competitive price advantage over its rival distributor. It may need this advantage to maintain its market share if Walker Brothers switch to Farm Fresh at lower prices.

Hence price pressure on Daily Milk is inevitable in the negotiations for a new supply contract. Also, the exclusivity clause is likely to be attacked by Door Step Deliveries, which might want to create some flexibility in its choice of suppliers, including the possibility of adopting a dual supply policy from both Daily Milk and Farm Fresh. This would enable it to take advantages of the likely price competition between the suppliers, if its negotiators are firm in their resolve.

Door Step Deliveries may also wish to take stances on:

- advantageous payment terms
- returns policies
- joint marketing and promotion campaigns
- investment by Daily Milk in Door Step Deliveries' capital expenditures for the delivery of bottled milk (new milk vehicles, etc).

Door Step deliveries might be tempted to go for an exclusive contract with Daily Milk to eliminate Walker Brothers as a Daily Milk distributor. While this tradable should be considered seriously, Door Step Deliveries would need to recognise that this might push Walker Brothers into alliance with Farm Fresh giving them a price advantage of at least 3 pence a litre. They could expect some spirited competition, though the three Daily Milk depots give them an advantage in early coverage and in restocking during the day. If these advantages are unique to Daily Milk distributors then the exclusivity issues could enable Door Stop Deliveries to increase market share at the expense of Walker Brothers.

Again, a potential vulnerability is no cause for panic, and certainly not for becoming submissive.

13.3 What negotiating stance should Door Step Deliveries adopt with Farm Fresh?

If the 3 pence per litre price cut is Farm Fresh's first offer, Door Step Deliveries should press for deeper price cuts – never accept the first offer!

Door Step Deliveries should also attempt to cover its concerns about Farm Fresh's intentions on price. Farm Fresh's attempt to enter the milk market may lead to a price cutting war between it and Daily Milk, and Door Step Deliveries would want to remain flexible to be able to take advantage of any other competitive consequences of Farm Fresh's entry to the market.

Therefore, Door Step Deliveries would want, as a minimum, a commitment from Farm Fresh not to raise prices for some foreseeable period ahead, and preferably a clause in the supply contract ensuring that the only price changes were downwards – a 'downwards only' price review clause.

Door Step Deliveries might try for a price formula based on the market average that automatically reduced prices as the suppliers' competitive pressure on prices takes effect.

Door Step Deliveries would also want a non-exclusive deal with Farm Fresh, enabling it to take supplies from Farm Fresh's rivals, with no minimum volumes to be purchased in a given period. It might also try for a commitment from Farm Fresh not to directly distribute milk in Bristol.

It would certainly want to raise the issue of a Farm Fresh bottling plant in Bristol and an early commitment made by Farm Fresh to invest in such a project. If such a commitment was not forthcoming Door Step Deliveries could use that as a 'hook' to turn down the Farm Fresh offer, providing its negotiations with Daily Milk were progressing satisfactorily.

Despite the vulnerabilities occasioned by the Farm Fresh initiatives, there is a lot that Door Step can do to protect its future interests.

13.4 How can Daily Milk protect its interests in its agreement with Door Step Deliveries?

Clearly the Farm Fresh competitive threat is serious. The 3 pence per litre offer produces significant gains to Daily Milk's customers (in the case of Door Step Deliveries this is worth £3,000 a month). If Daily Milk responds to Farm Fresh's price reduction (and any more to come) it would directly cut its own revenue by the amount its customers gain – a classic zero sum distributive bargain.

Without details of Daily Milk's costs we cannot speculate

what room there is for Daily Milk to respond to Farm Fresh's price cuts. If Farm Fresh initiates a price war, at the very least there will be downward pressure on supply prices of bottled milk – whether that filters through to consumers or is taken as windfall profits by distributors is an open question.

Daily Milk's negotiating positions would depend on the ambitions of Door Step Deliveries. Daily Milk would prefer to tie Door Step Deliveries into an exclusive contract for at least 3 years, 5 if possible. Whether it would concede to Door Step Deliveries (or, indeed, to Walker Brothers) the exclusive right to distribute its products in Bristol – effectively by not renewing its contract with one of its distributors – would depend on a careful assessment of the opportunities and threats of doing so, and what Door Step Deliveries or Walker Brothers were willing to offer in return.

Daily Milk could agree to price determination by way of a formula linking supply price to some industry average – retrospective or delayed in some way. It should resist any non-exclusive contracts with the distributors and would insist on high minimum volumes being taken by them to block off any encroachment by Farm Fresh or any other new supplier for the duration of the new contract.

It should leave itself the option to enter the distribution market direct, using its depots in Bristol as a base for supplying its own network. It should consider directly supplying large shops and stores with bulk supplies of milk, leaving itself free to respond direct to the residential market to cover any loss of volume through distributors or their customers switching to Farm Fresh and thus, perhaps, lowering to uneconomic levels the volumes of bottled milk passing through its depots.

To incentivise Door Step Deliveries, it could consider offering low interest loans to buy new delivery vehicles and perhaps to jointly promote milk sales to customers in Bristol. Its best defence would be to reach a mutually profitable agreement with Door Step Deliveries.

153

13.5 If Daily Milk moves on price how does it justify to Door Step Deliveries its past pricing policy?

This is always a problem for existing suppliers who respond to price cutting by new entrants. While Daily Milk will be pleased to gain from a price cut per litre, it is bound to be resentful that the price cut was not available to it before Farm Fresh came onto the scene. It could conclude that the £3,000 a month extra revenue had been siphoned off by Daily Milk for the past three years (£108,000). It might wonder just how much revenue is still available to it if Farm Fresh cut its prices further and Daily Milk were forced to respond.

This places Daily Milk in a defensive bind. If it does not respond it loses distributors; if it does respond its distributors resent the implications from the past! It's like someone demanding a raise from their boss or they take another job offer. If the boss raises their pay to keep them, they wonder why they are worth more today and were not worth more yesterday.

Daily Milk's justification could be developed around the theme that Farm Fresh's predatory pricing is a short–term ploy to enter the market and remove Daily Milk as a competitor. Having achieved this goal there is nothing to stop Farm Fresh raising their prices back to the old levels, or even higher.

Daily Milk could also suggest that, given that Farm Fresh would have to relocate their depot from 21 miles away, it would need to invest in a refrigerated bottling plant in Bristol. This would cost, say, £250,000. Daily Milk could plausibly imply that Farm Fresh would want to recover this investment from Door Step Deliveries and other local distributors, which would mean higher prices per litre.

Daily Milk could also argue that Door Step Deliveries would be opening the door to its own demise because once Farm Fresh had a plant up and running, it could enter the distribution market, starting with the profitable bulk market among local stores for bottled milk.

It could argue that Daily Milk, on the other hand, was not intending to do the same and would undertake to stay out of direct distribution for as long as its customers, Door Step Deliveries and others, stayed with it.

In order to show Daily Milk's good intentions, it was accepting a lower price per litre to compete with Farm Fresh, and once this threat was out of the way it would restore its policy of charging 'sensible' prices for bottled milk.

Some such plausible justification would be necessary if Daily Milk was not to lose its distributors in a bout of resentment.

SELF-ASSESSMENT TEST 14

1 You are a package-tour operator negotiating with a Spanish hotel chain on the terms for next season's bookings. The price they are asking per person per week in their hotels is £30 higher than your current offer. They offer to 'split the difference' 50–50. Do you:
   (a) Suggest, say, 55–45 in your favour?
   (b) Say you can't afford to split the difference?
   (c) Agree to their offer?
   (d) Agree, if it is a 75–25 split in your favour?

2 Do you see negotiating as being about:
   (a) A fair and equal transaction?
   (b) Compromising?
   (c) Making a joint decision with the other person that meets as many of his and as many of *your* interests as possible?

3 You are engaged in extremely difficult negotiations with a Lebanese-based construction consortium. After much haggling over finance for a road project, they make a small unilateral concession on their demand for irrevocable lines of credit. Do you?
   (a) Note the concession but otherwise ignore it?
   (b) Reciprocate with a concession of your own?

CHAPTER 14

The negotiator's most useful two-letter word

or how to make your offers count

When asked what they think is their most useful two-letter word, many negotiators suggest:

NO

This answer is not surprising if the question is posed *after* they have heard the story of Bjorn McKenzie's infallible system for coping with wolves (see Chapter Nine) or about the Law of the Yukon (see Chapter Twelve), as these tend to leave a somewhat negative impression of good negotiating behaviour.

However, while 'No' isn't the right answer, it isn't entirely wrong.

The question asks for the negotiator's *most useful* two-letter word and 'No' merely qualifies for the status of *being useful*.

The most useful two-letter word in the negotiator's vocabulary is:

IF

Why is *if* such an important word to a negotiator?

The answer lies at the heart of the negotiating process itself and fully explains my unrelenting hostility to unilateral conceding under any pretext whatsoever, or for any purpose.

The *Oxford English Dictionary* – that final arbiter of literacy

– defines conceding as, *inter alia*: 'to *grant, yield* or *surrender*'. For this reason I begin this chapter with the quiet but firm statement that readers are not reading this book to improve their skills in commercial *conceding*.

Your only interest is to improve your performance as a *negotiator*, which has nothing to do with surrendering. If you have to surrender there is no need for the other person to negotiate: you will be told what to do by the person with the whip. On the other hand, if you choose to surrender by unilaterally conceding *when you don't have to*, you are less than suitable to be in charge of protecting anybody's interests (including your own).

How do you know when you're in a negotiation and when not?

It isn't always obvious to begin with!

It is possible for a negotiation to be almost over before you realize you're in one (that's when you'll regret those early free-gift goodwill concessions), just as it is possible to abandon hope of negotiating about something too soon (that's when you start cringing instead of cold-eyeing them).

You find out sooner or later, of course, whether you can, or should, negotiate your way to a better deal. One thing is certain, though – at the outset always test the situation before you assume anything about the relative power of the other party.

We will discuss this in more detail later, but for the moment do not assume that the sound of a whiplash is proof positive that they have the power and you don't. They may just be good at sound effects.

If you identify the elements that make negotiating different from the alternative means of making a decision, you can use that knowledge to see if the conditions for negotiation are present. Essentially, negotiation can be defined as:

A transaction in which both parties have a *veto* on the final outcome.

159

If you don't have a veto (which includes the right to walk away and do business with somebody else) then you will have to accept whatever is on offer.

Each party in a negotiation has to consent to the outcome if it is to be implemented and each has an interest (not necessarily an equal one) in the other agreeing to it.

Thus by negotiating we make a *joint decision*.

If you don't like the other person's proposal as to what that joint decision should be, and are unable to agree on an alternative, you have the option of *not* agreeing to what he proposes, because:

Negotiation involves the *voluntary* consent of both sides to the decision.

If you are compelled to agree *against* your will, it's *not* a negotiation (the sharp sting on your back *is* the whiplash!).

What does this view of negotiating imply?

CONCEDING AIN'T NEGOTIATING

A package-tour operator in London (Costalot Travel Ltd) had occasion to meet the sales manager of a Spanish hotel chain to discuss next year's terms for block booking the resorts. The meeting opened with a long list of changes that Costalot wanted following widespread complaints from their clients about the hotels and also several lapses in service contrary to what the hotels had agreed to provide.

The Spanish manger (Señor Paco Eminos) started through the list item by item and agreed to most of them as they stood or in a slightly modified form. Eventually, he stopped his progress through the list with the exclamation:

'Señor, I thought this was a negotiation but I am making all the concessions.'

'True,' replied Mr Costalot, 'and when you stop conceding I will start negotiating!'

First, that the parties can have different preferences for which of the available outcomes is suitable as a joint decision. Naturally, you prefer the joint decision to be more rather than less favourable to yourself. If you don't, you've no business negotiating because, if you negotiate, you'll soon have no business:

If you are selling, you prefer high prices, if buying, low prices.

You prefer longer time to pay back than you do to get paid.

You prefer large simple orders to penny packets with precise specifications.

You prefer less up-front money if you are buying than you do if you are selling.

You prefer sale or return if you are buying and no-returns if you are selling.

If he wants delivery everywhere in awkward loads, you'd prefer he paid extra for it.

And so on.

It's not simply a matter that you gain what he loses. If you've negotiated successfully, the total package gives you more on the swings than you 'lose' on the roundabouts. That is what is meant by it being more favourable to you.

A trade-off in one area for something in another may give a differential advantage to you but this in no way implies that he directly loses what you gain. His swings may be your roundabouts; his willingness to give on price may be tempered by your willingness to accelerate on payment.

On the other hand, if you lose more on the swings than you get back on the roundabouts, your negotiating moves ought to have ensured that the final package isn't even less favourable to you than it might have been if you had been less skilful.

Secondly, this view of negotiating implies that your most favourable outcomes (the ones you would choose in the absence of having to consider the other person's interests) are not often available to you because he can veto any and all of your propositions. Nor are his most favourable outcomes available to him by virtue of your veto.

Hence, you both have to choose a joint decision, from among the many that may be attainable, that meets sufficient of the interests and expectations of both sides not to provoke a veto by one of you. If you cannot reach a settlement by joint decision, you must deadlock and, excluding the possibility of arbitration, take your business elsewhere.

Part of the work of negotiating consists of the careful search for outcomes that are veto-free or can be made veto-free by one means or another (of which more later). Some of the proposals for a joint decision or settlement are more favourable to both of you, some less, and some others may not have been considered during the negotiation.

Which outcome is finally chosen depends on a lot of factors, not the least of which is your view of the prospects (including the cost in time and energy) of negotiating a better outcome than the one presently on offer and the consequences to both of you of deadlock.

If you view negotiating as surrendering – in whatever form your surrender takes, including a proclivity for unilaterally conceding in the futile search for goodwill – then it is predictable that the deal will be less favourable to you and more favourable to them. This is not to say that poor negotiators can't get deals. They can, but they tend to get lousier deals than good negotiators.

How then is a negotiation to progress if there is a prohibition on surrender? Surely, if we merely stick where we start we will never get a deal? This is a case where we must not assume that the alternative to 'no surrender' is a fight to the death.

It is not the necessity for movement that is denied here. What is most emphatically denied is that movement must take the form of unilateral concessions.

Negotiating is about *trading*.

It is when you view negotiation as a process of *exchange* that you see the importance of *never* conceding anything without getting something back for it. In effect, as a negotiator, if you have to walk towards the other person you *must* ensure that he walks towards you as well.

Better still, your aim is to get him to walk *faster* towards you than you do towards him! Is negotiation a matter of give-and-take?

Not quite.

The idea of give-and-take is acceptable as a broad-brush concept of negotiating only as long as you do not make the mistake of *giving more than you can afford in order to get back less than you need*. There are no 'rules' that say you have to make *equal* moves towards each other – the idea ought to be anathema to negotiators – nor is there anything that says you have to move at all just because he moves.

This leads us to the most important single principle of negotiating:

NOTHING, ABSOLUTELY NOTHING, IS GIVEN AWAY FREE

I know of *no* exceptions to this principle.

This principle is the foundation of effective negotiating behaviour. The fact that it may not be guiding the other person's moves is not relevant to your behaviour – if he wants to give you things for nothing that is his private business and you should accept them without a quibble. You are under no obligation to look after his best interests!

Thus, if you are negotiating with a unilateral conceder (should you be so lucky!) your best response to his conceding is to sit tight where you are. And when the other person requires you to move you must insist that he moves too, preferably by much more than you do.

This might be considered to be 'unfair' (why it should be considered so is one of life's minor mysteries), for you might think that in negotiating we 'ought' to aim to make equal moves and sacrifices from our opening positions.

To my mind that is a mistaken view of negotiating.

Just because you reduce your demands it does not follow that I must improve my offer by the same amount. Perhaps you can afford a 20 per cent 'cut' in your price – which shows just how much you padded your opening position. I can't afford to reciprocate, and that's that! You see, I don't subscribe to the 'equity theory' of negotiating and neither should you.

IMPULSIVE CONCEDERS

The worst thing about unilateral concessions is that they weaken a negotiating position much more than the amount of the concession.

Consider the following cases:

'How much for the video recorder system?'
'£300.'
'As much as that?'
'I could let it go for £275.'

'I see you have requested a starting salary of £25,000.'
'Yes.'

> 'This operation cannot afford to pay that amount – in fact it would make you the highest-paid accountant in credit control. Would you consider less?'
>
> 'I'm willing to be flexible but I must get at least £19,000.'
>
> These concessions are got for practically no effort at all. The drop of £25 in the video negotiation after a single question tells the buyer that the owner has plucked his price out of thin air. He should (and did) push on price even harder (it eventually went for £250). The out-of-work accountant dropped her price by £6,000 almost without a whimper, and also demonstrated her total unsuitability to be employed (she wasn't) in a credit control operation – she will never get money out of debtors if she is a compulsive conceder.
>
> In both cases, the use of *if* conditions on the concessions would have protected the negotiating position:
>
> 'If you buy a set of tapes, you can have it for £295.'
>
> 'If you pay me a commission on the debts I collect and you pay my petrol account I will accept a salary of £19,000.'

'Fair exchange is no robbery', but that says nothing about a fair exchange being equal in some way. In fact, no trading exchange is an *equal* transaction.

When you buy a Mars bar from a kiosk for 35 pence there is no question of an equal transaction between you and the kiosk company. The Mars bar is not *equal* to the 35 pence. If you believe that it is, try eating the 35 pence!

When you hand over your money to the person in the kiosk for the Mars bar it is a *fair* transaction. If you believe that it isn't, take your business elsewhere. Nobody in a free society compels you to eat Mars bars. At the moment of purchase you need the Mars bar more than you need your 35 pence – you have money but no Mars bars. For the kiosk company, they need your 35 pence more than they need the Mars bar – they have a warehouse full of Mars bars.

For the soundest of motives, i.e. profit, they prefer to fill their till with cash and empty their warehouses of Mars bars. Hence, the trade can be fair without necessarily being equal.

If the best way to conduct a negotiation is to make absolutely no concessions without getting something in return (though we can accept concessions if they are offered for nothing), how then do we avoid deadlock?

This is where the power of the negotiator's most useful two-letter word – *if* – comes into its own.

The most important guiding principle of negotiating – even if you forget everything else – is to preface *all* your propositions and concessions with the word IF:

IF you drop 20 per cent on price, I can sign an order
IF you accept liability, we will release your shipment
IF you waive on-site inspection, we can meet your schedules
IF you pay the courier, I will despatch the plans tonight
IF you place an order immediately, I can meet your price

By using the word *if* you protect the integrity of your proposals. They cannot regard a movement as a unilateral concession on your part precisely because you have tied it to your conditions. As they say: you can't have one without the other.

Get into a the habit of using *IF every time* you make a proposal and the other person will get the message:

The IF part tells him the *price* of the offer.
The offer part tells him what he is *getting* for the price.

Do this in negotiating and you will also help to educate the other negotiator (you are doing the community a social service once again, for if you didn't help educate them who would?). Even the dumbest Donkey will get the message, eventually.

In one of the university campuses in the United States, a psychology professor taught a pigeon to pick out the ace of spades in a deck of cards. Now your average negotiating Donkeys are always going to have bigger brains than those belonging to pigeons – even Texan pigeons – and you can stake your last shilling on the prediction that they will eventually get the message.

If they want something from you it is going to cost them.

Perhaps in future they will ask for less?

COMMENTS ON SELF-ASSESSMENT TEST 14

1 a) Better than (c) but you are a Fox in too much of a hurry to compromise.

b) By far the negotiator's best Owl-like move. Why should you split the difference whether you can afford it or not? By making this offer they expose that their price is padded by at least £15 a person (and probably much more). Conceding to split the difference by £15 on 10,000 holiday weeks, costs you £150,000. Does this compromise look so equitable when grossed up?

c) Never. If you show negotiators that you practise 'split-the-difference' compromises they will give you bigger and bigger differences to split! As a Donkey you wouldn't know that.

d) Definitely better than (c) and more challenging for a Fox than (a). A possible move for an Owl much later, after you have tested the padding in their £15 with (b).

2 a) Negotiation is always fair, but seldom equal, unless you are a Sheep.

b) No. We negotiate to deliver our interests not just to compromise. As a joint decision the agreement must be acceptable to you both and better than the available alternatives. If it isn't, there is no future in compromising. Your choice suggests that you have the resolve of a Sheep.

c) Yes. It is your interests for which you are negotiating and their interests for which they are negotiating. Knowing this makes you at least a Fox.

3 a) Yes. If they make unilateral free gift concessions no Fox is obliged to respond in kind.

b) Not unless you are a Donkey.

SELF-ASSESSMENT TEST 15

1 You are a corporate finance manager and are trying to put together a deal with the Financial Director of a major customer. He starts browbeating you for the fee you have quoted for arranging the transaction. As the exchanges progress he gets more and more abusive, threatens that he will take his business elsewhere, makes slighting remarks about your professionalism and interrupts you constantly. Do you:
(a) Respond in kind to his language and tone?
(b) Respond in complete contrast to his language and tone?
(c) Walk out?
(d) Ignore his behaviour and press for your fee?

2 Your employees have gone on an unofficial (and illegal) strike. Do you:
(a) Demand they return to work before you will negotiate with them?
(b) Seek a court injunction (interdict in Scotland) to force a return to work?
(c) Accuse them of threatening the existence of the company?
(d) Tell them the strike will be a long one but it won't affect the outcome.

3 Your colleague is tyrannical, abusive, and sarcastic. Do you:
(a) Take her aside in private and tell her how her behaviour upsets you?
(b) Ignore her behaviour and get on with your job?

CHAPTER 15

They have a right to behave badly

or how to handle difficult negotiators

Extremely difficult people exhibit problematic behaviours for many negotiators. Being difficult includes demanding movement from you while offering none from themselves, being intransigent and expressing their intransigence abusively.

Mainly, they are domineering, bullying, threatening and outright abusive, and they seem to think that being 'tough' negotiators gives them a licence to behave badly. In fact, they are just plain ill-mannered and think negotiating is about them taking and you giving. Trading never enters their heads because they use their behaviour to intimidate you into weakening your resolve.

The problem of how to handle difficult negotiators is raised at so many *Everything is Negotiable Workouts* that it sometimes seems as if all of the people attending are the victims of difficult negotiators. (It is also interesting that this is always raised as a problem of how to deal with somebody *else* who is difficult, and never themselves!)

Among the common remedies for dealing with difficult people are whether to choose to **match** or **contrast** their behaviour? I always warn negotiators that this is one of those false dichotomies (like whether to be tough or soft).

Matching a difficult person's behaviour is an unsatisfactory response because it usually exacerbates their bad behaviour. It becomes a trial of strength because they react by raising the stakes. Their original intransigence is stiffened and, with enough provocation, they become even louder in their intransigence – the behaviour of the archetypal domineering bully. Each level of matching begets still louder intransigence, until the gloves come off – no more Mr Nice Guy – and it is a clash of the titans until one of you gives way and quits.

Starting off by contrasting difficult behaviour with your politer behaviour is no bed of roses either. Difficult negotiators see contrasting behaviour as a sign of your weakness (and your *naïveté*). They believe that you are about to give way. One more push, they believe, and you will roll over and play the patsy.

Hence, they intensify their bullying rather than abate it. If this does not work, because you are provoked into switching from contrasting to matching their behaviour, they blame themselves for not being tough enough with you in the first place and they increase the pressure even more.

It seems that whatever you do, match or contrast, or any combination or sequence of them, does not work.

What then is it to be: match or contrast?

My answer is neither, which is often treated sceptically by those who ask the question. Surely, they say, you must behave in one or other manner? I prefer to step back and approach the problem from another perspective altogether.

Their behaviour is the major determinant of our perceptions of their intentions. It is, after all, what we witness and guided by our feelings that arise from our perceptions we react, as we must, one way or another in response to the difficult negotiator.

We either stand up and fight back to deadlock or give in after a nominal resistance. We rationalize our reactions by some version of 'it is more important to get on with my life than engage in "macho" games for trivial ends' – some things, we conclude are just not worth fighting over.

This is an inadequate response but it goes to the heart of the problem. Other people's behaviour influences the outcomes we accept. But are we as impotent to deal with difficult behaviour as our eventual climb-down suggests? Must we quit and forego what we want? Not necessarily.

We simply disconnect their behaviour from the outcome.

This involves a determination on our part that whatever their behaviour – difficult, accommodating, or otherwise – *it will not affect the outcome.*

Repeat that mantra until it is hard-wired into you. Convince yourself and you will be immune to the intended effects of anybody's difficult behaviours.

You can choose, all circumstances considered, to tell them that their behaviour will not affect the outcome. Whether they believe you does not matter – your assertions, anyway, are unlikely to have quick results. After all, their behaviour works with other people and your assertions to the contrary may not sound so convincing to them – at first. So stick at it.

It is important that you understand the full implications of what the mantra asserts. If, as far as you are concerned, their behaviour truly is going to have no effect on the outcome, it must follow that their behaviour is not, nor must it become, an issue between you and them.

They may behave how they like, but as long as it does not affect the outcome, how they behave cannot be an issue for you. This contradicts some assertiveness training which insists you tell people how you feel about their behaviour. I disagree. Feelings schmeelings! – focus on the outcome 'cos that's where you get 'em.

Not every negotiator I have put this to sees it this way and they pay a price as a result.

For example, employees go on strike. To add to the issues that caused them to behave this way – which may be fanciful or vindictive – managements often mistakenly make an issue out of their employees' actions.

They utter the classic lines: 'no negotiation under duress', 'no negotiation until you return to normal working', even adding 'no negotiation until you give a written undertaking not to strike, etc, again'.

The result? The strikes continue. Why is this so? Because, if the management make an issue out of the strike, the strikers perceive that their strike must be hurting the managers, which is precisely the purpose of striking. If it was not hurting, you would not bother making an issue out of it and as they strike precisely to hurt you (sufficiently, they hope, to make you more compliant to their demands) your bleatings are to no avail.

This same intention lies behind a child's tantrum, a lover's walk-out, a worker's strike, an act of war or an act of terrorism. If their behaviour has no effect on its target they would not contemplate it so often. Terrorists in an airport hijack are demoralized more by the authorities getting the airport back to normal – even arranging somebody to cut the grass (just outside rifle range) as if nothing untoward was happening, than they ever are by senior government ministers pontificating on television about the evils of terrorism.

Observing industrial disputes over the years, I am always unimpressed by the tactical stupidity of managements (and governments) when they pontificate about strikers' behaviour.

Dutifully, the media reports 'how damaging' the stoppage is to those affected by its consequences – loss of business, loss of customers, loss of money, loss of jobs, loss of public sympathy, etc. The intention of such silly pronouncements is to warn the strikers that their actions are having detrimental effects on others and that unless they stop striking they will cause 'severe damage' to their company.

The message received by the strikers is entirely counter to the intended effect of the message sent by the management!

The reason why people behave in the way they do – difficult behaviour, bullying, strikes, overtime bans, work to rule, terrorist acts, etc – is precisely to inflict enough damage on the other side to undermine their willingness to support the outcome they chose initially. (I have attended enough board meetings during a dispute to be an expert in how individuals wobble when push comes to shove!)

These news reports and sound bites from people detrimentally affected by the consequences of such behaviour strengthens, not weakens, the resolve of strikers to continue with their behaviour.

In any group of people, opinions for or against any particular action vary right across the spectrum from keenly in favour, through various shades of warm to lukewarm in favour and neutral and out through lukewarm against to various shades of keenly against. Monitoring the shifting sands of opinion is a valuable investment for a 'beleagured' management.

To shift opinion for or against a proposition it is not necessary to win over every one of the people involved. You should not address your campaign to the extremists who are most in favour or those who are most hostile. It is much more effective to address yourself to the larger number of people who are lukewarm or neutral. In fact, concentrating your responses to those most passionately opposed to you is, in my experience, a common tactical error.

Whenever you show somebody that their actions are having an effect on you, you reinforce their current behaviour and you strengthen their resolve. The greater the effect of their behaviour, the greater their determination to continue with it until it gets them what they want.

What do we do then, if we neither match nor contrast difficult behaviour?

We must enforce, instead, the stance that the behaviour of the difficult negotiator will not affect the outcome. By being resolute we insist that the only criteria by which the outcome will be decided are:

- the **merits** of their case
- the principle of **trading**

or some combination thereof.

The selection of merit and trading as the sole criteria for a negotiated decision is a practical consequence of dealing over the years with both individual and multiple difficult negotiators.

Consider the difficult negotiator you are dealing with (remember you believe that it is always somebody else who is difficult!). Why are they 'difficult'?

Some people, habitually, are difficult to deal with because they believe that their behaviour gets them what they want. They are takers through and through, and they take from you whatever you are intimidated into giving to them. Put this group to one side for a moment.

What other reason could cause them to be difficult? Surely, it is possible that they are being difficult because of what they believe you have done to them?

You need to separate, therefore, habitually difficult people from the uncharacteristically difficult person who is behaving this way because they believe they are your victim.

Assessing the merits of their case is an essential step to separating the two types from each other. To do so, you have to refrain from imputing motives to them because it is more important that you listen than that you stoke the fire.

Years ago, Hamish, then a hotel manager and now a director of the hotel chain, explained to me his method of dealing with irate and, thereby, difficult customers. When a guest 'blew their top' at the front desk, he would invite them into his office and say, without pausing to obviate interruptions, three things to them:

'First, I unreservedly apologise for the stress we have caused you, second I am going to listen to what you say, and third I am going to put it right.'

He said this before he knew what the problem was and before he had assessed whether it was a genuine error on his staffs' part or merely a guest's tantrum. He told me that in almost every case, the guest calmed down and the problem was sorted out quickly to both sides' satisfaction. I recommend the Hamish approach to you.

To decide on the basis of merit there must be a discussion, with you listening to them. If you decide that you have made a mistake, put it right. There is little point in defending the indefensible. Of course, they could have contributed to your mistake and, if you have created the right conditions, you can discuss the implications of this for the eventual outcome.

For a negotiator, decision on merit is part of the debate phases of negotiation. The search for a solution is by way of listening to their statements, reporting their version of events and defining their criteria for their solution. Scoring points, sarcasm and direct rebuttal etc. are not useful behaviours for this purpose, nor is rolling over and playing the patsy.

It is seldom the case that the entire problem is susceptible to a decision by merit only, though merit inevitably plays a role whenever the parties attempt to influence and persuade each other. Decisions arising from the trading principle are quite distinct from decision by merit alone.

Take a consultancy case I was engaged in during 1991.

Harry was an irascible union official. By all accounts he was a difficult person with whom to negotiate (they called him the 'Dentist' because his favourite call at union meetings was to 'pull 'em out'). His behaviour was aggressive, physically dominating, loud and very abusive. His manners were not much to write home about and his language was unsuitable for hypersensitive people.

On this occasion, he arrived at one the company's depots and demanded that the toilets be cleaned up immediately as they were 'flooded with urine and excrement' (not the exact words he used!) and that his 'long-suffering members' (his regular 'catchphrase') 'were forced like animals to wade through [filth]'.

Normally, this approach would have provoked a row, with the manager insisting that his complaint be put through the official grievance procedure, which usually took two or three days to produce a decision, causing Harry to erupt into an even louder rage.

On this occasion, however, the manager was prompted to immediately accompany Harry to the toilets to see the extent of the problem. Not surprisingly, it was nowhere near as bad as Harry had described it – more a thin smear of leaking effluent that only an ant would need to 'wade through'. However, the toilet was leaking and it was unacceptable that this disamenity should take three days to fix. The manager judged that immediate action was merited and he ordered the supervisor to have maintenance re-plumb the toilet bowl and clean up the mess.

When Harry left the depot he appeared to be satisfied. The manager was also satisfied with the merits of the case and he thanked Harry for bringing the problem to his attention. (He said nothing about the manner by which Harry had raised the subject, nor of his threats about what would happen if something was not done 'pretty [sexual intercourse] quick'.)

An example (among many others) of a traded solution, dealt with by another manager in another depot, was slightly more tricky because the manager did not think Harry had any merits in his case at all. Briefly, Harry arrived at the depot with a demand that 'my long-suffering members' be given Saturday off with pay so they could go to a cup tie at a local football club. The work they normally did on Saturday, said Harry, would be done on Sunday at premium overtime rates.

Now, while cup ties are important local events, they are seldom so important that everybody would want to attend one. Moreover, it is unlikely that in a depot of 120 men and women that all of them were interested in football. In this case, the town had two football teams, United and Rovers, and the chances of them all being Rovers supporters was so remote as to be risible.

Harry, as usual stood his ground: it was 'Saturday off, Sunday on'. Anything else would be 'typical management tyranny to prevent my members enjoying a unique local cup tie'.

The manager did not argue with Harry even though he had strong grounds to reject the claim as spurious. Instead, he offered Harry a deal: 'If all deliveries are completed by 12 noon, then everybody can take the afternoon off with a full day's pay. Those who want to, can go to the cup tie. Nobody is coming in on Sunday.'

Harry protested at this 'miserable' offer and went off to report to his members on the management's 'totally inadequate' response to his 'legitimate claim'. The members, however, voted to accept it!

Harry alluded to allegations of managerial 'intimidation' and warned that the offer was a trap 'to get them to do a day's work in half a day and so create a precedent for redundancies' (itself, you may note, a fine example of his own intimidatory style).

The manager avoided being drawn into the ridiculous charge of intimidation – he had not left his office nor had he spoken to any supervisors about the offer to Harry. He had concentrated on planning the delivery schedules and other details necessary to implement the deal. He also stated that there was no precedent to be set.

The manager had resolved a problem by trading. He had not been influenced by the usual bullying, abusive and accusative behaviour of Harry.

He retained control of the remedy through a traded solution rather than make concessions merely to seek peace with an obstreperous union official. As far as he was concerned, whether the offer was accepted or rejected it did not cause major problems for him but he was not surprised that the union meeting voted overwhelmingly for the offer he had made. 'Folk around here,' he asserted, 'do not look gift horses in the mouth.'

Now, it ain't all that much different when dealing with difficult individuals who do not have the 'power' that Harry wields, usually with total indifference to his members' real interests. As long as you remember that it is not part of your mission in life to combine negotiating experiences with correcting their admittedly appalling behaviour.

As far as you are concerned, how people behave is entirely up to them and not really part of your business. Your role in life is not to take what they say or do personally. As a negotiator, their behaviour does not and will not affect the outcome. Once you have got that clear, everything neatly falls into place.

As consultants, we have had occasion to confirm to the shop stewards that they have an absolute and unfettered right to strike, and that any attempt to take that right away from them would meet with our strictest and most vocal opposition. However, we make it clear to them that the strike will not affect the outcome of their grievance, nor the extent to which we can meet their aspirations. In fact we usually tell them (and the employees) that any strike 'will be a long one'.

Likewise, with commercial negotiators whose behaviour and manners are beyond the pale. One director of a company we know theatrically removes his hearing aid when he doesn't like what he is being told about the terms of a deal and in between times swears and abuses the luckless bearers of, to him, bad news with absolutely no restraints.

However, as long as the negotiators stick to the deal, the merits of his case and the prospects for trading, they have no need to be upset by how he behaves. Their behaviour is not determined by his behaviour – nor should it be – because their resolve is self standing on the merits of their case and the willingness to trade for a deal.

If you remember and practise that principle, then difficult negotiators will become a minor irritant, and no more than that, on your way to a deal that is better for both of you.

COMMENTS ON SELF-ASSESSMENT TEST 15

1 a) What will that achieve, other than raise the temperature as he slugs it out with you? Sheep allow other people to dictate how they should behave.

 b) What will that achieve, other than raise the temperature as he puts more pressure on you because he thinks he has your measure? Sheep allow other people to dictate how they should behave.

 c) Might make you feel a better Donkey but won't change the outcome.

 d) The choice of the Owl.

2 a) Now you have two disputes – the issue that led to the strike and their right to strike – which is one too many for a Donkey to handle.

 b) Now you have three disputes – the issue that led to the strike, their right to strike and the use of the law in an industrial dispute – which is two too many for a Donkey to handle.

 c) No. They strike to get what they want even by threatening the existence of the company – if their strike had no deleterious effects on the company there would no point in striking! Donkeys can't see that.

 d) Owls know why the answer is 'Yes!'

3 a) Maybe you give her cause to behave this way? Sheep always think somebody else is responsible. No doubt you moan about her behaviour with your other colleagues.

 b) Sign of a clever Fox.

SELF-ASSESSMENT TEST 16

1 You are looking for a job and see an advertisement for out-of-work truck drivers to attend for interview at 2 p.m. on Friday at the personnel office of a local haulage company. When you get there at 1.55 p.m. you join a long queue outside the office. Do you think your chances of getting the job are:
   (a) Diminished?
   (b) Not affected?
   (c) Better?

2 You are in Accra (Ghana) and are loking for a 'Mammy Truck' that is going to Kamasi. You find one and the mammy tells you it will leave as soon as it is full. You note that there is only one seat left vacant on the truck and decide to take it. When will the truck leave:
   (a) Immediately?
   (b) Later?

3 You act as a go-between in the sale of a light aircraft. The buyer pays by cheque and the owner is willing to accept this and release the aircraft once it is cleared by the bank. When settling up your fee, do you:
   (a) Press for payment in cash?
   (b) Send in an invoice?
   (c) Accept a cheque?

4 An Arab with six camels approaches an oasis in search of water. Standing by the spring there is another Arab and a sign (in Arabic): 'Water: all you can drink – price one camel'. Who has the power:
   (a) The Arab with the camels?
   (b) The Arab with the water?
   (c) Impossible to say?

CHAPTER 16

Who has the power?

or how to get leverage

A thousand or more years ago, Viking raiders regularly slipped out of the beautiful fjords of Norway in magnificent sailing ships bound for the coastal settlements of Europe. Today, from those same fjords, their descendants use nothing more lethal than the fax machine to run highly efficient worldwide shipping operations.

Lars is the Vice President of a shipping company operating out of Bergen. He does scores of deals a year, buying or selling ships, negotiating contracts for newbuilds in Europe and the Far East, handling repair contracts (one of the toughest sides of a tough business), bunkers, freight and charter rates, crew wages, and agency fees. He's a busy man and after 40 years in the business he still has a romantic attitude to 'his' ships.

In the matter of negotiation, Lars is anything but romantic. In fact he is downright single-minded when it comes to handling his company's business.

Some of the managers – they range from clerks who learned the hard way, through graduates who learned the smart way, to 'retired' Masters who learned it anyway – occasionally discuss their negotiating problems between fax messages. If Lars happens to overhear such a conversation, while passing through the open-plan offices, he is likely to proffer the summary of his negotiating wisdom:

In any deal, ask: Who is buying and who is selling?

To Lars, the answer tells him who has *the power* and, as far as he is concerned, having power is an asset, not having it a handicap, which is a pretty sound approach to this aspect of negotiating.

It follows that Lars believes that his managers should seek power *before* a deal in order to exercise it *during* the negotiation.

What does power consist of?

If we haven't got it, how do we get it and from where?

First you must rid yourself of any lingering illusions that power doesn't matter. It does. The quaint view that power doesn't matter is often expressed in the belief that the act of negotiating somehow shelters the parties from the crudities of power.

REMEMBER, WE HAVE AN ALTERNATIVE!

A major European car manufacturer exports its vehicles all over the world in specially designed roll-on/roll-off ships owned by independent shipping companies.

There is a delicate power balance in the annual negotiations over freight prices. If the manufacturer squeezed the shipping companies too hard on price, one or more of them would go out of business or shift their activities elsewhere.

This would reduce the number of shippers and place the surviving companies in a more powerful negotiating position.

On the other hand if the shipping companies push their prices too high – by overt or covert collusion – this will

---

> encourage other shippers to join in the trade, or perhaps
> encourage the manufacturer to purchase its own vessels.
>
> A clear understanding of the need to contain the power
> conflict within 'reasonable' bounds is implicit in their
> negotiating relationship.

This is altogether wrong. Negotiating merely expresses the power balance in a different form!

The understandable preference for Jaw-Jaw rather than War-War has nothing to do with the excision of power from the relationship between the two contestants; it merely expresses a preference for one form of the power balance rather than another.

Lars is absolutely right in one thing:

power is the very essence of the negotiating process

It is through our perceptions of power – ours *and* the other person's – that we conduct ourselves as negotiators. This leads us to the most important single characteristic of power in a negotiation: it is entirely *subjective* and like the wind, power is felt rather than seen.

In short: power is in the head.

And remember, in negotiating there are *two* heads – yours and the other person's – not one!

NICE ONE, TOKYO

In Australia they have lots of iron and coal. In Japan they have none and import the lot. Who then is in the strongest bargaining position?

Right, the Japanese?

How do they achieve this remarkable result? By making

184

the Australian negotiators go to Japan to do the deals. Once there the Australians are negotiating at a Japanese pace with their minds operating at an Australian pace.

The Japanese are in no hurry – they live there!

The Aussies are in a hurry because they don't.

Australians like Australia. Hence, after a short while they like their affluent and sunny selves to be firmly planted back in Oz near the pool, the beach, the barbeque, and the kids.

The Australian coal companies have not always exercised their strength as seen by the Japanese – they have most of the coal Japan needs and this ought to be reflected in the price.

Instead they have gone for their own needs, seeing Japan more as a means to their *own* ends than as a customer desperately anxious to get its hands on long-term coal supplies.

Hence, it is what happens in the heads of the parties that determines how power impacts on the outcome of their negotiation.

'How so?', you might ask, 'surely power has an objective dimension too.'

I am compelled to agree, of course, that a world surplus of tanker capacity is an objective circumstance of some relevance to the power relationship between a tanker owner and a chartering agency. That cannot be denied. But what can be, and is, asserted here is that:

The negotiator's subjective perception is *more important* than the objective circumstances in themselves.

It is what the negotiators *believe* is true that counts, not what a panel of independent assessors could tell them if they sat long enough and reviewed in minute detail all the so-called objective evidence. (And note that their review of that evidence is itself subjective, as is your interpretation of their assessment.)

Negotiators instinctively understand the importance of subjective belief – that's why they spend so much time trying to convince us that their perceptions are so much more credible than ours.

If a shipowner sees a fleet of unchartered tankers riding at anchor in the bay, it does not follow that he rolls over and plays dead when he gets a bid for a time charter. He will attempt to convince the charterer that the vessel he has for hire is somehow different from the others in the bay.

If they believe what they hear and persist with the negotiations, this will reduce their apparent negotiating advantage.

Alternatively, suppose your business requires additional computer programming staff. What will they cost you? 'That depends', you answer; 'on how many computer programmers are in the market looking for a job.'

Now in an economics class you would get a bonus point for such a brilliantly obvious conclusion – though, not surprisingly what you have alluded to is of little consequence in the real world.

How many job-seekers make it a hirer's market? We could as productively ask: how long is a piece of string? Moreover, we don't negotiate with markets. We negotiate with people.

You cannot *safely* assume that the people you negotiate with are as well informed about the 'market' as you are, or think you are. Nor can you assume that what you know about the market is correct. Even majority opinion of the state of a market is a notoriously poor guide to its actual state – as you will find if you ask anybody who has been caught short when they played the market.

In fact the way to wealth in the Stock Market is to know better than the market about its prospects: when the market believes shares will go up and you think you know better, you sell out and take your profit; when the market believes shares will fall and you think you know better, you buy-in and wait for your profit.

If you wait for the market to form an opinion you could be buying when you should be selling and selling when you should be buying. Setting aside how you know at any moment that the market has got it wrong and you've got it right, it is certainly true that if you get it right more often, and for bigger stakes, than you get it wrong you might retire owning a fortune, and if you don't, you won't.

All economists assume that something called *the* market makes decisions about prices and quantities and that they (and their students) have a bird's-eye view of the entire market mechanism.

FLY ME

An oil company that operates several rigs in the Mexican Gulf hires $70 million worth of helicopter services a year. Most of the business is placed with one of the largest helicopter operators in the world. It is highly efficient, competitive in price and has an excellent safety record.

However, the oil company does not place all its business with this operator, and about 20 per cent of it goes to three other much smaller companies.

They are run by 'two-men' outfits (mainly ex-pilots for the major company who branched out on their own) and are slightly more expensive than the corporate giant.

Why does the hirer do this if it costs more? Because the oil company does not want to drive out of business the smaller suppliers in case this gives its largest supplier ideas about the power balance.

But in a negotiation you don't have a bird's-eye view because you are not a bird – you're part of the mechanism!

Suppose, as an out-of-work computer programmer, you walk into the personnel department of a company that has advertised a vacancy in its computer department and the waiting room is crammed full with other applicants.

Are you stronger or weaker as a result?

Your natural reaction would be to feel less confident of your chances – clearly there is a lot of competition for the job.

Or is there?

The answer is, and ought to be: how do you know?

How do you know what they are queuing for?

How do you know that you're not the only computer programmer they have seen all week?

You may be weaker with competition around but on the other hand it may not be competition at all. They could be queuing to be interviewed for a receptionist's job in the word-processing department.

But if you *believe* they are computer programmers you will feel weaker and are likely to end up a *cheap* programmer. It could be that the employer has hired a group of actors from Rentacrowd to intimidate you into accepting £5,000 less per year.

THE CIRCLE OF NEGOTIATING RELATIONSHIPS

Negotiators for Third World governments and Western mineral corporations over the past 50 years have seen a significant shift in their relationships.

The balance of power has changed since the first 'concessions', were granted during the 'colonial' period.

In the first stages of the relationship, the company was

given a 'concession', i.e. an absolute right to remove from the territory primary resources for a fee or a royalty per ton removed.

Several 'revisions' have been negotiated, basically concerned with the demands from the host authority for a greater share of the income from its mineral resources. The major inhibitions on the rapid spread of these revision agreements was either technological or monetary.

The more the mineral operation concentrated on simple ('steam shovel') operations or the greater the facility for raising necessary funds from international agencies, the greater the bargaining position of the host government.

The other major barrier to host country development has been the lack of access to Western markets, without which there is not enough demand to justify a host monopoly.

But the picture is patchy across the extraction sectors in Third World countries. Some countries manage to tie their contracts to the establishment of local 'down-stream' capacity, others to local participation in the equity of the mineral companies.

In addition the government has renegotiated both royalty and taxation liabilities with the mineral companies.

The final stage has been the movement over to 'management' agreements where the corporation manages the exploration, commissioning and extractive contract for a fee from the indigenous (usually nationalized) company and arranges the marketing of the output (again for a fee).

This reverses the original relationship but the parties have found a way of living with these changes.

In general then, we cannot be sure that what we think in the situation actually pertains in practice.

If counterparts persist in seeing the situation differently, we have the classic negotiator's dilemma: we can't be sure that their apparent position reflects the true power relationship between us and is not just a tactical stance on their part to convince us to change our perceptions.

Indeed, we can conceive of all negotiating moves and tactics as attempts in one degree or another to structure how the other party views the power relationship. The more skilfully we structure their subjective views of the power relationship in our favour, the less relevant to the outcome of the negotiation the objective power balance of the market.

In other words, if you believe *they* have power then nothing more need be said: they have it (and they have you too!). For this reason, I tend to (respectfully) disagree with Lars on the importance of who is the buyer and who is the seller, if by the answer he implies an *automatic* conclusion that buying puts us in a more powerful position than selling.

It does not matter whether we are buying or selling *if* we get the power dimension to work for us rather than against us.

It all boils down to how you and the other person see your relationship. If you can influence his perception you get a better deal.

What factors influence our perception of the power relationship?

The answer could open up that most complex of subjects – what makes people think the way they do? – and would fill volumes rather than close off this chapter. For the moment let us confine our discussion to the perceptions we form *before* we meet the other person, for these are often the most influential on our approach, our manner, our demeanour, our confidence and, eventually, our deal.

Almost all sellers suffer from a twin obsession: the *power* of the buyers and the *extent* of the competition. Given the slightest encouragement a seller will catalogue the atrocities committed by buyers or the competition on his good self.

Any five people from sales mixing socially regale each other with ever-more incredible tales of perfidy among buyers and 'the dirty tricks of the contemptible competition'. In short, they psyche themselves into believing in their own weakness by assuming the buyers' strengths.

THE MARKET MAMMIES OF MAKOLA

When Ernst Weinbanger went to Ghana as the marketing manager for a large Dutch oil company, his first assignment was to visit dealers, many of whom lived up country. He wanted to see as much as he could of Ghana and meet as many people as possible and he was advised by colleagues that there was no better way to learn about the 'real' Ghana than to travel by 'bus', which in Ghana means the back of an open truck.

Ernst's colleagues did not warn him about the business standards of the 'bus companies', and he made the mistake of assuming that Ghana ran its public transport with the same attention to timetables as the honest burghers of his native Amsterdam.

He innocently believed a mammy in the Makola market who said her truck's departure for Kamasi was imminent and that as soon as the truck was full it would depart. Ernst could see that every seat in the truck was full except for one and concluded that he would soon be on his way to Kumasi. So, as it was his first visit to Ghana, he paid his fare and got on board – only to see the person next to him get off!

That is how the market mammies use Rentacrowd to fill their trucks with cash customers.

Eventually, it dawned on Ernst from the number of times the mammy repeated her sales routine that he was not the *last* but the *first* fare-paying passenger to get on to her truck that morning.

If it happens to you, it's no good trying to get your money back – when a market mammy says 'no' in matters relating to business, you had better believe that she means it!

Ernst Weinbanger learned a lot on his first tour. So much in fact that for years he sent newly arrived managers, without a briefing, to see Ghana by 'bus'.

'Nobody,' he is wont to say over drinks in the bar of the Ambassador Hotel in Africa, 'warned me, so I didn't warn them, but what they learn in a month about how they do business in West Africa is worth a year at Harvard.'

Yet buyers can see things differently. For instance, I know a buyer for a large mainframe computer company who buys millions of pounds' worth of components for his company's assembly plants each quarter and who firmly believes that sellers have the power.

How did he draw that conclusion?

There was a time when he knew his company's computers inside out (he used to make them) but the technology has moved so fast in the past ten years that he feels at a disadvantage because ten years out of computer engineering is several generations too long.

He buys thousands of different components in large and small lots for the entire range of his company's computers and he claims that the manufacturers' representatives have an advantage over him as they are specialists in their own components, while he, as a buyer, knows little about any specific item.

He must rely on the seller to guide him on technical matters regarding their products.

It all comes down to perception. If you are selling and believe that the buyer has the power, you could be filling your head with the buyer's ammunition.

How do you know whether a specific buyer has more power in a negotiation than you do? Do you believe what he is saying about the competition just because he says it, or worse, do you believe you are up against tough competition before you have even met him and found out what it is he wants?

Think less about the buyer for a moment and think more about the alleged competition. In the ordinary run of events in business, people deal with more than one company. Their experience of a particular company can vary from satisfactory to absolutely hopeless. It is just not true that every other company that sells similar products or services to you is set to get the order you seek from a buyer.

The buyer may have dealt with your competitor before and been given cause to weigh his products or service in the balance and find them wanting. In which case, you are stronger than you think. Competition is only strong if every firm that is knocking at the buyer's door is equally competent in providing what the buyer wants. Experience of business suggests that it is very unusual to find firms competing on exactly the same terms (it's so unusual that in most countries they get very suspicious if it happens!).

The buyer may prefer to deal with firms that are close to his own plants or are owned by fellow Bostonians. This reduces his power if you're local or from Boston, but enhances it if you're not.

The buyer may operate a company policy that excludes certain firms – perhaps they didn't deliver what they promised, or chased too hard for their money, or antagonized the staff in some way – and this too weakens the buyer's power as long as you are not one of them.

The buyer may be buying to a departmental specification that reflects the preferences or training of the people who will operate the machinery. This also weakens the buyer's power.

You can bet your last ten pence that if the programmers were trained by IBM they will tend to specify IBM plug-compatible products. If that is what you are selling you need not collapse your margins *just because* the buyer has a Digital catalogue on his desk.

(The first car that people buy tends to be the same make as the one they learned to drive on, which must give a lot of negotiating leverage to driving schools when they buy their fleets.)

Conversely, if you're selling non-IBM products you ought not to feel weak just because the users have specified IBM, providing you sell products as good or better than IBM.

Also, the buyer may be willing to look elsewhere for other reasons and override the preferences of his engineers.

The buyer's choices can be constrained by all kinds of things – he often works to a policy set by other people (not always considerate of the economics of their decisions) and he is often at the mercy of his company's specialists who seldom consider his problems with suppliers. He may be under instructions not to give all the business to a single firm in case he gets too dependent on it – that could be your chance to get in – or he could have instructions to always buy bulk – hence you're chasing a big order.

Therefore, don't forget that buyers do not automatically have the power, unless you give it to them.

And what of sellers? Do they have the power?

Not necessarily: it depends on what they choose to believe.

If the buyer convinces them that the competition really is strong, this must weaken the seller's power. For this reason, a caution is appropriate: learn to recognize the buyer's theatre 'props' (for that is what they are) as he performs his version of the long-running off-Broadway play, *Oh, What a Lot of Competition There is Today.*

Among the props that alter your power perception are:

1 Catalogues from your competitors, preferably with page markers sticking out of them.
2 A pile of papers on his desk showing their letterheads (but not their contents) – handy to tap when he utters the well-worn (but still devastatingly effective) seven-word-killer line:

'You'll have to do better than that.'

Buyers use these props because they work – The League of Gullible Sellers has always had a mass membership!

Sellers can fight back against these tactics.

If your price is challenged you ought at least to work hard at defending it. One thing you can do is ask, 'Why must I do better than I have proposed?' The reply can give you information about whether it is a bluff or not – the vaguer, or the more heated, the response the more likely it is a bluff.

If you have such insufficient confidence in your price that your first thought when it is challenged is to think how you can drop it without starting a rout, then there is no reason why the buyer should have any confidence in your price either.

Buyers always challenge prices – it's in the nature of the beast! Many sellers always back off from a price challenge – hence it pays buyers to challenge their proposals with the 'killer' line.

Buyers are not entirely defenceless against sellers who are in, or feel that they are in, a strong position. Nor do they always need to stoop to deceit to alter the seller's perception of his power.

They can adopt tactics to convince the seller that they do not need his products – perhaps by showing there are other suppliers anxious to do business with them, or that they have large stocks, or that they might set up their own production facility to make it. If this is credible, the seller will lower his perception of his own power.

Buyers can hint about the longer-run benefits of the seller going easy on price just now – 'sell cheap, get famous' – and the longer-run consequences of exploiting negotiating power –

'screw us now and we'll screw you later'. This can curb the seller's use of his power. It is seldom in the longer-term interest of a business for it to screw the other person to the floor with stiff demands.

Sellers know that high prices (and high profits) attract competition, and that the one great law of the market is that if you want to sell more, you have to reduce your price or raise your marketing costs, or both. This puts pressure on the seller's power.

You can strengthen your power by persuading him that there is a lot of competition for your business – certainly you will never strengthen your power if you tell him otherwise.

WHO'S LAUGHING NOW?

A cabaret comedian had just finished his first act for a (far) off 'the Strip' Las Vegas nightclub and the owner came up to him backstage with tears running down his cheeks – he had started laughing at the first joke and didn't stop for 20 minutes. He told the comedian: 'You're the best act I've seen this year. They're still rolling in the aisles back there. You were fantastic!'

The comedian told the owner he was glad he liked the act.

The owner said: I'm gonna show you how grateful I am. Just name it, and you've got it. The tab is on the house.'

The comedian, who had a fine sense of timing, replied: 'Well, the first thing I want is a raise to $1,000 a show.'

The owner agreed – still laughing – at least until he got back to his office.

If the owner had been less enthusiastic about telling the comedian what a great act he had, he would probably have kept him working for a month for three shows a night at a $500 a throw.

By exuberantly praising the comedian's performance he changed the power balance between himself – a hardened nightclub boss giving an untried comedian a break – into a more than satisfied customer vulnerable to a soft touch.

Moral: don't praise your suppliers unless you want to be charged more for the same service!

Don't confide that your warehouse is full and the alternative to his placing an order is for your plant to go on short time.

If he feels there is competitive pressure upon him even when none is being directly exerted, that is bound to reduce his power and raise yours.

Hence, as a buyer, you can let him see that you are aware of his competitors' products, know their special features and benefits, and show that you are in regular contact with them.

You should never explain *why* you are not doing business with the seller's competitors or *why* you want to switch from them – and above all avoid the temptation to knock those who have let you down as it merely strengthens the seller's power.

Conversely avoid telling him how much you *love* his products – it might be just enough to give him the courage to raise his price!

Even if your business relationship with a seller is secure, you should keep him unsure of it, by showing interest in switching your buying policy to rivals on any credible grounds such as:

Price ('they're cheaper').
Delivery ('they're offering CIF against your FOB').
Quantity ('they are offering bigger discounts').
Patriotism ('the boss wants to buy home produce only').
New features ('their machine bags the cement too').

Security of supply ('they guarantee all the cocoa we can take for three years').

Credit terms ('they offer 90 days' interest free'), etc.

This will reduce his power over you, or at least keep him from getting big ideas about his relationship with you.

Who then, has the power?

You do, if your opponent believes you have it. And if he believes that you have the power, you can extract a premium off him for your services.

On the other hand, he has the power if you believe he has it and you can be sure that your perception of the power balance will cost you something extra above what you would have paid if you had been less influenced by what you thought you knew about the other guy's position.

If you need the deal more than you can cope with the prospect of not getting it, you will be less powerful in the negotiation. The converse is true for him – if he needs to settle more than he can face a deadlock, you have power over him.

The main point to remember is that who has the power is not decided by the calculation of a formula of relative ability to do without the deal. It is your *perception* of the pressures on him to settle compared to the pressures you feel upon yourself that will influence your reading of the power balance.

If you get this wrong because you are misled by your assumptions, you will award him with a greater power than he might have in fact – that could cost you something on the final price that you needn't concede. And this is true whether you are buying or selling.

COMMENTS ON SELF-ASSESSMENT TEST 16

1 a) How do you know that they are all out-of-work truck drivers? The response of a Donkey.

b) Owls are not influenced by what they think they see.

c) Obviously competition inspires you – you must be a very clever Fox.

2 a) You have a tendency to believe what the seller tells you and in Accra, as elsewhere, that is a Sheepish mistake. When the truck goes to Kamasi depends on whether you are the last passenger – the mammy did not lie to you – or the first, with the rest a rentacrowd.

b) Clearly, you have been caught out before but are Sheepish enough to accept your fate again and wait.

3 a) Sound advice from any Owl. Get paid while you have some influence on the seller.

b) Your services are valued less after they have been performed than beforehand – as every hooker knows but Donkeys don't.

c) Only if given to you in his bank and made out for cash. Otherwise, no way! Another mistake by a Donkey.

4 a) How many camels has the man with the water got? Feeling Sheepish?

b) What if the man with the camels is the only one with a loaded rifle? Also feeling Sheepish?

c) Correct, as any Owl would tell you.

SELF-ASSESSMENT TEST 17

1 You are a real estate agent and have been assigned to sell a downtown property by its owner. Your instructions are 'get the best price you can'. Do you:
   (a) Get on with the search for a buyer?
   (b) Insist on more specific instructions?
   (c) Decline the assignment?

2 You are selling a piano that has cluttered up your garage for several years. A prospect appears to be interested in purchasing it and asks how much you want for it. Do you:
   (a) Give her a figure at the top end of your expectations?
   (b) Ask her what she will offer for it?
   (c) Tell her the amount your spouse told you to get?
   (d) Go in lower in case she backs off?

3 You are interested in buying a used 12-foot dinghy and ask the seller how much she wants for it. She tells you that her boyfriend told her to get at least £1,400 for it. You find that she is reluctant to budge from her price. Do you:
   (a) Give her your phone number in case she changes her mind?
   (b) Take the deal after a haggle?
   (c) Ask to see her boyfriend?

4 You respond to an advertisement in the trade press offering a salmon-fishing estate for sale. The advertisement insists on 'principals only'. You find in discussion with the other side that you are dealing with an agent of the owner. Do you:
   (a) Insist on dealing with the other principal?
   (b) Ask if the agent has power to settle without reference back to the owner?
   (c) Carry on negotiations on a wait-and-see basis?

CHAPTER 17

If you haven't got a principal – invent one!

or how not to have negotiating authority

Every week in Britain thousands of readers purchase *Exchange and Mart* and scan its pages for bargains. Many thousands of others look through the small ads in their local papers to see what is for sale, or what is wanted.

To indulge in this weekly search you needn't have anything other than curiosity in mind. If something strikes your fancy you can try to buy it, or, seeing the prices offered for certain items, you might be induced, if you have similar items, to try to sell them yourself.

Some papers actually draw the attention of prospective sellers to the market prospects of goods they may possess but no longer have a need for. A paper could carry a notice like the following:

TWENTY COMMODE PURCHASERS INCONVENIENCED

The gist of the pitch is that an advertisement to sell an antique commode attracted 21 buyers willing to buy at the asking price of £1,000 and, presumably, this left 20 buyers still without one! Clearly, by implication, any reader of the paper with a spare commode could contact the 20 disappointed buyers by paying for a similar advertisement.

Whichever way you make known your desire to sell an item you still face the problem of actually negotiating a price for it.

Getting a prospect to look at your article is a big step towards a sale, but it is only a first step to actually negotiating the price.

Prices in the 'household goods' market are not always specified in the advertisements, which is one way of avoiding the ONO mistake! This creates for both the buyer and the seller the problem of what price to open at.

Alternatively, if a price is mentioned, the buyer can decide to ignore it and see what concessions he gets when the seller believes he will lose the sale if his price does not come down.

It is typical in these types of informal transactions for the buyer, with disarming innocence, to ask:

How much do you want for it?

This can embarrass a seller who has no recent experience of haggling and is unprepared for the question. The most common counter is to reply:

How much will you offer for it?

More than likely, both parties avoid eye contact during the exchange of parried questioning, and each desperately examines the sale item as if it might give them a clue as to what to say next.

This behaviour is a natural product of unfamiliarity with the market for used household goods – only professional dealers conduct similar transactions every day of every week and, consequently, have the confidence to quote a tough opening price.

Unfamiliarity with the market comes from a lack of information about the 'proper' price for a used car, a desk, a plant pot, a wheelbarrow, a commode, or whatever.

The seller wants to sell but does not know what to ask for: the buyer wants to buy but does not know what to offer; and each tries to pass responsibility for the first move onto the other.

The ritual 'sword fencing' of what-do-you-want/what-will-you-offer is as spontaneously discovered by people as it is inevitable, because, essentially, haggling consists of:

The seller trying to ascertain the maximum that the buyer is willing to pay without disclosing the minimum that the seller is prepared to accept.

All negotiating problems involve the perplexity: how to uncover the other party's upper boundary while keeping one's own well and truly camouflaged.

This chapter discusses one common solution to the problem, namely, the tactic of the 'mandate'. It is stumbled upon by gifted amateurs, as well as being the basis of a lucrative career for some professionals. After discussing its help to the former, we will look briefly at its role with the latter.

Negotiators use the mandate tactic in an attempt to build a negotiating position. It requires only that the parties refer to some absent principal as the person who, allegedly, has determined the terms they must stick to in the negotiation. By implication, these terms are mandatory.

The negotiator will say something like:

My brother says I must not accept less than £615

This can be countered by:

My husband told me not to pay more than £555

Clearly, if a deal is to be agreed one or both of the (often fictitious) mandates has to be ignored.

An entire conversation between two would-be traders could be constructed, in which the actual principal parties to the transaction shelter under alleged mandates from their relatives who, conveniently, are not present.

You should be wary of an absolute inflexibility when using the mandate tactic – after all it is a negotiation – because you could provoke the 'organ grinder' sneer: 'If you can't make your own decisions, I prefer to speak to the organ grinder and not his monkey.' (You should only tease *him* with the organ-grinder sneer when *(a)* you are in a very strong position, i.e. he needs your business; or *(b)* you don't care about deadlock, i.e. you don't need his.)

But, if you are not sure what to do next when asked about your price, and don't have enough confidence to go in tough, try the mandate tactic.

In the case of used household goods it is not normally worth hiring agents to negotiate the sale of, say, a used washing machine (though the author, on occasion, has done so for friends).

You can use the mandate of a principal not present in the negotiations as long as their influence on the outcome is credible. I was once floored by a man who exclaimed: 'What will the wife's mother think of me if I sell to you at *that* price?'

Managers, of course, use the mandate of their absent bosses all the time:

If I shave any more off the price, *they* will go bananas upstairs

or, in a slightly different version,

It's simply against company policy to agree to those terms.

Selling a house clearly requires the consent of your spouse to the terms, as does selling most household items. So use his or her mandate in the negotiations, which effectively turns you from a principal into an agent of the 'absent principal'!

An invented mandate could give you that margin of confidence you need for the moment you seek eye contact just before the other person responds – a most off-putting behaviour if he is under pressure.

The mandate tactic can be used:

1 To support your demands that the quality of the goods is of

a certain standard (enabling you to draw attention to flawed features of his product).

2 To demand that the deal must include, say, the leads and spares (enabling you to back-off the sale if these are not included or to demand that the price be discounted in lieu of them).

3 To insist that it must be *demonstrated* to be in working order (creating the prospect of a discount for anything less – given the 'time and trouble, not to say expense, of putting things right'). And so on.

There is almost no end to the issues that you can confidently raise under the protection of a real or imaginary mandate.

Of course, in return, the seller can quote 'his brother's' opinion that he must get cash only (suggestions of a discount for cash, or, perhaps, a premium for a cheque?), and that if you want spares you must pay for them separately ('it being normal in these cases').

By displacing the source of our demands onto others, it is easier (in the sense of less embarrassing) to introduce them into the negotiation, and easier to back away from buying/selling on this occasion if the terms are not right.

In this respect, never underestimate the unwillingness of non-professionals to tell you that they don't want to buy an item:

I didn't want to tell him his car was no good, so I told him I would think about it, which got me out of the house.

Professionals are no less coy about saying 'no', as in the classic:

Don't call us, we'll call you.

With an invented mandate we act *as if* we are *agents* in the transaction when, in fact, we are *principals* and, by distancing

206

ourselves from the issues, we achieve a kind of neutrality about them. This makes us very difficult targets if things get tough.

Of course, in the used-household-goods markets we are the principals – and the other party knows this – but the *fiction* that we are only an agent of our spouse is often credible enough for it to be accepted, so:

IF YOU HAVEN'T GOT A PRINCIPAL – INVENT ONE!

Thus, we get a line of retreat if we need it, a bolster to our price defences if they are under pressure, and less chance of tension if deadlock threatens; after all, 'it is not *me* you have to convince but my wife'.

Mandates (real or imaginary) protect the negotiator from taking personal responsibility – and thereby personal hostility from the party – for the demands they make.

Union leaders are adept at using the mandate demand, as are all negotiators who are representatives of absent principals (such as lawyers who insist on referring everything back to their clients). For instance, union officials often preface their claims with remarks to the effect that the 'members have instructed me to demand' whatever it is they are formally asking for.

Mandates also give those who use them a means to limit the number and size of concessions they can make:

It's not up to me, it's in the hands of my members.

Or:

My client will never accept less than a full rebate, etc.

A mandate can also give you a first look at their price, particularly for large-value items like houses and cars, and also a note of any concessions that the other party prematurely offers.

You can see a house alone and ascertain what is in the mind

of the seller, and then 'escape' politely to 'consult' your spouse. You might be able to extract the seller's best price and also get an idea of the extra items they might include in the purchase (fittings, carpets, kitchen furniture, etc.).

This leaves the way open for a joint visit, if you decide that the house is potentially suitable, and gives you an opportunity to assess the available extras you want included in the deal. Finally, you can go to a *third* round by shunting the negotiations, *plus the early concessions*, onto your estate agent!

Husbands and wives going round houses 'oohing and aahing' together is no way to buy a house. (I once got priced out of a house sale because my mother-in-law told the owner on the first visit that it was the 'most beautiful house she had ever been in', which certainly firmed up his soggy ideas about price because three weeks later he was still quoting her statements to me in the negotiations – after that she went under a strict gagging rule!)

Another Class A mistake is to be hurried into house purchase by real estate brokers who are more concerned with their take from the deal than saving you money. (I am often asked how to tell the good guys from the bad guys in brokerage. Well, one thing for sure, the bad guys don't all wear black hats!)

In general, rushing into deals is bad news for your bank balance.

One reason why house owners use agents to conduct the sale is precisely because they can shelter behind the mandate. When asked, 'What price would you accept for the house?', you can neatly sidestep with the reply, 'All that is handled by my agent.'

The mandate tactic is not just used in negotiations for household items. Some of the world's biggest deals are negotiated using a sophisticated version of the mandate tactic. Professional agents often negotiate the outline of the deal subject to the approval of the principals, *who are not present*.

It is common in business for advertisements to include the phrase:

This is sometimes an attempt to save time and money.

However, giving an agent a mandate is likely to strengthen his negotiating position. He is arm's length from the deal, and you, as principal, can accept or reject what may have been put together by much haggling with the seller: you were not party to the pressures and compromises of the negotiating process and thereby can reject out-of-hand elements of the deal you don't like.

In other words, you can repudiate a deal through an agent at no emotional cost, and, as a result perhaps, get it improved as well.

Naturally, the greater the distance between you and the negotiation the easier it is for you to say 'no'. That is why if you want to say 'no', use the telephone – or a letter – and avoid personal contact if it is fatal to maintaining a tough posture.

The other party has no way of knowing the extent of your agent's authority and consequently he has no way of knowing whether a little more conceded here or there will secure the deal. This might produce bigger concessions in your favour than otherwise.

The mandate can be used by agents to secure better terms:

> If it was up to me, I might agree with you, but my client insists on a full penalty clause for late delivery.

Or:

> I'm sorry but there is no way my client will accept that proposal.

Both these statements can be very difficult barriers to get round.

If you are negotiating with an agent, you have no control over how he reports the proceedings to his principal – or even whether he reports anything at all. This is the greatest weakness of negotiating through agents (though I strongly recommend their use when the stakes are high and the market is unfamiliar to you).

The agent, for all you know, may be working to bump up the price in order to increase his fee, while the other principal may be quite willing to settle if he only knew about the offer you've made.

Again you just don't know.

Hence, in seeking to bar agents from the negotiation, the advertisers are trying to meet face-to-face with the person who has full authority to settle and who, by his physical presence in the negotiations, must perforce be directly subject to their pressures.

However, professional agents at the *Everything is Negotiable Workouts* often wax eloquently on an apparently common complaint among their number. In real estate, for instance, an agent can be undermined by a principal who instructs him to accept the other party's last offer even though the agent advises him, on the basis of his experience, that the other party can be pushed to a better price. In fact, the worst instruction an agent can get is to be told:

Get the best price you can, but above all get *a* price.

This complaint is the reverse of the suspicions voiced by some principals about agents:

I believe that agents always hold out for a higher price from the other party merely to get a bigger fee.

This suspicion can be fed when the negotiations are conducted in semi-public. Competitive business takes place in a relatively small community in any one place. To lose one's commercial reputation in the City of London is as devastating as it is to lose it in Edinburgh, Hong Kong, Bahrain, Sydney, or Los Angeles.

In all serious competing businesses, everybody knows everybody worth knowing in the rival companies, and nudge-nudge-wink-wink 'confidential' whispers travel round the trade like fire around a prairie; there is nothing closer to greased lightning than the tittle-tattle of business (with the possible exception of politics). Nothing is more deserving of being true than a good piece of in-the-know scandal – and, anyway, if it isn't true it's almost certain to be funny!

GETTING YOURSELF AN AGENT

In some cases you are better off with an agent, especially if the stakes are high and the market is unknown to you. Your first problem is to get a good agent and this is a lot harder than you might imagine. True anybody can get *an* agent – there are plenty of people doing precious little for either themselves or their clients.

What you need is an agent who will work for you and not somebody who expects you to do the work for them. If they never return your calls within a reasonable time (you can't expect them to be in their offices *and* selling your filmscript), do not keep you informed of progress and show no evidence of making any, constantly argue with you when you ask reasonable questions, are totally conservative about what they should go for on your behalf, and prefer to haggle with you than haggle with whomsoever they are supposed to be dealing with, you ought to get out of the relationship.

The best agents are always in demand – I know one in London who only takes *five* clients at a time and if you want her you have to wait until one of them goes off her books.

Agents cannot produce miracles – at least not on a regular basis! Nor can they be left to get on with it without help from you. My rule for judging the worth of an agent is I know I need him as long as he suggests we go for a deal way beyond the very best I had hoped for. If he doesn't, then I know I know as much about the business as he does and would be better off holding onto my ten per cent!

In negotiating through agents, the other party can seek to undermine your position by trying to contact your principal. Of course, this could be construed to be unethical, etc. (indeed, most professional bodies frown at such conduct) but there is more than one way to achieve this end without becoming an outcast.

The other party can leak 'news' to the trade press, such as by asserting that only your personal intransigence on 'minor' points is preventing the deal going through. If your clients read these press reports (and copies can be brought to their attention) they might be conned into believing them, particularly if they already half believe you are holding out for an extra commission.

This causes them to insist on an early settlement, which, presumably, is why some negotiators go semi-public in this way, hoping that it will sow doubts in the (sometimes) anonymous principal's minds about the probity of his agents.

Apart from trying to avoid time-wasting and the possibility that over-zealous (or greedy) agents are manipulating the settlement terms by provoking an unnecessary deadlock, the demand for 'principals only' can increase the bargaining advantage of the parties.

Suppose the property for sale is a large company, and the seller ends up face-to-face with a prospect who has authority to settle – it's his own money – but little experience of handling transactions of this size. If the seller has been the owner of similar properties for long enough to be less than intimidated by them, he must have an advantage over a keen and vulnerable buyer moving into the 'big league' for the first time.

It is also possible that the advertiser is himself an agent for the real owner and is fishing for 'principals only' precisely in order to smoke out would-be entrepreneurs with little professional experience of what they are doing.

More than one hotel has changed hands in recent years on terms less than favourable to the first-time buyer, who arrives at the negotiation clutching a recent legacy or a large redundancy cheque.

For these reasons, reputable agents are a good protection for an unsure and inexperienced buyer.

What constitutes a good agent is another story. In real estate there is some safeguard in the professional status of Chartered Surveyors, and in other commercial sectors many people make an honest living by acting as agents between principals (but watch out for 'Jaws' – he and his cousins swim in the smallest ponds and strike without warning).

But in the absence of an agent, or where the value of the transaction does not justify their expense, your best bet is to become one!

COMMENTS ON SELF-ASSESSMENT TEST 17

1 a) If you're new, hungry and a Sheep, you will. Such instructions are nothing but trouble because no matter what price you get the owner will be dissatisfied.

b) Correct. The Fox always seeks the client's bottom line when given negotiating instructions, if only to protect her bushy tail.

c) More than hasty, even for a Donkey.

2 a) A toss up with (b). Foxes are confident of their prices and state them without hesitation and 'um ah-ing'.
   b) A Sheep isn't sure, but you will have to work hard if her price is on the low side.
   c) The 'mandate' demand has credibility. A good lead for a Fox into (b) or (a) depending on their response.
   d) Never pre-judge their offer price, otherwise you will always cut yours like all Donkeys.

3 a) Possibly, if she refuses (c). A Foxy option.
   b) Not unless you are a Donkey and desperate for her dinghy.
   c) Correct – what every Owl would do.

4 a) Surely what any Owl would do if it's 'principals only'?
   b) A second-best protective move for a Fox.
   c) Too Sheepish, as he will always refer back to the organ grinder.

SELF-ASSESSMENT TEST 18

1 You are in Bergen (Norway) and want to buy toy trolls for your children. You enter a *very* expensive souvenir shop which sells trolls. The ones you want are priced at 165 Kroner each. You want three. Do you ask the clerk:
   (a) How much for two trolls?
   (b) How much for three trolls?
   (c) What special offers are there on trolls?

2 You are in a store buying a freezer and the one you want is marked at £800. You ask for a discount and the clerk tells you that it is company policy not to give discounts off the goods as they are already marked down to the lowest possible price. Do you:
   (a) Ask to see the manager?
   (b) Accept what he says as being plausible?
   (c) Press your case for a discount with the clerk?

3 In a survey of buying behaviour of customers over three months in a major European store chain, what percentage of people do you think paid the price shown on the tag:
   (a) 97?
   (b) 37?
   (c) 11?

CHAPTER 18

There ain't no such thing as a fixed price!

or how to haggle for a lower price

Why do shops have price tags on their goods? I have heard many explanations for this phenomenon:

To save everybody asking the price of every product.
To save time in the onerous task of shopping.
To speed-up the buying decision.
To avoid mistakes at the cash desk.
To help the consumer make choices.
To treat all customers the same with the same price.
To avoid making losses on small-margin goods.

Most of them sound plausible but all miss the point. The real reason is much more subtle: the overwhelming majority of consumers are brought up from an early age believing in fairy stories, Santa Claus and fixed prices.

The first two are quite harmless and, sadly, pass with the age of innocence. But once the belief in fixed prices gets its barnacle-like grip on your brain, it hardly ever lets go. It manifests itself in the enslavement of the consumer to the price tag.

And the stores know this, which is why they use them.

In other words, they know that customers, almost totally without exception, will part with their cash for the printed price.

And what a power this gives the owners of stores! They know that most consumers would never dream of questioning a price tag – far from it, because most consumers believe that if it's on the tag then it's *gospel* – and so the stores can choose the price to put on it.

If events prove them wrong, and not enough consumers jump at the chance to buy whatever the store is selling, they hold a 'Sale' and put *another* price on the tag. One would expect consumers to be outraged at so-called 'Sales' where the evidence is as plain as can be that the stores have been padding their prices.

But no!

The belief in fixed prices appears by some weird logic to be *reinforced*, not shaken, by the visible drop in prices! Stores even leave both prices on the tag to make you think they are doing you a big favour. Instead, you ought to realize what a sucker they were taking you for before the 'Sale'.

Ironically, the greater the drop in price the greater the 'bargain' consumers feel they have achieved. But the bigger the 'bargain' the more unchallengeable is the evidence of the humbug of fixed prices.

Barnum, of Barnum and Bailey Circus fame, confessed that he made his (wholly deserved) fortune on the willingness – nay, insistence – of the great American public to pay to see his totally improbable spectacles. They were humbugged – and loved him for it.

Yet Barnum only reflected the humbug of business life. He sold tickets to dreams that could never be fulfilled – his 'products' were always a fantasy.

In retail stores the products are real – many of them are excellent – and there is little or no humbug in the claims that are made for them (give or take the 'occasional' exaggeration!). The humbug lies in the price. It claims to be real, and you believe it is real – but it is only a childhood fantasy that was reinforced with every transaction you made since you bought your first stick of candy in the corner shop.

That is why the message of this chapter is:

There ain't no such thing as a fixed price!

Gilbert Summers knows all about the fragility of fixed prices. He runs a store in Texacana, Texas, and has done so for 20 years. He never had any trouble with his prices until 1985. Up to then families loaded up the carts in his store with their weekly shopping, waited quietly while the clerks at the checkouts totalled the price tags, and then paid with cash, cheques or credit cards.

If there were any 'rows' they were over delays while a price was checked because the tag had come off, or if the clerk suspected it had been 'accidentally' changed, or a drunk had wandered in and wouldn't go home, or a couple were fighting over an incident at last night's party.

Most of the time the only noise was that of the cash registers, the piped music wafting overhead, the kids screaming as they larked about. Nobody, but nobody, ever asked to see Gilbert Summers about a price tag.

That was until Hang Ha Dong and family moved into the neighbourhood. Hang Ha Dong brought with him his entire family – all twelve of them, including his wife's sister and her aged mother.

He also brought with him the habits of a lifetime – one of which is a total incomprehension of the phenomenon of fixed prices. The first time the Hang family (en masse) visited Gilbert Summer's store was nearly their last.

Dutifully they loaded up their carts with their requirements and when they got to the checkout, Hang picked up a tin and asked how much the clerk wanted for it. The bored clerk checked the price and drawled '$2.25'. Hang delved into the cart and asked: 'How much for two tins?' The clerk looked puzzled and said, irritably, '$4.50'.

It was Hang's turn to look puzzled and he spoke to his wife in Vietnamese. Whatever she replied, Hang told the clerk that he would offer him $3.98 for the two tins. This was obviously a bit much for his wife because she let forth a gale of Vietnamese at him – and her mother joined in too. The clerk wondered what was happening.

Hang next lifted out of the cart four string bags of oranges. The clerk said: '$1.30, each.'

'$1.05,' said Mr Hang.

'$1.30,' repeated the clerk, adding 'Can't you read? It says a dollar-thirty on the tag. Where did you get a dollar-five from?'

'$1.10 and that's my best price,' said Hang.

'$1.30,' replied the clerk.

'S1.12, if you throw in the bag of rice at $4,' said Hang.

'It's a dollar-thirty for the oranges and five-forty for the rice, as it says on the tag.'

'But how much for two bags of rice?', asked Hang.

'Jesus!' exclaimed the clerk, by this time losing his cool. 'Are you nuts or something?'

CHEAP BUT LUXURIOUS

Travel is often a large proportion of the expense for a holiday, especially if you want to reach exotic places.

A travel agency in London specializes in rock-bottom luxury holidays. Clients can get a two-week cruise in first-class accommodation for as little as £550 all in.

Or they can safari in Kenya for ten days on the 'millionaire's circuit' for £600, first-class air fare included.

Or how about three weeks in the Caribbean in a sun-soaked paradise for £370?

How do they do it?

The agency contracts to buy up all the cancelled holidays at the top end of the market for a nominal sum and they sell the holidays at a knock-down price to their clients.

The clients state the months when they are free to travel and they must be prepared to go on holiday at 72 hours' notice.

But the deal certainly proves that even high-priced services can be consumed at rock-bottom rates – if you look for the deal!

He decided to explain in simple English (he knew no Vietnamese, having spent his army service in Colorado Springs) how the Texacana store run by Mr Summers operated, which he assured Hang was no different to every other store in the United States of America.

'*You* have to pay the price on the tag. *I* have to check it here. When you've paid, you take the goods home. Until then they stay in the store. Got it?'

Hang and his family began speaking at once. Some to each other in Vietnamese, picking up and turning over items to look at the tags, some to the clerk in English, trying to get the haggle under way again.

The din rose considerably and other shoppers crowded round to watch what was going on (watching people shouting at each other is a common trait in the West).

At this point Gilbert Summers arrived at the checkout. The clerk explained to him that he was dealing with some weird people who didn't appear to understand how the world was organized.

'What do you mean?', asked his boss.

NEVER MIND THE WINE, WHAT ABOUT THE MONEY?

A discount wine chain in the UK made a name for itself for many years in selling good-quality French and Italian wines at knock-down prices.

In fact the prices were so low that people wondered how they managed to make a profit.

True, the wine company bought up vast stocks of wine and sold it virtually at cost to the customer.

How did they make their money?

On a large volume for a small profit?

Not at all.

They weren't interested in making a profit on the wine—that's how they beat the competition.

They made their profits by having a constant flow of cash into their bank accounts which they loaned to the banks for 30 days until they paid their invoices. The interest of ten per cent on the money exceeded the profit they would have got if they had sold the wine at regular prices.

'They want to haggle over every goddamed tin of peas and packet of soup,' he told him. 'Christ, Gil, they're offering me deals left, right and centre, for two of this and one of that, or three of this or one of the other. I don't know what's going on. Can't they read the frigging price tags?'

'H-o-l-d-i-t,' bawled Gilbert above the row.

His whole store stopped.

The checkouts, crowded with carts and people, stopped ringing up the dollars, which in Gilbert Summers' world made it **an emergency**.

He ordered Hang to take his family out of the store and not to come back. He told the clerk to run their carts into the shelf lanes and then get back to his desk 'pronto'.

Hang didn't move. He was clearly completely bewildered by the strange behaviour of the Bossman. He knew about hard bargaining from the market square at Lang Foo, but had never had a merchant snatch away his goods and order him off!

This was clearly a time to try another tack. He put his hand in his coat to take out his wallet.

Gilbert Summers, the clerk and a half-dozen others, hit the floor as if to get through it. When they saw Hang was holding his wallet and not a Magnum revolver they got up sheepishly.

Hang shoved a piece of paper towards Gilbert. It was his honourable discharge as a cleaner from the US army back in Vietnam. (Hang was using the 'returned soldier' ploy, or rather a 'Vietnamese ex-cleaner' version of it.)

He explained to Gilbert Summers that he had always liked the Americans and had wanted to be in Texas ever since he had seen a John Wayne film where everybody in it spoke Vietnamese. He had heard that Texas was a land of opportunity where anybody could make their fortune if they worked hard and knew that 'a dollar saved was a dollar earned'.

'Damned right,' said Summers, 'as my daddy told me, you'all work hard and live like decent folks and you'all get by.'

'OK,' said a beaming Hang, happy to have resolved the mis-understanding with such a fine Texan as Gilbert Summers (though he didn't understand why he spoke no Vietnamese). 'Now about these oranges at $1.30. I'll give you $1.15 if you throw in two tins of tomato soup at 35c each . . .'.

It took many months for Gilbert Summers to get used to Hang and his family. Likewise for Hang, who found that if he waited until 5 pm each day he could get his fruit and vegetables from the Summers' store much cheaper than they were in the morning (giving him a unique insight into the American concept of the 'happy hour').

He also found if he bought soup by the case he got a few cents off the per tin price. Sometimes he sat outside the shop with his family for hours and made trial runs inside to see if the price of tins of soup had fallen in the past hour. Occasionally, the clerks would give in to the Hangs just to get rid of them.

Other times, Hang chose to go in when the shop was busiest and delay the checkout while he haggled over the price of three loaves of bread, or fruit cake (for which Texacana is famous), or the weekend's groceries.

Gilbert Summers and Hang Ha Dong have got on fine since 1985. Their families became related after the eldest Summers' boy began courting Hang's daughter at the 1987 Thanksgiving.

They now have three grandchildren between them and several of the Hang daughters also work in the store. Although Gilbert resisted until recently letting them loose on the checkouts (!) he encouraged two of the Hang sons to develop their own delivery service to local restaurants and motels, where they can indulge their proclivity for 'special deals' without compromising his store's pricing policies.

What worked for Hang Ha Dong can work for you. His advantage is that he never believed in fixed prices – they were unknown in Vietnam, until, ironically, the Communists took over.

Communist fixed prices are the final proof of the idiocy of them. No Communist knows the *real* price of anything because their accounting 'systems' do not recognize supply and demand or the value of what is contained in any product.

How then should you tackle a fixed price?

The simple way to do so is to challenge it! If you don't ask for a discount for cash, you certainly won't be offered one. (If you are offered five per cent discount ask for 7.5 per cent.)

If you can think of a way to change the deal you might be able to change the price. For example, what does the deal include?

Delivery and installation: how much off for uplifting and/or installing it yourself?

Parts and labour warranty: how much off for foregoing your rights to these? (You can be sure they cover themselves for repairs and defects in their price.)

Pay now or later: if there is a delivery delay, how much off for paying cash now – you get the use of my money?

New or 'as new': if it's £1,500 for a brand-new deep freeze, how much off for a demonstration model, a window model, a slightly bashed-in or scratched model?

Price for one: how much for two – or three? This will tell you something about the margin on the price for one.

Compatible purchase: suppose I buy the desk *and* the chairs together? ('OK, I'll take the suit *if* you throw in a tie.')

Non-compatible purchase: how much off if I buy the lawn mower *and* a set of pans from the kitchen department? ('How much off the rent of the office if I use your fax?')

Related service: how much off *if* I clean up after you and dispose of the rubbish?

Gross account: how much off the price for the pipes if I agree to place all my business with you this year?

You are unlikely to get very far with the counter clerks in a store. Higher management deliberately give them absolutely no discretion over the price – though it is worth testing this assumption just in case they do have a small margin to work with.

In clothes stores, the counter clerks sometimes have discretion over small things like the price of alterations. Almost certainly, even in big stores, you can get the alterations done free if you make that a condition of purchase, particularly if you have already taken up their time looking at lots of suits.

Naturally, they will tell you that it is company policy to charge for alterations – and so it should be if you are daft enough to accept this. Hence, you must be prepared to ask to see the manager when you are approaching a 'buy' decision. If you can't do that you're sunk.

If the clerk tells you that he cannot give you a discount, ask him who can, and invariably he will tell you to see the manager.

Now, either this is a way of telling you that if you don't believe him about the company's policy on discounts you had better hear it from the boss, *or* he is telling you that only the boss can/will give you a discount. Either way, you must be prepared to test it.

Why should the boss give you a discount?

Firstly, it's likely that he has the authority to do so, and people who have authority like occasionally to exercise it, especially if they like to impress their subordinates from time to time of the distance between them.

Secondly, you have probably brought him away from much more important work and the amount you are haggling for is not 'worth his time' to fight over. If he gives you five per cent off a suit or a table, he still has a 40 per cent mark-up left for his profit. And if he believes you will not buy without a discount he knows he loses the entire sale.

What is the rational thing for him to do? Agree to a discount! He didn't get where he is by being silly over 'trifles'.

Thirdly, people who have 'graduated' up from the counter like to keep their hand in when it comes to individual selling. They get promoted because they are good at selling and they are good because they enjoy it.

In management they seldom get a chance to show themselves (and their subordinates) how good they are, so your request to see him could be music to his ears. You are doing them a favour!

I always go to the top person when making a purchase, though I met my match a few years back. I went into a clothes store in Princes Street, Edinburgh, to look at their suits. When it came to the buy decision I asked for a discount off the price tag.

The assistant couldn't give me it, so I asked to see the

manager. He came along with a smile and a 'what-appears-to-be-the-trouble' look about him.

I told him I liked the suit but not the price and asked him for a ten per cent discount. He started chatting and soon had me trying on suits again, and he indicated that I could have five per cent off the grey suit I liked but said he thought I 'looked better in the brown one'.

He also offered me five per cent off the brown one *and* hinted at a bigger discount if I bought them both.

That is what eventually I agreed to.

It wasn't until I got home that I realized I had ended up spending more than twice what I intended, had two suits instead of one (I narrowly escaped from buying a winter coat too), and had been given a 7.5 per cent 'discount' off an amount I hadn't intended to pay.

And I wore the brown suit once only! That is what comes from chasing a discount and forgetting the budget.

However, I still challenge those fixed prices. You should too. It could save you hundreds of pounds a year.

The fact that most people don't bother to challenge fixed prices is no comfort. Sure, there is a time penalty for haggling and for much of the time we simply do not have any to spare.

TWENTY-FIVE WAYS TO TAKE ON A FIXED PRICE

1 Throw in the accessories and I'll take it.
2 At that price I must get the display unit free.
3 What discount is there for a standing order?
4 I'm a new/old customer and should get an introductory/loyalty discount.
5 What is the discount for cash payment? (At 18 per cent per year it costs them 1.5 per cent a month for credit.)

6 If you give me 90 days to pay I'll buy now. (At 18 per cent per year, that's worth 4.5 per cent to you.)

7 What will you take off for a demonstration model?

8 If you give me a special price, I'll order right now.

9 I want a year's free maintenance, which will cost you nothing if your product is as good as you claim.

10 I want to test it for 30 days free of charge.

11 How much off if you use non-returnable/returnable crates?

12 How much off if I take the bin ends?

13 I'll take last year's stock if you take off 15 per cent.

14 I'll try it if you guarantee my money back if I am dissatisfied. ('How much off for a no-come-back deal?')

15 How much off if I recommend it to my friends/colleagues?

16 What's the discount for a repeat order?

17 What's the discount for an exclusive supply agreement?

18 How much off training if your people come to our place?

19 How much off if we collect?

20 How much off if we order but you deliver when we need it?

21 How long will you hold your prices if we order today?

22 As we are the first/fiftieth/last purchasers, we should get a 20 per cent discount.

23 As you can quote me as a reference, I'll require a discount.

24 As this is a risky/new product, I'll need ten per cent off.

25 If you have the power to give me a special price, I'll order now.

But one consequence of *never* challenging fixed prices is that we do not know how to when we want or need to. It's no good waiting until we are about to make a large-value purchase before we get experience in taking on a fixed price.

In Texas they say that business is about people with money meeting people with experience; the people with experience get the money and the people with the money get the experience.

But as Hang Ha Dong puts it: he didn't go all the way to Texas just for the experience!

COMMENTS ON SELF-ASSESSMENT TEST 18

1 a) Good. You are now able to push for an extra discount for three trolls. Very Foxey.
  b) Not so good. You now have no leverage for a quantity discount. A Donkey move.
  c) Excellent, but, as an Owl, you already knew it was the best move because there might be special offers available that you ought to know about before you press for a quantity discount.

2 a) Yes. If you can't face this step (sign of a Sheep!) you certainly won't get a discount, and, then you would hardly be a Fox.
  b) You are a Sheep – and are obviously easily persuaded.
  c) If you ducked out of (a) I doubt if you will get very far with this Donkey approach!

3 a) Right. (You can see how many Sheep there are in Europe.)
  b) Not on this continent – but about right for Australia, where Foxes are supposed to be scarcer than Sheep.
  c) Are you serious or just another Donkey?

CHAPTER 19

Mustapha Phee's Jamboree

This is the fourth of the Negotiating Scenarios for you to practise some of the lessons of *Everything is Negotiable!* As with
the other scenarios, they are a lively way for you to learn in the
'safe' environment of your private reading.

Read through the scenario a couple of times, making notes
in whatever way suits you. Then think about what you would
advise Mustapha Phee as he prepared for meetings with Costalot Tours to negotiate for the Annual Jamboree presentations.
How would you put together a negotiating strategy, remembering what you have covered so far in Chapters 1 to 18, and,
perhaps, as always, what your gut feelings tell you about the
negotiating situation.

There is no point inventing 'facts' about the scenario to settle
the case your way. If it is not stated in the scenario, it hasn't
and won't happen. Simply stick to the storyline and prepare
your responses from there.

So have some fun – and good luck.

NEGOTIATION SCENARIO 4: JAMBOREE FOR COSTALOT TOURS

Costalot Tours are to hold their Annual Jamboree in Penang, Malaysia in three months time. They have a reputation for aggressive promotion and marketing in the charter tourist business and they drive for business growth through ruthless pricing strategies. The annual jamboree is to re-motivate employees selected from the company's performance appraisal system.

A major feature of this year's jamboree will be some special personal motivation sessions, linked to Costalot's business plan. Several companies who specialize in this type of event have submitted bids to run the session.

You are Mustapha Phee, Managing Director of Barnton & Rose, one of the bidders, and Costalot has invited you to a meeting to discuss your proposals. As one of the leading firms in the motivation business you have a deserved reputation for high quality presentations with high fees to match. Your bid price for presenting the motivation sessions is £35,000. You regard Costalot Tours as a way into the tourist business for your seminars.

You know that the senior people at Costalot are not shy at demanding compliance with their requirements, nor are they unassertive in their negotiations, especially on price. You also know that the MD of Costalot recently attended a negotiation seminar well known for its advocacy of 'streetwise' negotiation techniques.

Your world-class motivation seminars are always on an all-inclusive price basis with no extras charged. You do not normally give breakdowns of your bids and your fees are inclusive for presenters, use of all audio and video facilities, staging, lighting, all travel to the venue, accommodation of your people, course materials, company margins and local taxes. The fee you quote is the fee they pay.

Now try some questions to practise your negotiating skills on the problem and to explore, using your experience to date and drawing on your reservoir of common sense, how you might set about negotiating with Costalot Tours. You can work from your notes on a separate sheet of paper, or from brief notes and highlightings you have made in the text.

Remember, Foxes cheat without prompting, Sheep need to be prompted to cheat and Donkeys skip the exercise altogether. Owls makes notes on their answers *before* they compare them with my own comments in Appendix 1.

QUESTIONS ON NEGOTIATION
SCENARIO 4:

19.1 Upon what area of your bid do you expect Costalot Tours to concentrate and why?

19.2 What sort of package deal might you suggest to Costalot and why might it be attractive to them?

19.3 If they deserve their reputation, how might the Costalot people behave in the negotiation?

19.4 What price challenge ploy might you expect and how might you respond?

COMMENTS ON NEGOTIATION
SCENARIO 4:

19.1 Upon what area of your bid do you expect Costalot Tours to concentrate and why?

You would expect that they would make a price challenge against your bid price of £35,000. In fact price challenges are the most predictable reaction of buyers, as the price is the obvious focus of the negotiation.

Even Donkeys would be expected to challenge a price, albeit by different means to those adopted by Owls.

Price, of course, is not the only element in a negotiated agreement, nor is it the only factor on all occasions by which a buyer decides to purchase a product or service. There are also issues of quality (is the product/service fit for use?), delivery (will the product/service be available when I want it?), satisfaction of my needs (will the product/service meet my needs?), ethics (does the product/service and the supplier of it act ethically?), and income (can I afford to buy the product/service given my income or budget?).

Experience suggests that price is the main focus for most people, especially when the product/service meets the other criteria. Every point that Costalot Tours reduces the price it has to pay for its Annual Jamboree, it is pounds better off (subject, of course, to some critical minimum level where the purpose of the jamboree is compromised by too skimpy an event). Given that it has grown by aggressive marketing in a highly price competitive business, this suggests that it has held down costs while increasing its revenue. The MD would therefore be highly sensitive to ensuring that any costs he is asked to meet are fully tested by vigorous price challenges. After all, this is certainly what they regularly do when they are purchasing flights and hotel services around the world for their tourist customers.

19.2 What sort of package deal might you suggest to Costalot and why might it be attractive to them?

A price challenge can be contested in numerous ways. Looking at Costalot's business sector which Barnton & Rose is seeking to enter, it is noticeable that some of the necessary inputs into providing the presentation services that it is supplying, are also outputs of Costalot Tours business. Holidays and tourism are serviced by air flights, hotels, hospitality and leisure activities. Costalot Tours sells these at (low) cost plus a profit margin. As it is successful in this business sector it must have a wide range of destinations and travel routes at its disposal, including Penang.

Suppose Barnton & Rose has a need for such services – and as a leading firm in the international seminar business it is more than likely that you do – it could be possible to reduce your inclusive jamboree fee by the amount by which it costs you to fly to Penang and what it costs to accommodate your presenters and the back-up crews, who set up the stages, lighting and audio facilities for your presentations. This is a cost rechargeable to Costalot (and is presently buried in your total fee of £35,000) and neatly fits in with what they could supply from their own services.

For Costalot Tours, the flights and accommodation it can supply do not cost as much to them as they would when purchased on the open market by Barnton & Rose. The difference is in the gross profit Costalot Tours includes in its prices. Also, being as big as they are in the business, there is every chance that they benefit from volume discounts from the airlines and the hotels in which they place their business.

If the discounted cost of these services is insufficient to reduce the £35,000 price as far as Costalot might desire, it is possible for you to develop this idea further. You could reduce your presenter's fees by offering them cash plus some highly discounted prices for their holidays, courtesy of Costalot Tours,

233

and pass some (all?) of the savings to Costalot Tours. More, you could also take a slice of your £35,000 fee in the form of holidays for your own staff.

Suppose you were to charge Costalot Tours, say, £13,000 for presenting the motivation sessions at the annual jamboree, with Costalot Tours flying the presenters and crew and accommodating them at no charge (normally costing, say, £12,000), and you were to accept from Costalot Tours a package of holiday facilities worth, at list price, £10,000, for redistribution to your staff, the real cost of the jamboree presentations to Costalot Tours would be the £35,000 quoted fee less its profit margins on the travel and holiday facilities it provided to Barnton & Rose personnel. The value to you would be £13,000 in cash as the jamboree fee, plus £10,000 in holiday facilities for your staff. The free travel and accommodation to present the jamboree is neither a cost nor a benefit to you as it is paid directly by Costalot, to whom it would normally be recharged anyway.

If your staff were allocated holiday facilities at times and in places where demand from the public was below sellable capacity, then Costalot Tours would gain even more from the package (ignoring taxation of 'benefits-in-kind' for your staff!).

19.3 If they deserve their reputation, how might the Costalot people behave in the negotiation?

Costalot Tours is reported to have a reputation for 'aggressive marketing'; its people are reported to believe in 'ruthless pricing strategies'; they are 'not shy in demanding exacting compliance with their requirements' and nor are the directors 'unassertive in their negotiations'. This suggests a hard-headed approach to business dealings.

On the basis of this information, what behaviour will they be likely to use to obtain their objectives? There is a need to be careful, for it is too easy to assume that their reputation indicates an aggressive manner.

If Costalot Tours' personnel normally adopt predominantly

aggressive behaviour in their negotiations with the airlines, hotels and leisure companies from which they buy services for their own customers, you would expect to see them hammering away on price and related issues to ensure that their company got the biggest slice of the available 'pie'.

If, however, they adopt more Owlish behaviour in their negotiations, you would expect to see them working to create a bigger pie across as many issues as possible to ensure that there was more pie to share with you. For example, in their normal business negotiations they may offer to exchange early payment to their hoteliers during the off-season, when the hoteliers are low in cash, in exchange for keener prices, or greater flexibility in bookings and rebookings, etc during the peak holiday season. This why your suggestion for them to take on all the travel and accommodation costs of your people for the event would be welcomed by them, if not proposed by them in the first place.

The aggressive Fox's behaviour would generally be overbearing, bombastic and, perhaps, devious. It is the effect on the outcome that they seek which determines their styles of behaviour – if they want to 'win' at all costs, you will no doubt be subjected to a lot of pressure. Aggression is used to exploit weaknesses in those with whom they do business. This can have a negative effect on your commitment.

It is essential that you are prepared for these different styles of behaviour from Costalot.

19.4 What price challenge ploy might you expect and how might you respond?

Given his attendance at a streetwise negotiating seminar, we would expect the MD to try the 'Mother Hubbard'. Fortunately it has a counter and can be neutralized.

The 'Mother Hubbard' is an obvious opening for Costalot. They can tell you that they think the motivation sessions look fantastic and that they really would like Barnton & Rose to win the business, but unfortunately the £35,000 price tag is well above Costalot's budget for the event – all of this supported by their body language, showing the deepest sorrow and resignation at their inevitable disappointment. What they would be trying for is to get you to reveal that you have some flexibility in price (being buyers, 'all prices as padded').

You might attempt to demonstrate that you have no flexibility in your price by revealing your detailed costs. What a mistake that could be, because once these costs are revealed it creates opportunities for them to challenge individual items to force the price downwards. They could challenge the fees paid to the presenters, the shipping costs of audio and video facilities ('why not hire locally?'), and the specifications for the staging ('change the quality of the carpentry, use cheaper paint, fewer lights, no back-up generators, use local roadies, cut out the glossy course materials, simple handouts will do') and so on. As you defend the need for quality you are pushed on price, cutting something here, something there.

True, if you have padded your prices – which, in anticipation of the MD's Mother Hubbard, you may well do so – the relentless questioning of every item of cost will reveal this to be the case, hence the MD will feel justified in what he is doing to your padded price and you will feel justified that you took the precaution of padding in the first place! Alternatively, you could challenge the limitations of the budget, escalate your challenge beyond the MD to the board, establish that the bid is a total package deal and cannot be cut away in parts.

The MD could go directly for the 'killer', by telling you that you must 'do better on price' if Barnton & Rose wants the business (he could do both, of course, using the Mother Hubbard to strip out alleged padding and then to the 'killer' to pull down your reduced price). Again this ploy stems from the view that all prices are flexible – downwards.

Faced with a killer challenge to the £35,000 – cut it down or else – you are in a difficult position. If you cut the price you confirm you have padded your prices, if you do not cut your price, you face losing the business.

The 'reverse killer' is to challenge the MD's 'killer': tell him he must raise his sights on the realistic cost of running this world-class event or use a lower quality substitute seminar provider and thereby fail to motivate his staff. And, whatever he pays for an *el cheapo* is a total waste of his money and whatever he thinks he has saved by using them.

SELF-ASSESSMENT TEST 20

1 You are on a sales tour of South Africa arranging dealerships for your range of industrial pumps. In Johannesburg you are told that your pumps are 'too expensive', in Durban, your prices are 'unrealistic' and in Cape Town 'the dealer's margins are too low'. Do you:
   (a) Fax head office to say the marketing people have got the price structure wrong?
   (b) Carry on your tour as normal?
   (c) Request discretion on the margins?
   (d) Give discounts off the list price in exchange for the order?

2 You are negotiating the supply of heavy pumps to a power station project and the contractor tells you that your prices are about 15 per cent above the quotes he has from a competing German firm and 35 per cent above the prices he is being offered for a totally reconditioned set of pumps. Do you:
   (a) Assure him that your pumps are the best in the world and known to be such by everybody in the business?
   (b) Tell him that the price is negotiable *if* you get the order?
   (c) Remind him that your pumps are regularly serviced and have a 24-hour emergency repair service behind them?

3 You are faxed by a construction consortium that they will accept your tender for earth-moving equipment to be shipped to Jordan if you can reduce your prices by five per cent. Do you:
   (a) Offer three per cent only?
   (b) Agree?
   (c) Suggest that it is possible only *if* the tender terms are varied?

CHAPTER 20

The Walls of Jericho

or how to stop conceding

Faint-hearted negotiators, faced with a challenge to their price, change their price rather than risk deadlock. They have the resolve of a wet paper bag.

Price is a predictable target in any negotiation, and you don't need to be a genius to appreciate why. Price is divisible – it's counted in pounds and pence – and many buyers (rightly) believe it pays them to try to shave prices a little.

Hypermarkets that cut a penny off per delivered bottle can share the savings with their customers, or add directly to their profits.

A wine negotiator who concedes a 'mere' penny a bottle cuts his own company's cash flow on 50,000 cases a year by 600,000 pence, or £6,000. That is equivalent to two months of his salary. (Even a penny off per case is worth £500.)

If he concedes a penny a bottle with six of his accounts, he doubles what it costs the company to employ him!

Conversely, if he could get an extra penny a bottle from six key accounts he costs his company nothing and can spend the rest of the year earning pure profits.

A Middle East 'go-between' on a modest three per cent 'commission' (some get nine per cent) makes £900,000 on a £30 million Turnkey Project – if you can get him down 'only' a half of a per cent, you save yourself £150,000.

Is it worth trying a price challenge to save your company £150,000? Of course it is!

Is it worth his while trying to raise you half a per cent on your offer of three per cent?

Sure it is. If he gets you to agree to 3.5 per cent, his commission for acting as a 'go-between' goes up to over a £1 million.

Pennies and half per cents do matter.

That is why you must expect the opposition to try some form of price challenge – they wouldn't be doing their job properly if they didn't – and if you are not ready for them you aren't doing your job properly either.

If price challenges succeed they provide big benefits to the asker. The faint-hearted always crumble to a price challenge, and they are a cause of their company's losses – which proves that employing them as negotiators is an expensive luxury.

Of course, if you are buying you should always make a price challenge. Never accept his first offer: test his resolve! If he crumbles, you gain – if he doesn't, you haven't lost anything.

But what of your own propensity to crumble? What can be done about it?

Quite a lot.

You can eradicate the propensity to crumble to a price challenge by learning how to fight back without provoking deadlock.

One immediate way to stiffen your resolve is to stop thinking about price in the same terms (and sometimes even in the same currency) as the other person.

He will ask you to drop your price by so much a unit, or to raise his fees by so much a day. He certainly won't talk to you about the total cost of his price change or the annual cost of his services.

Why?

Because by looking at his price challenge in the small, you forget to think about what it's going to cost you in the large.

241

He encourages you to think of a single bottle rather than the warehouse full of cases stacked from floor to ceiling. Are you going to think a penny doesn't matter when you multiply it by the half-million bottles of wine in your warehouse? That is the *real* cost of giving in to his price challenge.

Use a calculator if you want to see the real costs of conceding to price challenges – and let him see you using it too.

But seeing the real costs *and* avoiding them are not the same thing. The 'per unit price' ploy is aimed at making the cut more acceptable to you and is not an end in itself.

The other guy's real objective is to achieve a larger slice of the cake for himself, and therefore you need to have some weapons to hand to resist him reaching that objective entirely at your expense.

Take the case of Helmut Weber on his first overseas negotiating tour. Representing a German firm of high technical reputation, he went to South Africa to negotiate new supply and service agreements with his company's existing local distributors and some new outlets.

Helmut Weber knew something about pumps; he had graduated in engineering. However, he knew next to nothing about negotiating, and nothing at all about price challenges.

South Africans as a whole are not reputed to be handicapped in business matters. The distributors didn't know much about the technical side of pumps but they knew how to buy and sell them (and most other things) in their territories.

THE SQUARE ROOT OF NOTHING!

The last air freight price war in the North Atlantic routes saw extensive price slashing by air-cargo carriers.

If one carrier cut rates to get business, another would go below the cut immediately. This led a third to follow suit and a fourth to jump in with yet lower rates.

Something akin to panic set in when one cargo handler was filling space for an airline at 25 per cent off the already slashed kilo prices of the main cargo carriers.

Not surprisingly this handler's client went bust.

But the heavy pressure on rates continued.

Except for one company, British Caledonian.

To the surprise of almost everybody, they refused to join the suicidal scramble to cut prices.

'It is the easiest thing in the world to go out and fill an aeroplane with the square root of nothing,' was how a company spokesman put it.

'We have refused to dodge the issue,' he added. 'If shippers do not wish to pay our rates they do not get our services. We are not in a rate war on the North Atlantic in any shape or form.'

The result?

BCal's air freight revenues rose 36 per cent during the price war as it made an aggressive marketing bid for traffic at economic prices.

It was also able to expand its facilities and capacity when all around it other carriers were in severe financial difficulties.

British Airways was forced to withdraw from the cargo business altogether and other giants had to revise their rates upwards.

Obviously, BCal was not managed by price crumblers!

A classic negotiating asymmetry!

You might wonder why Helmut's company sent him on such an important mission when clearly he was less than qualified for it. That was precisely the question I put to the company president, and he said that his wife had insisted that their *son* show what he could do!

Helmut's progress across South Africa was monitored by the long trails of fax messages that accumulated on his father's desk. If they were read in sequence the trend was obvious to even the untrained eye, but his father did not need the normal German passion for order to see the pattern of his son's negotiating behaviour.

Helmut was a price crumbler.

Not that Helmut saw it that way. He was working extremely hard in what he considered the most difficult of circumstances. If asked, Helmut would have summed up the problem in one word: 'competition'.

Within two days of arriving in Johannesburg he was convinced that South Africa was the most price-competitive economy in the world.

Nobody denied the technical excellence of Weber pumps – though nobody praised them outright either – but everybody told him that Weber's ex-works pump prices were 'too expensive' and that the dealer margins 'were too low'. He faxed Hamburg that he had been forced to cut the ex-works price by five per cent just to hold the current order level with their largest Johannesburg distributor.

Durban was much worse: 'Weber prices are too high and your pumps will never sell at the list prices even if I take no cut myself,' was how the boss of the largest engineering parts stockist put it. Helmut faxed Hamburg: 'Our prices unrealistic. Have increased the distributor's margin by ten per cent and opened up a new dealership.'

A new distributor asked him why Weber pumps were costing more this year compared to last, which puzzled Helmut a little as he didn't know they had sold pumps to that outlet before – he would check when he got home – and as far as he knew Weber pumps had not risen in price for 15 months. He agreed however to a 15 per cent discount and faxed home that he had opened up another new dealership and an order for one of each pump type was enclosed (the dealer wanted 'to try the market' first).

Another distributor told him that he wanted to stock and sell Weber pumps but: 'The competition quotes me keener prices than yours and trade is so bad at the moment that I am not re-ordering anything.' This got the distributor a 20 per cent discount.

Helmut got different versions of the same story wherever he went, and he faxed Hamburg that he was 'compelled' to make discounts of between 15 (if he was really lucky) and 30 per cent (when he wasn't).

By the time he returned to Johannesburg he was utterly convinced that Weber pumps would never keep a foothold in South Africa if he stuck to the company's 'ridiculous' overseas pricing policy.

TRAINING STAFF IN 'PROFIT AND LOSS'

The founder of a long-established family firm was puzzled by the lower than usual profits earned in the previous six months – they sold non-food products to large supermarkets. While his product ranges were under competitive pressure, sales were still healthy compared to those achieved in the recession 30 months earlier.

Investigation soon disclosed the source of the problem: the sales staff were discounting to get business. While the individual discounts they gave away (often merely because the buyer asked for one) were not large in themselves, they were huge when added together. In fact, discounts were costing this company £850,000 a year, or putting it another way, they were reducing profitability by exactly the same amount. Moreover, as his company paid the sales staff commission on their achieved sales volume targets, he was losing twice over!

He called in the field sales force and gave them a five-minute course in How to Avoid Bankruptcy and Keep Your Job. Briefly, he revealed to them the facts of business life. 'Every ten per cent discount you throw away,' he told them, 'halves your contribution to the company's profits'. His arithmetic was impeccable (so was his reminder that those who persistently damaged profits in this way would soon be judged to be unprofitably employed): 'If you sell £100 worth of our products to the local store,' he told them, 'we do not make £100. We have to pay out to our suppliers what it cost to buy in the goods and what it costs us to sell them (including your wages).'

'My accountant,' he continued (one of his sons in fact), 'calls this the Cost of Sales. I call it £60, which taken off the £100 sales you made leaves us with £40. But before you run off with the delusion that we have made £40 profit, you should know that we still have to fork out yet more cash out of that £40 to pay for our warehouses, our offices, and our administration staff (most of whom earn a lot less than you do). These costs come to £30. They cannot be avoided according to my administration manager,' he said, mentioning another one of his sons, 'who assures me that these costs must be paid irrespective of sales and irrespective of market conditions.'

He paused while he wrote the figures on the wall: £100 less Cost of Sales at £60 equals £40, less overheads at £30 equals £10. He underlined the final £10 and wrote beside it the word PROFIT. 'We can just manage on a profit rate of ten per cent,' he assured his listeners, some no doubt calculating how much of it they could argue for in their next performance review.

'However,' he continued, 'when you throw away a 15 per cent discount, often for no better reason than that the buyer asked for one, what happens to the company's profits?' He did not wait for an answer but returned to the numbers on the wall. This time he wrote '£85 less Cost of Sales at £60 equals £25, less overheads at £30 equals minus £5.' He drew a red circle round the £5 and wrote beside it the word LOSS.

'That, ladies and gentlemen, is what all of you are doing some of the time and what some of you are doing all of the time. It is costing the company £850,000 a year. We need that £850,000 to grow the business, to refurbish the regional warehouses, to introduce new brands, and,' here he paused for effect, for he intended to appeal to their keenest sense of self-interest, 'to pay your commission.'

He was mortified when a distributor in East London rebuked him for 'attempting monopolistic exploitation of South Africa's need for good pumps' and he reported by fax that he had conceded a 30 per cent discount because the distributor said that 'his budget for pumps does not enable me to take on your series'.

A Cape Town distributor's accusation of 'price skimming' (as Helmut wasn't even sure what this meant he asked Hamburg for an explanation!) left him depressed and the distributor with a 15 per cent discount.

When an admittedly somewhat sloshed buyer in Bloemfontein charged him with 'bare-faced profiteering', he realized what it was like to feel guilty *and* framed at the same time, so in response to the claim that 'my customers would not pay that price for a pump' he made the usual price concession.

He got to the point where he dreaded anybody referring to the high prices of Weber pumps. So much so that he got in first to discuss his prices almost as soon as he opened the negotiations and kept referring to his prices whenever he thought the distributor was about to raise the subject himself.

THE COSTS OF COMPETITION

Getting back from a suicidal freight-rate policy to an economic one is not easy in shipping.

Customers do not like taking price increases, especially when other lines are holding their rates down below yours.

One container shipping line decided to break away from the crazy prices that operated in the business in 1982 and imposed a surcharge of $275 a TEU (Tons Equivalent Unit).

'Rates must rise today, to avoid dramatic increases tomorrow,' they announced, for rates had to reflect a reasonable return on investment.

'We re-invest our profits to increase efficiency,' they claimed, and it was from efficiency that 'you the customer benefit.'

They asked customers to think what would happen to their freight rates in a year's time if the rates war drove the line out of business.

That is what price wars are about: driving the weakest companies out of the market.

But you have a choice before the price war begins: keep out of it, and run your business without price crumblers!

He had no doubts that he had identified price as the barrier to securing a foothold in South Africa.

He reported by fax to his father that the marketing men had got this one completely wrong, that the competition was fierce, even cut-throat, and that he had been able to maintain interest in stocking Weber pumps with dealers but only at the cost of discounts off the list prices and other concessions.

He faxed home shock-horror stories galore about 'pump

dumping' by the Japanese, the French, and the British. They were all at it! They were going into the dealers and selling them pumps at 'below cost' just to keep out Weber's pumps. The representatives of one Japanese firm – he was told this 'in confidence' by a Somerset West distributor – had been instructed to 'always go below whatever price Weber quoted for their pumps'.

'How can honest men compete with such rogues?' Helmut wanted to know when he faxed the distributor's story to his father and asked for a similar freedom so that he could get Weber pumps into that distributor's warehouse. 'If the Japanese stoop to low price tricks of that sort, we must show them what a low price looks like!'

When his father read this particular fax he held his head in his hands in despair and refused to see anybody for an hour while he recovered his composure. Then he rang his wife to tell her what an idiot of a son she had given birth to and he faxed Helmut with immediate instructions to return to Hamburg.

When Helmut got back to the office – after a few days' rest, during which his father thought carefully about what he was going to do with him – he was told to report to Fritz, the marketing manager, who gave him a thick pad of paper and a pencil and told him to write out his experiences in detail.

His reports, client by client, were read carefully and sent back to him with comments and questions in the margin. He was told to identify what each distributor had told him regarding the prices of Weber pumps ('their *exact* words please').

Long after he had wearied of this seemingly pointless task, he completed it and was ushered into Fritz's office. He realized that he was to be the object of a special grilling and naturally got apprehensive about making a fool of himself.

Fritz put such fears to rest by opening up with the statement that after what Helmut had done to the company in South Africa there was no possibility of him ever making such a fool of himself again as long as he lived. Everybody had made similar mistakes (though never on such a scale, he added to himself) and they had all learned how to avoid them.

'In your opinion, what is the big problem with Weber pumps in the South African market?' he asked.

'Undoubtedly the fact that our prices are too high,' replied Helmut.

'OK, let's accept that view for the moment and ask how you know they are too high.'

'Because the distributors told me they wouldn't buy pumps at our prices.'

'Did they all tell you the same story about our prices, or did they vary their stories?' asked Fritz.

'The same story.'

'Interesting,' said Fritz thoughtfully. 'How then do you explain that in your reports of each client, you mention being given not just one, but several reasons why they think our prices are too high?'

'I don't follow what you are getting at,' said a puzzled Helmut.

'OK, I'll show you.'

Fritz turned over the top sheet of a flip chart that stood in a corner and read down the page:

'Weber pumps are too expensive ex-works and therefore the distributor's margins are too low.'
'That is more than I paid for similar pumps last year.'
'The competition quotes me keener prices.'
'My budget for pumps won't stretch to your range.'

When he had finished he asked Helmut if he agreed that these were sentences from his reports. Helmut muttered: 'If you say so,' and nodded, though he couldn't remember specifically.

'Are these sentences the same?' asked Fritz.

'They are all about our prices being too high!' offered Helmut.

'That, Helmut, is where your mistake is being made. They are not the same. They are all different notes in the same song: "Get Your Prices to Tumble Down". And like Joshua at the battle of Jericho, the dealers only had to blow a note and your prices did precisely that – they came tumbling down.'

Helmut thought that a little unfair but said nothing and allowed Fritz to continue his lecture.

'Price was their vehicle for putting pressure on you to make concessions. The fact that you responded by reducing your prices does not make price *the* barrier to the deal, nor does your collapse on price automatically secure you a deal, as we can see from the number of times you offered a price concession and did not secure any business.'

'How do you mean?' asked Helmut. 'All the deals I got required me to make a price reduction. Perhaps with the others I did not go far enough down in price!'

This provoked a visible sigh from Fritz, but he continued patiently. 'Ask yourself what interest a distributor has in getting you to reduce your prices to him – leaving aside the question of whether he is telling the truth about the state of the market?'

'Well, I *suppose* it is possible that he would gain an extra margin if I reduced my price to him and he was able to maintain prices in the market, but that is not how it is in South Africa as the competition is fearsome.'

COMPETING OURSELVES OUT OF BUSINESS

Looking back on the 1980–82 North Atlantic air-cargo carriers' pricewar, it might be thought that they did not realize what they were doing.

That is by no means the case.

The boss of the US Flying Tigers Corporation had no

doubt where it would lead.

In 1981, he warned customers and carriers alike: 'The shipper in the short term may think he has the benefits of getting low rates, in the long run he will suffer because if the free-enterprise carriers are driven from the market, he will be stuck with the government-subsidized carriers who are well able to sustain losses.

'These are the inefficient airlines and in those circumstances the price of the service will rise steeply if we are not around to discipline them.'

This situation, he added, was caused by the 'unreasonable situation where airlines are trying to protect market shares at all costs at prices which are totally uneconomic'.

'How do you know it is fearsome?'

'I could see it, of course,' replied a by-now irritated Helmut, 'and the distributors know best about the market.'

'OK, let's take the distributor's budget-for-pumps example. How do you know what his budget was limited to?'

'I remember that one. He told me he had only five per cent of his sales in pumps and showed me the racks where he kept his stocks of that Yahatsu range. They took up only three shelves out of the entire warehouse,' Helmut replied triumphantly.

Helmut thought he heard Fritz mumble something about 'Frau Hubbard'.

'And the one about the keen prices from the competition?'

'I heard that from practically everybody,' replied Helmut.

'I am sure you did, but did it not occur to you that they say the same thing to everybody? If they told you that your competitors' prices were higher than yours, would you want to raise or lower your own?'

'Raise them,' began Helmut and then realized the implication. 'I see what you mean,' he mumbled.

'Yes, I hope you do. Now consider the one about the customers not paying our price for a pump. How many pumps do we sell each year from this factory – 10,000, plus all the spares? Who buys them? Is price a barrier for those customers?'

'No, but that doesn't prove we can sell them at our prices in South Africa,' suggested Helmut.

'Maybe, maybe not, but I think the chances of South Africa being a different market to the rest of the world are pretty slim, don't you? After all, allowing for exchange rates, I should think that our pumps are more expensive in the USA at the moment and that is our second largest market. We even sell our pumps in Japan, not a million miles from Yahatsu's main plant.'

'So, I overdid the discounts a little. Next time I'll be wiser,' said Helmut.

'The discounts were only part of the problem, Helmut!', replied Fritz. 'You conceded discounts, credit terms, sale or return, free inventories, CIF shipping – the only thing you didn't give away was a promotional budget. All these concessions on top of the price concession. Have you any idea what they add up to in cost? No, don't bother guessing. I'll tell you. As of now, Weber Pumps is giving its products almost free to the richest country in the whole of Africa, meanwhile we sell at a profit to everybody else in the African continent, including the reconditioned jobs we sent to Chad. It would be cheaper to dump our pumps in the Rhine – that way we'd save on freight to South Africa!'

There was silence for a full minute. Eventually, Helmut spoke quietly: 'What should I do now?' he asked, resigned to the worst.

'How about getting a job with the competition?' whispered Fritz.

Poor Helmut. It was a heady baptism indeed. It took his company several years to get out of the mess he had got them into.

It wasn't just the price concessions he had made but the way he had crumbled on price and everything else *once he believed that price was the obstacle to a successful outcome for his negotiation.*

Handling a price challenge is one of the two skills of the successful negotiator – making a price challenge is the other.

COMMENTS ON SELF-ASSESSMENT TEST 20

1 a) Every sales negotiator believes this is true when they start and occasionally now and again when they are having a bad day. Invariably they are wrong. Anyway, marketing will not change its policies because of a single fax from a Donkey.
   b) Yes. What you are hearing is what buyers say everywhere, as I am sure a Fox like you realized a long time ago.
   c) You are weakening like a Sheep under pressure and could end up a price crumbler.
   d) You are a price crumbler! And definitely a Sheep.

2 a) Every Sheepish seller claims something to this effect. If true, they know it; if not, you only annoy them.
   b) The first step of a Sheepish price crumbler.
   c) Could be a Fox-like move if it highlights benefits that separate your pumps from the competition.

3 a) You are a modest but Sheepish price crumbler.
   b) You are a rampant crumbler with Donkey tendencies.
   c) Much better and more Fox-like.

SELF-ASSESSMENT TEST 21

1 You are a specialist in deep-sea oil exploration and have been
approached by a consultant engineer in Singapore to join his
staff on a two-year assignment. In their letter offering you the
post, they quote a salary that is within a few dollars of what
you are earning from a company in Stavanger. Do you:
   (a) Tell them you want a higher salary?
   (b) Quote a figure that you would settle for?
   (c) Quote a high figure and suggest a compromise between
       that and their offer?

2 A client expresses strong objections to a price proposal you
have submitted. He makes no suggestions as to what could
be done about it. Do you:
   (a) Say 'no' to price cuts?
   (b) Suggest he makes a proposition?
   (c) Ask him why he is objecting to the price?
   (d) Make a proposition yourself?

3 You are negotiating an off-site sales-training seminar for an
insurance company. They are worried about the aggregate cost
and are pressing for a reduction. They hint that unless the
price comes down they cannot run the course, nor the three
follow-on courses they had planned to use you for. Do you:
   (a) Go over the proposal with them and see what items they
       can provide from their own resources to save you charging
       them for hiring in?
   (b) Take a firm stand on price, given your outstanding quality
       and the improvements in sales they will get from the high
       numbers they intend to put through the programme?
   (c) Find out what their 'best price' is and go for that if it is
       close to your own?

CHAPTER 21

Don't change the price, change the package!

or how to shape up to better deals

In 1801, when Lord Nelson's small fleet hove-to in sight of the Danish island forts, armed hulks and ships defending the entrance to the harbour at Copenhagen, there was more than one palpitating heart as his men gazed in awe at the menacing ferocity of what was waiting for them.

Characteristically, Nelson wrote of the Danish preparations that they 'only look formidable to those who are children at war'.

Similarly, the opposition in a negotiation is seldom as formidable as it looks and almost always looks invincible only 'to those who are children at negotiating'.

Those who feel that the competition they face is formidable ought to mind Nelson's judgement and, perhaps, emulate his grit!

Of course, it does not follow that Nelsonian grit is enough by itself for success – Nelson almost lost the Battle of Copenhagen, making it one of Britain's bloodiest naval contests – you also have to be good at what you are doing, but if you surrender, merely because of what you are up against, then they will ride all over you.

This chapter is about a key negotiating skill: handling a price challenge from a skilled and formidable negotiator.

From the last chapter we know why people invariably challenge your price – it's the obvious thing to do! Helmut Weber's response was to crumble like the walls of Jericho. The people he negotiated with saw how he crumbled under pressure and, inevitably, they didn't confine their pressure only to his prices – they pushed on everything else too: credit terms, shipping and insurance, spares, returns, training, and so on.

If you concede, you open the door to an across-the-board challenge to everything in your package (and possibly some additional issues you had not even thought were negotiable).

THE KAMIKAZE AEROPLANE BUSINESS

One of the world's most highly competitive businesses must be that of aeroengines. Three or four large corporations dominate this market and the competition is murderous – almost kamikaze!

It began when General Electric fought Pratt & Witney for the engine contracts of the Boeing 767 and the Airbus A310.

The 'giveaways' they offered the planes' users reached 40 per cent of the initial prices of the engines!

The Saudis were 'persuaded' with offers even they could not refuse. They chose the Pratt JT9 over the Rolls Royce RB 211. Rolls accused their competitors of 'buying business'.

They claimed that Pratt offered cheap spares, training, free maintenance, tooling, free rebuilds on existing engines, free access to worldwide maintenance bases for their aircraft and even special finance.

And all this to the richest country in the world. Naturally, the Saudis took the deal – if people want to give them millions of dollars for nothing it sure beats giving them oil for it!

Once the price walls tumble down, so does almost everything else! Hence, it is important to hold to your price if you possibly can.

How do you do that?

By repeating 'no'? By doing without a deal? By having a policy of fixed prices only?

Not at all!

The idea of fixed prices implies fixed packages, and the reason why there is no such thing as a fixed price is because:

There is no such thing as a fixed package.

Everything that is negotiable has different attributes for different people. Take a chair, for instance:

I see a means to comfortable seating.
Somebody else sees an item for decoration.
A third person an antique.
A fourth person a stage prop.
A fifth person an investment.
A sixth person some firewood.
A seventh person a pile of old junk.
An eighth person a wedding present.
A ninth person a hole in his bank balance.
A tenth person part of her image.
And so on.

The attributes that people see in the same object are as endless as there are people. And as each person's perception of the object is subject to change, the possible attributes of the object for any one person increase through time; today's fashionable furniture is tomorrow's junk (and among the 'trendies' the exact reverse!) etc.

Also, a black chair may not qualify as a wedding present but might as a stage prop. Offer to sell her a white chair and the uses may reverse – and may change again when the price is quoted!

People do not purchase objects – they purchase the *services* that the objects provide for them, and these may be tangible or intangible, specific to the person, or general to everybody. Sometimes we put up with an object that meets our needs imperfectly and other times we insist on a most exacting match of our needs with the services derived from the objects on offer.

This is the foundation of all good selling and buying practice: find out the needs of the customer and fit what you have for sale to those needs and you'll get their money: find which object provides the services you need and you'll not regret your purchases.

In principle, the price of any particular object, when all else is said and done, is what somebody is prepared to pay for it: you match the service provided by the object to the price they want for it.

If they press you on your price that may be because they don't think the services they derive from the object are worth what you are asking for them. Alternatively, if they believe the services they obtain from the object are very valuable to *themselves*, they may be willing to pay a great deal more for it than they tell you.

On the other hand, there are other reasons why they may not agree to your price:

1 Most commonly, the other person may just be testing how firm you are on price.
2 He may just be mean – some people abhor spending money.
3 He may genuinely believe you are ripping him off.
4 He may not be able to afford it (the cupboard really is bare).
5 He may like to bargain for its own sake (good man!).
6 He may want to use your price concessions against your rivals – (a 'Dutch Auction').

7 He may be using price as a camouflage to back out of the deal.

Now you are not likely to know beforehand which of these is behind the particular price challenge you face in your negotiation – yet another dilemma for you as a negotiator!

The first thing to do when you hear a price challenge – as in other critical moments in negotiation – is ask: 'why?'

You don't naively need to accept his answers but they are a better start to handling the challenge than to assume that, because he tells you your price is too high (or too low for that matter), this is necessarily *the* barrier to the deal and therefore you must cut your price to get the deal.

Cutting your price because of a price challenge could be the worst thing you can do. Looking at the reasons for his challenge we can see that a simple price change is not your best move in any of them – this was Helmut's real mistake in South Africa.

If they are testing your resolve with a price challenge, it does not make a lot of sense to show them that you have none. They will only press for more, until they are convinced that you have nothing left to give – and as they still may not agree to a deal, you ought to stick where you start.

Meanness is a very difficult attitude to cope with and it flourishes in small pockets all over the world. It is not confined to any class, race, political system, religion or nation, nor is any grouping you care to name entirely free from it.

It is most often prevalent among people who know the price of things but not their value, and because reducing the price of something does not increase its value there is little point in you doing so.

As for the person who believes that you are ripping him off there is no surer way to confirm his suspicions than to reduce your prices! The person who cannot afford the deal you are offering may be open to another deal and it is up to you to find it (of which more in a moment) and the person who likes to bargain for its own sake is not really a big problem – indeed in a sense he is the easiest of the lot to deal with.

When you suspect that the other person is using you as fodder for a 'Dutch auction' with the competition, you will not frustrate this tactic by cutting your prices – as that is exactly what he wants you to do it must be self-defeating – so don't.

The same is true of the person who is using a price challenge in order to get out of the deal. Nothing you do on price – except in a totally humiliating fashion – will keep someone in a deal who doesn't want to be there.

It's more likely to give him yet another excuse for not agreeing – 'If your boat is now reduced by 20 per cent in price, you were obviously ripping me off in the first place.'

How then do we handle a price challenge?

Few deals are decided solely on price. There is almost always more than one variable in any deal and where there is a variable there is a possibility of a negotiation. Therefore a price challenge is a challenge to only one of the, possibly numerous, variables available for negotiation.

We know already that to give way to a price challenge is to invite a challenge to the other variables. So consider the consequence of using the other variables to protect your price. If they want to change the price variable in the package, it is legitimate for you to adjust the other variables. Indeed, make it a condition for the change in one variable, that some others must be changed in compensation.

You can sum up this strategy by:

For this package there is one price, for another price there is another package.

I can illustrate this strategy with the subsequent career of Helmut Weber. After his debacle in South Africa, he decided to resign and start again, not with the competition, as the mar-

261

keting manager had sarcastically suggested, but in an entirely different line altogether.

The spur to Helmut's redemption was the German passion for chocolate. The Germans are very competitive with the Austrians and the Swiss in the production of chocolate delicacies, for chocolate is to the Germans what cheese is to the French – there are hundreds of different types, many eaten only in the locality where they are made.

Chocolate is made from cocoa and cocoa comes from West Africa. The cocoa beans grow in Ghana, Nigeria, Togo, Ivory Coast, and Cameroun, and are shipped in 130lb sacks to Europe. There they are processed and sold to chocolate manufacturers who add their own ingredients (mainly milk and sugar, but also nuts, raisins, cream and jam) from their own recipes.

Some of the chocolate is made into popular products for the supermarkets and some into local varieties. The packaging and marketing of these brands is a highly diversified business, with some large companies and lots of smaller ones.

It was into this business, as a cocoa broker, that Helmut threw himself, originally in a quest for his father's approval but latterly because he enjoyed it. This was how he discovered packaging. Not the stuff they wrap the chocolate in, but the way that negotiators go about getting a deal.

Chocolate, like pumps and most other products, is no stranger to prices.

In a market economy, price is a great storer of information; it is an efficient indicator of a product's standing in relation to supply and demand.

But man does not buy chocolate only on price, any more than he lives by bread alone. The cocoa processors who buy tons of beans a month are not just concerned with price. If they were they might very well end up producing an inferior product, and if they won a reputation for inferior – or even variable – quality, their sales would plummet.

Thus, the quality of the beans, and the consistence of that

quality, is an important variable in the deals they negotiate with the shippers of beans from West Africa.

Quality is a variable in a technical sense, for not all variations in quality are critical to the production of highly consistent output in each type of chocolate. It depends on the type of chocolate a particular batch of processed cocoa is to be used for.

Helmut had to learn in buying processed cocoa to get the right trade-off between price and the minimum quality required in each process. For instance, cooking chocolate can take a lower-quality cocoa than confectionery chocolate. Top-class table chocolate – the kind you would give your loved one – requires top-class cocoa.

With some processors the quality control is so reliable that you need fewer sample inspections and risk fewer rejects than with those others whose quality is a bit of a lottery and whose output generates substantial wastage during the making of chocolate.

The quality variable throws up several other related variables: inspection criteria, rejection policy, credit or replacement for rejected batches, payment on delivery or after processing to take account of acceptance levels and so on.

These variables had to be considered when prices were negotiated. If the processor pushed up his prices, Helmut learned to adjust the package he proposed to take account of the risks his company ran and the appropriate compensatory measures it required either before or after delivery and payment.

It could be that for a particular reason he would agree to a higher price per ton of cocoa if the supplier agreed to accept later payment and a higher inspection standard, and sometimes he did the reverse.

He certainly did not just change his price upwards or downwards because the processor told him how 'fearsome' the competition was or how lousy his prices were.

This does not mean to say that Helmut was not interested in

the competition. On the contrary, he made it his first objective to learn about the business he was in and how the industry was organized. He knew about the real competition and how it was faring because he studied it and consequently he was never hustled by processors or manufacturers and their fairy stories.

In this respect, he lost count of the times buyers told him ('in confidence', of course) about a Dutch, Danish, or Swiss company – the nationality varied each time (he even heard it once about a Japanese supplier) – that 'was given instructions to beat whatever price Weber's company offered'!

Helmut took an interest in processors out of a healthy concern for ensuring continuity of supply for his customers, the chocolate manufacturers. If a processor was totally dependent on cocoa supplies from a single West African country, then this was of significance to Helmut, particularly if political conditions in that country were unstable.

The prospect (highly probable) or actual occurrence (frequent) of a military coup influenced the way he approached a supply contract both as a buyer and as a seller. With those processors who were not dependent on a single source for their cocoa but had several sources, he had to face the question of the compatibility of their cocoa from the different countries that they got it from.

Blending compatibilities could be reflected in the price he was prepared to pay per ton or the credit terms he sought and the prices he could get from the manufacturers – who insisted, like art dealers, on knowing the provenance of the processed cocoa he supplied to them.

Sometimes, in periods of tension or calamity among the West African growers, the payment terms switched one way or another between Helmut and his suppliers. If supplies were unsettled the trade-off could be to shorten the payment period; if they were fine, the payment period might lengthen, or it might stay the same and the price per ton change.

There was always the possibility of longer-term contracts

for at least some amount of the output of certain suppliers. Helmut had to make a judgement about whether to get locked in at too high a price or risk being locked out if he didn't offer enough.

For each negotiation there was a different set of tradables to consider and the skill that Helmut developed was that of packaging the best deal he could out of the deals that were available.

The supplies that were earmarked for Helmut's company – and they could be counted in anything from thousands to tens of tons – could be stored with the processor (at whose expense?) or with Helmut (at whose risk?). It could be delivered in large silos (who paid for them?) or in containers (who owned the containers?).

The negotiators had to decide who was responsible for the processed cocoa when it was in their stores and what access to what minimum amounts was possible if supplies were needed urgently. These are only some of the many tradables that Helmut learned about in his new job as a negotiator with the cocoa processors, and this represents only *half* of his job.

He only bought processed cocoa in order to sell it to chocolate manufacturers, and while dealing with one side of a transaction – buying in – he could very well be dealing simultaneously with the other side – selling out. On occasion, Helmut also dealt direct with the retail outlets, though on a small scale (he has ambitions to produce his own chocolate brand – Weber's 'African Delight').

In selling, the same tradables emerge. Manufacturers require consistency and continuity of supply. They may want to vary the supply over a production cycle – they need more chocolate for Christmas than they do for the height of the summer, for instance.

The issues that have to be negotiated as part of a package include: who holds the stocks surplus to current requirements and who pays what for the cocoa, and when, between contract and delivery?

To what extent can a price variation be traded-off in the returns of inferior or damaged supplies? How much of a promotional budget would a manufacturer contribute for its branded products and what effect does this have on the order levels of the hypermarket chains?

And so it could go on. The tradables that emerge from a simple product like chocolate are clearly very numerous.

In your world, whatever it is that you sell or buy, there may be many tradables that you have not considered recently, or at all. It's time you did, because it is in the tradables that you will find the defence of your prices.

At the *Everything is Negotiable Workout* we require participants to identify all the negotiable tradables in their business. The results sometimes surprise even the old hands.

Routine approaches to their business can exclude glaringly obvious tradables from consideration which must diminish their negotiating ability to package and repackage deals. Constant reviewing of the negotiable tradables is a necessity for successful negotiating.

In one seminar, for a multinational company, the various national divisions produced from their syndicate sessions lists of tradables that directly contradicted each other!

It was an illuminating experience to watch the syndicates explain why they had grouped some tradables as 'non-negotiable' while their overseas colleagues considered them 'negotiable'. This was all the more interesting when the Canadians disclosed they were negotiating on some issues that the English traditionally held out on. The English were not slow to wake up to the real explanation as to why they had lost business over the years in the United States and Mexico – their clients had switched to the Canadian branch of the company instead!

TRADABLES AND CONSTANTS

What are the *negotiable tradables* in your business?

It is well worth spending some time writing down a list of the tradables you negotiate in your particular line of work. Then add to the list all the things you could negotiate over at present, but, for one reason or another, you don't.

The list should be a long one. If it isn't it may be you are missing opportunities for negotiating better deals. If you get stuck with a small list, start from the other end and write down all the *non-negotiable constants* in your business – the things you do not negotiate over.

Ask yourself why you don't negotiate over each constant?

Who said you shouldn't? What good reason is stopping you? Is it a matter of habit, tradition, custom? Is it an ethical matter?

As you ask these questions you will gradually find reasons to move those constants into the variables column.

The boss of one of Britain's largest life assurance societies said: 'You need a big crunch every now and again. Out of that you get a lot of ideas. In a big organization it is amazing how many sacred cows are created – and it is hard to slaughter them.'

How many sacred constants have you got around your organization and its activities in the competitive markets you deal in?

Once we stop seeing price as *the* issue in a negotiation we can really put some good deals together; deals that are good for us and good for them. All the tradables in and around the deal can be used to improve the deal and protect our interests.

How?

By concentrating our attention not on the huffing and puffing about price but on the total *shape* of what is proposed.

Consider some illustrative tradables that are present in most deals. They were present for Helmut Weber in South Africa but he didn't see them, and they are present for you in your negotiations if you look for them. Take *money* as a tradable. Can we adjust:

The way we pay?
What currency we pay in?
The credit terms – 30, 90, 120 days?
The discount for early payment?
In advance or in arrears?
The intervals between progress payments?
With revocable or irrevocable lines of credit?
To a third (neutral) party?
Cash on delivery or after acceptance? (Whose inspection?)
Consequences of default?

Or consider *delivery* as a tradable.

In what quantities can it be delivered?
Any advantages for smaller packs/larger loads?
Who pays for delivery and insurance?
If in a container, who pays for damage?
What packaging is used? Possibility of own branding?
How wind-, water- or rodent-proof are the storage materials?
Who stores surplus requirements?
Who pays for storage?
What minimum loads can be got quickly?
What and whose inspection of deliveries is acceptable?

What about the *specifications* as tradables?

What are the critical specifications?
Can they be varied without risking quality?
Do we need 95 per cent reliability?
Is a doubled working life worth a trebled price?
How much do we save by marginally reducing a spec?
Should the extras be standard or some standards extras?
Which features are attractive and which actually used?

What about the *relationship* as a tradable?

Is it worth anything to be a sole supplier?
Is it better to spread the business among several suppliers?
How long should a sole-supplier contract run for?
How long should any contract run for and what is duration
    worth off the basic price?
If we deal with them solely how much advertising and
    promotion will we get them to pay for?
What about joint promotion?

Is there anything tradable in the *risks*?

Who pays for insurance?
How much insurance should we go for?
Who pays for replacements and how are they credited?
Who defines *force majeure*?
What is a warranty worth?
Who guarantees quality and inspection?
What about performance measures and third-party liability?
Share of insurance payouts?
What expenses are covered?
Whose liability for patent breaches, copyrights, etc.?
Whose liability for local taxes, sundry debts?

Is *time* tradable?

> When is delivery to commence?
> Over what period is the contract to run?
> How late is late delivery?
> When do we get access to the product?
> When will proportions of the project be released?
> In what order will things happen?
> The timing of progress reports?
> The closing dates for inspection?
> How flexible is the completion date?

If you handle price challenges this way, the people across the table will learn from your behaviour that if they want to change the price, they will have to face the inescapable consequence that you will vary the package.

For you, everything must be negotiable!

There are no circumstances in which you agree to back off a price unilaterally. This is negotiation, not a Dutch auction in which you keep shouting out lower and lower prices until somebody agrees to take the deal.

If the person does not like your price for the package you propose, then you are happy to quote him another price for another package. It may be that the new package you propose meets his needs closer than the original one. In moving to alter the *shape* of one or more of the components of the deal, you could be moving closer to what he really wants.

HOW TO WIN PRICE WARS

Faced with stiff competition many negotiators turn first to price cuts as the road to salvation – it is in fact the road to ruin.

270

Every negotiator must eradicate the view that price cuts win business; they are often the first resort when they should be the last.

If the competition is tough it is the time to wage a relentless war on COSTS. All costs must be pruned to the bone. Inefficient plants should be closed or re-organized; all deadwood eliminated; sentimental symbols scrapped; workforces slimmed down and all expenditure that is not connected with the productivity of the assets postponed (in some cases for good).

As costs come down, profitability goes up. With higher profits the beleaguered firm has an alternative to a kamikaze price war.

The beer business is extremely competitive and it is getting tougher as younger people turn to other beverages.

In some cases, beer companies, having rammed down their prices to grab market share, seize a temporary advantage and provoke price crumblers to panic.

The firms that will survive resist joining in a price war. They go first for profits and use them to increase their marketing impact.

Distributors and retail outlets are trained in grass-roots financial management so that they can see for themselves the margins on each of their lines, the turnover per asset they use, the sale per customer, and even the profit per use of shelf space in their operations.

Everybody becomes cost- not price-conscious. Marketing support is demanded by the people selling the beer to the drinkers because they want to sell more of the most profitable beer brands. Their attitude changes from demoralized people looking for price cuts to people 'struggling to be humble' because they are proud of their profitable products.

His price challenge is a signal that there is something wrong with the proposed package. That is how you must interpret it. If the other person insists that he is flying a different signal, then, like Nelson at the Battle of Copenhagen, put the telescope to your blind eye and tell him you 'really don't see the signal'!

The rule that Helmut Weber had to learn ought now to be abundantly clear:

> *Don't change the price,*
> *change the package!*

COMMENTS ON SELF-ASSESSMENT TEST 21

1 a) Wouldn't we all! But is this a sign of your resolve or that you are not too fussy about the job? If you would like the job and more money, you should explain why you work for what they are offering in Stavanger but won't do so for them in Singapore. Your Sheepish resolve has got you into a little tangle.

  b) Better. The size of your demand will tell them how serious you are but watch out for a 'split the difference' ploy. As a Fox I am sure that you ready for that angle.

  c) No! Because your 'brave' high figure has no conviction in it and your speedy willingness to abandon it in the same sentence is clear evidence that you are a Sheep and need not be taken seriously. If they still want you they can get you either for a minor increase or for the original offer.

2 a) How Donkeys force themselves into deadlock – either they now back off or you don't do business unless you back off.

  b) Implies that you might Sheepishly compromise – certainly don't move until you know his entry price.

  c) Better. Foxes need more information about his reasoning.

  d) Oh dear! He said 'boo!' to a Sheep and you gave in.

3 a) Yes (you obviously read the answers in Chapter 19 like a good, if devious, Fox!).

  b) Better, because a strong defence of your prices is the best introduction to (b). As an Owl, you already knew this (which is why you got it right in Chapter 19 too – without cheating?).

  c) That only teaches them to make price objections. Now go back and read Chapter 19 which, as a Donkey, you skipped.

SELF-ASSESSMENT TEST 22

1 You are in the market to buy an executive jet for a small courier air service you intend to set up out of your hard-earned savings and small borrowings from a local bank. The company selling new and used aircraft of the type you want is located on the 72nd floor of the World Trade Center in Manhattan. The President's office is as big as an aircraft hanger and the carpet pile is up to your ankles. The elegantly dressed man behind the 20-foot mahogany desk sits in front of a Picasso original. There is a Henry Moore sculpture in one corner of the room and a fountain spraying quietly in the other. Do you:

   (a) Think you will get a bargain price?
   (b) Wait and see?
   (c) Believe you are likely to be pushed to the top price?

2 The man who has come to see you wears a beautifully cut Saville Row suit, a gold Rolex watch and Gucci shoes. If asked to rate his status, would you rate him:

   (a) Low?
   (b) High?
   (c) Indeterminate?

3 When he leaves, how would you rate him (high or low) if he:

   (a) Waited at the curbside for a cab?
   (b) Had your secretary call him one?
   (c) Got into a compact car he had parked round the corner?
   (d) Got into a chauffeur-driven Rolls Royce?

CHAPTER 22

All that glitters isn't gold

or how to resist intimidation

Have you wondered why some corporations go in for highly expensive waste space?

They locate themselves in glass palaces, downtown in the most exclusive real estate they can find, or out in the wide open spaces of the far-flung suburbs, surrounded by acres of pretty flowers and healthy trees.

The entrance to the glass palace is like a scene out of Cleopatra: vast columns rise towards the heavens, marbled staircases wind majestically upwards, fountains and waterfalls abound everywhere and there is solid dark wooden furniture dotted about like little fortresses on a plain. The only thing missing is a trumpet voluntary announcing arrivals.

Batches of people cluster at the mouths of high-speed lifts and the doors swish open and shut disgorging and swallowing their fare effortlessly.

Behind the front desks sit immaculately groomed receptionists chosen presumably for their perfect smiles and expensive teeth, and an ability to suffer boredom gladly.

Nearby, the security guards hover, looking busy but doing nothing much. Each is turned out like a Marine drill sergeant who has had nothing else to do since his last war. When a phone rings, it does so quietly and is answered with manic precision before the second bell.

When you arrive for an appointment you are treated as if you are in danger of becoming a lost parcel. And just in case you have an identity crisis while on the premises they give you a pass to tell you, and anybody else who asks, who you are.

If they are really pulling out the stops, they take a quick photograph, seal it with plastic and pin it on your chest so that you look (and feel) like an immigrant at Ellis Island in the 1920s. When you go anywhere you are escorted politely by a junior clerk (or a spare gorilla from security).

Lifts, corridors and waiting rooms are furnished to give you the impression that you are passing by Big Events that are taking place behind the closed doors that hum with purposeful activity. The way the staff move about is proof that *something* is happening.

When you get to the person you have come to see you enter an office that is as large as an aircraft hangar and has carpet pile up to your ankles. It also has the odd Picasso or Van Gogh on the wall and some tasteful sculpture in the corner.

This is the moment when you make your most important mistake.

You foolishly believe that all the trappings of corporate wealth you have seen are for the benefit of the people working for the outfit and are their reward for loyal service to the corporation and an exhibition of their successful endeavours.

Nothing could be further from the truth!

It has nothing to do with the comfort of, or praise for, the employees, loyal or otherwise. If they benefit from working in such munificent surroundings, that is an unavoidable and minor consequence of the main objective of all the splendour.

Everything you have seen has been put there specially for *you*.

It is your perceptions that they are working on.

Everything you see from the moment you step through the front door is pure theatre. You are being got at by props, all carefully designed to create the right impression in the minds of visitors.

The purpose of the design?

Simply to *intimidate* you!

And unless you are very strong-minded, or prepared, you don't stand a chance.

Why?

Because intimidation of this kind works.

The building oozes success. Power creeps out of its every pore. You are seduced into asking yourself: 'If they can spend that kind of money on this kind of foyer, what must they be making out there in the harsh competitive world that I am struggling in?' leading to: 'Boy, do I want to do business with this company!'

One thing you feel for sure. They are making a lot more money than you are. How do you know that? Because you are on your way to see them; they are not on their way to see you. And if they did visit you, how would your entrance and foyer compare?

A wee orange box of an office, an old desk and chair and last month's rent overdue? You either have a bigger glass palace than they have – in which case you wouldn't even notice the splendours of theirs – or you haven't – in which case you do.

BIG AND LITTLE CONS

Practically every known con starts with the use of props. That is why the use of props in business runs a thin line between probity and fraud.

Just because a person is living in a penthouse suite it does not mean that he is productively using the funds he collects each week from gullible investors.

He may just be using each week's 'contributions' to pay the bills for his exotic lifestyle so that he can con new contributors to pay his bills next week.

More than one real-life bankrupt flies the Atlantic by

278

Concorde – it makes creditors less anxious about their money if they associate the person with the trappings of wealth and power. If the bankrupt switched to economy stand-by tickets to save cash, the creditors would begin to worry about their money.

There is a constant stream of programmes on TV about dubious business dealers who drive Rolls Royces and Mercedes and live in small palaces. Hence, *caveat emptor*.

Also, there are several religious cons that involve substantial transfers of wealth to high-living 'saints' – the more material wealth they display the more their followers are convinced that they are divine.

The source of the problem is a logical distortion: the successful have high living standards and conspicuous evidence of wealth (yachts, helicopters, country houses, etc.) hence – so the 'logic' runs – people with high living standards are successful. Almost all cons rely on that sort of 'logic' in the minds of the marks (victim).

If you are intimidated by the other (honest) person's props you are a victim of a mild con. If this results in you settling for less you might as well be in a bunco booth!

If you notice it, you're half way to being conned.

It'll get to you and when it does it will influence your attitude to the way you go about doing business with them.

You'd better believe that it will.

It's your impression of their strength that they're working on. Why?

Because through intimidation they subtly get you to undersell yourself. In its extreme form this kind of intimidation can turn you into a cowering cheapie.

Once you've been through the intimidating treatment and are in the presence of the Very Important Person who has granted you some of his precious time, there is no doubt that you are likely to be grateful for whatever he feels you are worthy of.

And that is before he has even begun his 'pitch' (it doesn't matter whether he is buying or selling). Covert intimidation is the least-talked-about aspect of the negotiating relationship.

Screeds have been written on overt and actual intimidation through the use of threats and so on. Yet covert intimidation is probably more prevalent and is certainly more efficient in that the person who is intimidated in this way is less likely to realize it and, not realizing it, is less likely to resent it.

If someone bullies you to take a lower price, you resent their exploitative behaviour – especially if you might have to take the deal as well. But if they psych your perceptions through covert intimidation you cannot resent them for what you do to yourself, can you?

Some sales training programmes prepare the participants for some forms of intimidation by buyers, but not for others. They cover those aspects of buyer behaviour that are designed to intimidate the luckless seller who is unprepared for them.

The tactics used by such unscrupulous buyers are now well-known in the folklore of the downtrodden salesman. Ask anybody who has been out selling in the real world for his atrocity stories of how buyers can behave, and he or she is bound to include one or more of the following:

You will be kept waiting outside his office, or the appointment will be postponed, rescheduled or clash with another he has with a far-more-important person than you.

When you do get in to see him he directs you to a seat that is smaller than his.

It's also lower down – and probably wobbly as well.

Also you are facing a brightly lit lamp or the sunny window.

The door will be left open and you can hear people moving

about outside and the secretaries might walk in and out looking for papers.

The room is too cold, too hot, too stuffy, too open or too draughty (and guess who is sitting in one?).

The phone rings incessantly as you make your pitch.

There are other interruptions, such as staff knocking loudly on the door and entering to discuss business or social affairs with the buyer.

The buyer tells the secterary to hold his calls for a couple of *minutes* – indicating your time is nearly up – and he'll keep looking at his watch.

Other times he meets you in the foyer or waiting room with other people milling about and proceeds to conduct a conversation.

He gets your name wrong and that of your company (repeatedly).

He looks bored – painfully bored – and stares as if he is not listening.

If you hand him some literature he throws it casually to one side or doesn't study it at all (though he will certainly spot a blemish on it if it is torn, stained or written on).

He will avoid touching any samples of your product and only give them a cursory glance – he certainly will not show any interest in seeing them operate.

He will make disparaging remarks about you, your appearance, your weight, your hair loss, your teeth ('do you smoke a lot?'), your accent, your ethnic origins, your background.

He'll do the same about your product, your company, your deliveries, your quality control, your invoicing, your previous promises, your superiors, your employees, your track record and your chances this time.

He'll do the opposite about the competition, using their first names and personal details of their background. ('Did you know that Henry, their marketing boss, won a gold in the Olympics? Of course, he's a fit, good-looking man for his age, and never lets me down.')

He'll also praise their products, their efficiency, their accounts, their integrity and their prices.

He'll ask you questions aimed at identifying your social inferiority – which clubs you belong to, what car you drive, have you been to the Seychelles, do you know the president of the steel company in your home town, what do you think of the Hotel Al Khozama in Riyadh, how are your stocks going and which way will Dow Jones go, what do you think of the Archbishop of Canterbury's library, have you seen the price of gold this morning, who is your broker, your banker, your tailor? And so on.

He'll stall over decisions, announce that he doesn't make them and the person who does is not available.

Next time you go there you have to begin with somebody else; if he has higher status than the first person, you are in for a tough fight over the deadlocked issues and if he is of lower status it's going to be even tougher!

He'll require everything in writing and all your prices have to be your 'best prices'.

ON BEING HUSTLED

A young manager decided to invest his savings in land which he saw advertised in a New York paper. He visited the site where the broker assured him of the stiff competition for the lots, recently zoned by the State for housing development. He was not persuaded by this but was marginally interested in the proposition.

However, as he was talking over the deal another man entered the room and interrupted their conversation, asking to buy some of the lots (including the ones that he was interested in) for a house-building programme. The broker told the man, who apparently was a local builder, that he would have to wait a moment.

The builder replied that he was ready to place an order for the unsold lots there and then and he ought not to be kept waiting as he had the bank behind the finance.

The young manager hearing this realized that if building commenced on the site, any lots he owned would realize an early profit to him on his investment (and therefore he could afford to buy more than he had originally intended).

He told the builder that he had first option on the lots in question and that he was about to write a cheque for a signed title agreement. This he did.

The builder was not too happy about this and demanded to have the right to purchase the surrounding lots. The young investor left the two men in the office deep in argument about the remaining lots and their price.

He felt very pleased with himself, and this feeling persisted for about a year until it became obvious that no houses were being built in the area he had purchased. Had the builder changed his mind? Or was he the victim of a set-up by the broker and a so-called 'builder' to hustle him into believing there was competition for the unsold lots? (What do you think? No prizes for my guess!)

It took him five years to get out from under with a capital loss of three-fifths of his savings.

The purpose of these behaviours is to intimidate you into a submissive attitude and every seller has to learn how to cope with buyers who use these methods.

Fortunately, some sales training programmes show you how (and buyers' programmes teach them the counters!) and you'll pick up some ideas from Thank God it's Friday seminars with your colleagues.

But these well-known stress ploys of buyers are small beer compared to the self-induced intimidation that comes from down-grading yourself because of the way the other person's corporation spends its money on props.

These latter tactics are far more intimidating because they operate in your mind as 'own goals'. You see, deep down you really want to acquire the trappings displayed in the corporate headquarters yourself and when you see them around somebody else you assume that the other person has got them already because he is better than you, or has more power than you, or knows better what he is about.

I was given a very clear example of the power of subtle intimidation through the use of apparently expensive props when I was involved in negotiating the sale of a hotel in the Highlands of Scotland – just across the water from the Isle of Skye.

The owner had offered me a commission if I could close a sale with the third set of buyers he had tried to negotiate with, the other two falling out after meeting him.

I had driven up overnight from Edinburgh to be ready for the arrival of the prospective buyers the next morning, and five minutes before the meeting was due to begin the owner began to get anxious as the other side had not yet arrived.

We could see about four miles down the road towards Fort William and no cars were coming our way. Was it a no-show? I too was a trifle anxious as I was to get my commission for arranging a sale and without the other party there could be no negotiation.

At one minute to twelve, we heard a loud noise approaching and sure enough in swooped a helicopter right into the hotel's car park and set itself down a few yards from my Mercedes –

which the owner had been impressed with on my (quieter) arrival the night before.

There is no doubt that it was a magnificent entrance for the buyers to make. They totally upstaged me in the eyes of my client and in doing so weakened his resolve (but not mine!) on price.

I am certain that this knocked about £30,000 off his aspirations for what he thought he could get for his hotel. He literally fell over the buyers for the two hours or so they were there and clearly no longer regarded them as the 'mugs' he thought they were going to be in our conversation over dinner the previous night.

The helicopter had intimidated him.

He believed he was dealing with *real* money when he talked to those guys and was more than grateful when they treated him and his business with some respect. This made him feel, almost, like the kind of guy who one day would ride around in a helicopter!

If he had thought about it (as I did on my way home by car) the cost of hiring a helicopter for a round trip from Glasgow via Fort William was about £1600. If that knocked £30,000 off the top price the owner was looking for for the hotel, it had to be a good investment.

And it was. The buyers got extended credit on part of the sale price, a generous assessment of stock at valuation and were required to pay a very low deposit on contract.

Also, I had difficulty in getting my full fee out of him!

I had pressed hard in the negotiations for a price about 20 per cent more than the owner finally settled at and also for stiffer terms. He instructed me to accept the lower price and the softer terms and even suggested *publicly* that I was threatening *his* deal!

When the agreement was signed and it came to my turn to get paid, he had the impudence to suggest I should take a smaller fee as I had not got as much for the hotel as he had anticipated.

Fortunately, I had a signed letter from him confirming my fee and I waved it at him. Also, in view of his attitude, I insisted on cash or kind and told him I was quite prepared to load the Mercedes with Scotch if he didn't have the 'readies' to hand.

We settled on a bit of each, with the whisky valued on the same terms he had given to the new owners.

Intimidation through props is not easy to combat.

In business you make status judgements all the time. Practically everybody equates the trappings of status with the possession of power.

YOU CAN TAKE 'PRESTIGE' TO A BANK

A major Bank had cause to re-examine its methods of doing business when its share price fell to an all time low of £1.50, making it a take-over target from a couple of rivals in the UK and one from mid-Asia, who believed they could make it successful again.

The initial results of the investigation showed that 22 per cent of its corporate business customers were not contributing profits to the Bank from using its services, and of these a third were causing the Bank real losses (it would have been cheaper to pay them to take their business to other banks).

Detailed enquiries showed that one of its major clients with a strong balance sheet and consistent profits every year, had been receiving virtually free banking services for many years.

Why? Because, like many others, it was regarded as a 'prestige' customer, whatever that meant. Critics were

informed that prestige was something you either understood or you didn't (as close as you get to a 'put down'
in banking circles!).

When pressed, it emerged that the owner of the prestige
business was a very keen golfer – as were many of the
Bank's staff – and he was also the ex-captain of a very
prestigious golf club just outside the town.

The Bank's new management decided that there was a
confusion between which aspect of the owner's life merited
his prestige but fully understood which to negotiate
increased charges for, like they did with their other customers.

Three years later, when these unprofitable corporate
accounts were either in profit or re-banked, the share price
stood at an all time high of £6 a share and the Bank was
now the target for take-over by a rival bank, who wanted
to buy them for their success.

That is why there are so many burned fingers in the negotiating business and why so many people are conned every day
by acting upon what they think they are seeing.

Intimidation does not have to be projected by physical props.
It is also common through the subjective intangibles of supposed
reputation and prestige. Such has been the success of this form
of intangible intimidation, that it is inexorably driving prices
down in one area of business activity, with which I am familiar,
and of which I would have thought the 'victims' would have
known better.

Take the obsession that the big five accountancy firms have
with being the auditor of as many of the large corporates in the
'Footsie 100' (and their equivalents around the world) that they
can gain and hold on to.

Now, auditing is a 'distress purchase' – like when your
exhaust pipe falls off your car, you just have to pay to get it

fixed no matter how inconvenient it is to your cash flow. No exhaust, then distressingly, no driving. And no audit, as distressingly, no trading. In both cases, the police would take an interest in your continuing driving or trading without paying the price legally to do either.

You would think that something somebody had to have would ensure 'sticky' prices – those prices with an in-built tendency to stay where you first find them. But that is not the case. Audit fees have been coming down for several years, sometimes in jumps downwards of 30 per cent!

The big corporates are aware of how prestigious their audits are for the big five accountancy firms, so they pander to their auditors' feelings of dependency. If they can't negotiate an audit fee downwards, they threaten to put it out to tender, which usually produces the expected collapse in resistance to a fee cut. And, what do they find – when an audit fee does go out to tender, every firm's bids, including that of their current auditor, tumble down in a manner that makes Helmut Weber's errors seem minor peccadilloes.

Having dealt with four of the big five firms, I am perplexed with their obsessions. In fact, I tested it in their market place. At a conference on negotiation strategy I was presenting for financial directors, many from the top 100 UK corporates, I asked how many of them knew the names of the auditors of more than ten of the 'Footsie 100'. I got to 'how many knew three of the Footsie 100' before any hands went up!

They all knew their own auditors, of course, and some knew of at least one other corporate's auditor (only because they had worked for both) but the auditing firm's obsessions were not shared by the overwhelming majority of financial directors at the conference, almost all of whom came from their client base.

But like any sensible negotiator, if the other person regards the right to audit as many of the top 100 corporates as their main mission in life, then it is incumbent on the respective financial directors to let them stew in their obsessions and to take full advantage of their willingness – nay, angst – to cut and cut their fees to 'enjoy' the privileges they so ardently desire (and which nobody else, apparently, shares!).

Every hustler knows about intimidation. They know that you judge the quality of someone by the possessions they have around them. If you notice and are impressed by ostentatiously visible possessions, you are almost hooked and the rest is easier than it would be if you weren't.

What will intimidate the average negotiator? Any or all of the following:

A prestige headquarters exquisitely furnished.
A list of international offices.
An executive jet, or better still, two, or a helicopter.
A yacht cruising in the Mediterranean or Caribbean.
Rolls Royces and other big gas guzzlers.
Minions running around at the whim and behest of the
   boss.
Expensive clothes, accessories and gizmo gadgets.
An obvious ability to get other people to fawn.
A facility to talk in large numbers and work out
   percentages of awkward sums fast.
Association with 'important names' in society.
Evidence of cash resources, credit cards, and lines of
   credit.
The appearance of being unrushed, and unworried.
Evidence of constant international travel.
A much larger business than the negotiator's.
Some evidence of 'kindness' and 'respect' from the 'big
   guy' with a reputation of ruthlessness towards others.

All of these are pure intimidation. They are the business versions of see-through blouses and tight jeans (indeed, it is not unknown for ostensibly non-business intimidation to be used to facilitate a negotiated outcome).

The antidotes?

Recognize the signs of intimidation for what they are – don't psyche yourself into becoming a victim of your own fantasies. All that glitters is not gold and the apparent access to props is no proof of the actual power relationship between you and the big guy in the corporate suite.

If you are not intimidated you have nothing to worry about, no matter who you are dealing with. In a practical sense you can steel yourself against their intimidation by avoiding any overt references to their props. You give the game away if you make it obvious how impressed you are with the props for this automatically acts to strengthen the other person if he basks in your approval and you gratify his self-esteem.

Hence, do not exclaim how wonderful their building is or even make a remark about the view from his office (no matter how magnificent it is – that's why they pay for it).

If you are there to see a head guy, and you are kept waiting, always ask the receptionist to use the telephone to ring home, the office or your next appointment. That will change her atti- tude towards you (remember she is part of his team not yours) and when the boss hears what is delaying your admission it undercuts why he is keeping you waiting.

If the wait is likely to be a long one (he is delayed at an 'important' meeting, i.e. his lunch, a round of golf, or coffee and doughnuts with his girlfriend) make some more phone calls – think of the money it's saving you – and, if you really want to fight back, make a long-distance call by direct dial. Or better still ask to be connected to the fax room!

Whatever else you do, do not read the magazines they leave out for visitors in your predicament because that is your first step in the dance to their tune. I always bring a book to read in these circumstances and when he looks out of his door he sees me immersed in something from the Top Ten list (hardcover not paperback), but certainly not *House and Garden*, *Vogue*, or his company's *Annual Report*.

IT DOESN'T ALWAYS PAY TO BE AN MBA

A multinational shipping consortium faced a severe drop in earnings caused by a world trade recession. It decided to rationalize its operations and called on the various national components to submit survival plans.

The US end of the operation took the problem on board much in the manner of a Harvard Business School case study, i.e. a problem to be solved rather than a fight for national interests.

They set up a ten-man survival team, seven of them with MBAs, and produced a detailed survival report for the meeting. In presentation terms it was a well-produced document – stitch binding even! – and was supported by a slide projection programme.

The other members of the consortium were less than impressed with the hundreds of man-hours that had been used in producing the report and its obvious profession-alism. They recommended that the US office be demanned by 15 per cent as they obviously had too little to do if they could produce such magnificent reports with their available staff.

One man I know fights back by going to sleep, he says it gets him into the right unintimidated mood. Another only talks business with clients, never anything personal. That way he can't be intimidated by the (often entirely phoney) international jet-set image his clients like to create for the impressionable. He finds no need to explain himself as a person or to account for his wordly adventures. He just sticks to the deal, the whole deal and nothing but the deal.

So should you.

Beware, however, of trying to out-intimidate the other person with your own props and phoney lines. Stick to the use of your skill in negotiating and leave the manipulative moves to others, because it is sufficient for you *not* to be intimidated by what they do. It is not necessary for you to work out how to intimidate them by what you do.

If you're good at your job, that is all the intimidation you require, for there is nothing so awe-inspiring as a richly-deserved reputation for being good at your business.

COMMENTS ON SELF-ASSESSMENT TEST 22

1 a) Foxes are never intimidated by the props of power – though they sometimes use them!
  b) What an Owl would do. The props may camouflage an imminent disaster unless he can off-load some planes.
  c) You have been intimidated – the fate of all Sheep.

2 a) Low. Surely a bit perverse, even for a Donkey!
  b) You've been intimidated again. Baa! Baa!
  c) Correct. Owls do not judge status by props.

3 a) Indeterminate – perhaps his chauffeur-driven Rolls has not turned up on time?
  b) Indeterminate – a power prop is not a guide to status.
  c) Indeterminate – perhaps he is environmentally conscious?
  d) Indeterminate – perhaps, like Robert Maxwell, he can afford it because he is in charge of your pension fund!

SELF-ASSESSMENT TEST 23

1 You manage a small engineering plant and one of your large customers owes you for three deliveries. You feel you are getting the 'run around' from his accounts department and another delivery of parts is due next week. Do you:
   (a) Tell his accounts department that you will hold back the next delivery unless they pay up?
   (b) Continue to demand payment for the overdue accounts?
   (c) Tell the user department that you will hold back delivery until the overdue amounts are paid?

2 A small supplier of valves has delivered a batch which failed your quality-control tests and you put them into your own workshop for corrective machining. Do you:
   (a) Demand a reduction in the invoice for your machining costs and warn them about future quality?
   (b) Deduct your costs from the invoice and pay the balance?
   (c) Pay the invoice but demand a guarantee on future quality?
   (d) Wait until you hear from them about their unpaid invoice?

3 The supplier demands payment in full. He argues that your machining costs are excessive and that allegedly rejected work should be returned for their inspection and replacement. Do you:
   (a) Reject his invoice again and insist on your reasonable costs being met?
   (b) Tell him that if he insists on full payment you will cease to do business with him in future?
   (c) Pay the invoice but demand a guarantee of future quality?

CHAPTER 23

On being Russian-Fronted

or how to cope with threats

Consider young Lieutenant Wolfgang Mueller's predicament in Paris in 1943. He was dining with his girlfriend in a bistro just off the Boulevard St Germain, in the Rue De Bac, when his Colonel walked in and took a fancy to his companion.

He called Wolfgang over and ordered him to go for a walk, to which order Wolfgang protested. The Colonel told him: 'Either you do as I say, or I will have you sent to the Russian Front *tonight*.'

'Mein Gott,' said Wolfgang. 'The Russian Front! Anything but the Russian Front!'

And he went for a (long) walk.

Why?

Because Wolfgang believed that the Colonel fully intended to get his way or send him to the Russian Front, which, Wolfgang also believed, would be absolutely disastrous to his interests.

If you believe that the threatener fully intends to carry out his threat and has the capability to do so in such a way that you are damaged by the consequences, it is bound to influence your judgement about the appropriate courses of action for you to follow.

If this causes you to alter your previous intentions in any way, you have been 'Russian-Fronted'!

May I be permitted a small personal interjection at this point?

An author on negotiation has seen fit to traduce my naming of the Russian Front threat ploy and, normally, I would rather be traduced than ignored. But he went further.

He completely re-invented the origins of the Russian Front, misunderstood it, and arrogantly claims that my version is unlikely to be found in real world negotiation practice while, of course, his is!

The origin of the Russian Front threat is exactly as you have just read it in reference to Wolfgang Mueller in 1943. Well, my critic has moved its origins back to the Napoleonic invasion of Russia in 1812. So what? Well, for a start there was no such concept as a 'Front', Russian or otherwise, in 1812. But worse, his version of the ploy has nothing to do with threats in nego-tiation – it is something to do with long supply lines when negotiating.

Could, therefore, we be clear? The Russian Front is a threat tactic that is highly prevalent in negotiating practice, and my origination was loosely inspired by the 'B' movie scene of the credible threat to German soldiers being 'Russian Fronted' in Hitler's War. How Napolean got into the act, I have no idea, and what the relevance of long supply lines has for negotiation, I have even less of an idea, as, I suspect has my hapless critic, too.

Please continue to enjoy your reading!

When was the last time you were Russian-Fronted?

You may remember your feelings of resentment at being forced by circumstances to accede to a threat. True, you get a choice, but the choice is between something so unpleasant that the alternative, unpleasant as it may be, is less unpleasant than the Russian Front.

What is the role of a threat in negotiation?

The evidence is overwhelming that threats, sanctions and their counters are familiar features of negotiating practice. They are used frequently in many negotiations – industrial relations, international conferences, commercial disputes, domestic altercations, and so on. Sometimes they are used as pressure tactics in the aftermath of a deadlock and other times they are a part of the negotiation itself.

Threats and sanctions can be used as a substitute for negotiation, such as in hijacking and kidnapping, though the more you can get the hijacker or kidnapper into a negotiating relationship, the more likely you are to resolve the issue without giving in.

To see the tactical use of threats, consider the case of a small components firm that had not received payment for the last three deliveries it had made to a large Brazilian engineering corporation. All three deliveries were on time and all of them were accepted by the customer's quality-control people.

Naturally, it had chased the various departments concerned for its money and had been fobbed off by various managers, including the accounts department, each time.

The managers of the small firm were of the opinion that they were getting the proverbial 'run around' from the corporation's employees who gave no explanation for why payment was delayed – only references to 'it's in the system'. The failure to pay was causing a serious cash-flow problem and they did not have the resources to sustain themselves beyond a few weeks.

The next delivery of components was due in two weeks' time and a letter was sent to the head of the particular division that used the components, informing him that until the previous accounts were paid delivery would not take place.

The day before the delivery was due, a cheque for the outstanding amount arrived without explanation or apology.

The small firm had successfully *threatened* the larger firm.

However, threats can sour a good relationship, and make a bad relationship worse, by leading to outright warfare and mutually damaging behaviour.

Nobody likes to be threatened.

In fact the chances are very strong that a person who is threatened will resent it so much that they will make a counter-threat, *even if the implementation of that threat will lead to large mutual losses for both parties*. For once a threat/counter-threat cycle gets underway it is very difficult to reverse it into a reward/counter-reward cycle.

Threats beget threats, probably more often than they produce compliance.

A North American aircraft corporation, for instance, received a batch of valves from a supplier which failed to pass its quality-control sampling test. Following procedure, every item in the batch was individually inspected and the failure rate reached 24 per cent.

The rejected valves were re-machined on site and the supplier was notified that its charges had to be adjusted downwards to take account of the (itemized) additional cost of labour and machine time to the aircraft company. They were also issued with a warning on quality standards.

The supplier refused to accept a reduction in their invoice and insisted on full payment. Allegedly defective materials should be returned to them for re-machining or replacement, they argued, and they did not accept the customer's machining costs which they considered were 'overpriced' compared to the costs they would incur in their own plant for the same work (this also told them something about the cost margins between their work and their client's and suggested that they were quoting for work too cheaply).

The aircraft corporation threatened the supplier that unless they agreed to cut their invoice by the stated amount and guaranteed quality for the future, their contract would be terminated forthwith and they would 'never earn another dollar from them again'.

After a delay of some weeks, the aircraft corporation received an invoice for the same amount by certified post and a demand for full payment within 30 days otherwise the supplier intended to go to court over the issue.

A week later, the supplier received a cheque and formal notice of their removal from the list of approved sub-contractors.

Neither side have done business with each other since.

The corporation *threatened* the supplier and the supplier *counter-threatened* the corporation. The corporation *implemented* its threat (not to do business with the supplier); the supplier didn't have to implement its threat (to take the corporation to court).

But who, if anybody, won?

The capacity for people to act 'irrationally', i.e. against what a disinterested onlooker would judge to be in their best interests, is not related to the level of intelligence of the parties.

Geniuses can engage in mutually destructive behaviour when they are in contest over something – who 'discovered' something first, for instance – so it is not surprising that 'mad' behaviour is commonplace among the rest of us.

When threats appear in a negotiation there is a higher chance of deadlock than when they don't.

There is a lesson here: avoid making threats in a negotiation. They are often unproductive for being made explicit.

As a professional negotiator I almost always raise at least one eyebrow (two if the timing of the threat is utterly ridiculous!) when a threat is clumsily articulated by the other person.

Why?

Because I regard it as a sign of impatience, of amateurism, even, that the other person thinks I need to be reminded of the power balance between us. Threats are put-me-downs, like drawing attention to my accent or my clothes.

If he thinks I need reminding of the power balance he is trying to intimidate me, or he has no respect for me as a negotiator. On the other hand, when a negotiation is in deadlock – or stalled due to a party's tactics of prevarication – it may be that only threats will get things moving satisfactorily. In this circumstance the threatener regards the risk of upsetting the overall relationship as less damaging than letting things slide indefinitely.

It all depends on context.

Some types of negotiation involve the frequent use of threats and counter-threats by both parties. International disputes between countries and labour disputes with managements are two familiar contexts in which threats and sanctions (or implemented threats) are regular features of dialogue.

RUM DEALS IN THE POOL

A vice-president of a UK beer company was on a business tour of South America and was faxed by his head office to go to Jamaica on his way back and meet with the management team of one of the local rum exporters. His problem was that he did not have the correct visa required for a business visit to Jamaica, nor on his tight schedule did he have time to acquire one.

Hence, he went into Norman Manley airport, Kingston, as a tourist. His problems began at immigration, because it was obvious from his previous itinerary and correspondence in his briefcase that he had been on a business trip. He claimed to the officials that he was in Jamaica for a few days' recreation before returning to London.

He booked into his hotel and phoned the rum exporter he wanted to meet. Later at the hotel he was interviewed by an immigration official who accused him of being in Jamaica for business purposes without a proper visa. The official told him that he was being watched and that if he did any business at all he would be arrested, fined heavily and deported.

For two days a policeman shadowed him everywhere and forced him to spend the days and evenings like a tourist. The visit was clearly going to be a waste of time and money.

Before leaving, however, he met with the rum exporter and they did a deal right under the nose of the police.

The hotel has a patio bar, one side of which is built into the pool for swimmers to sit beside while in the water. While a policeman sat keeping a sleepy eye on him, he sat at the bar in the pool talking to the barman and a young woman who joined them.

The policeman assumed that he was merely idling his time talking to a barman and flirting with a guest. In fact he was negotiating with the head of the rum company who was behind the bar dressed as a barman. His secretary was the 'guest' undressed in a bikini in the pool.

Moral: initiative can beat any bureaucratic nonsense aimed at stopping people doing business.

In business negotiations threats are also common – much more than is admitted – though they are often disguised or buried in subtle hints and the parties can miss them when they are made.

Anyway, properly prepared negotiators are aware of their vulnerability in a deal without the heavy-handed needing to remind them. The purpose of every threat is intimidation and there are two ways to intimidate people by using threats:

You want the kids to cut the grass, so you threaten them with no television for a week.

This threat is a *compliance* threat that compels the kids to do it or else.

Your spouse wants you to stay home and sober, so you are

warned if you go out to expect the house to be deserted when you return.

This threat is a *deterrence* threat that deters you from doing it or else – you may do almost anything else instead.

To illustrate the difference between these types of threats more clearly consider the unhappy (for the hostages) experience of hijacking or political kidnapping.

An aircraft hijacker's demand for the release of terrorist prisoners (or similar) is a compliance threat; the passing of a law that requires a mandatory life sentence for hijacking is a deterrence threat.

How should we respond to threats? This is a very difficult question to generalize about. The question that must be uppermost in a negotiator's mind when contemplating making a threat is:

What is the likelihood of the threat succeeding as an intimidator?

That depends, as with much else in negotiating, on the context of the threat. Specifically, it depends on two interrelated but nevertheless distinct factors:

1 The credibility of our intention to carry out the threat.
2 The capability of the implemented threat to damage the other party.

These have both objective and subjective aspects.

If the threat has high credibility and its capability to damage us is extensive, we are likely to accede to the Russian-Front tactic. There is no point mincing words about this: if they have you by the 'short and curlies' the prospect of resistance to their demands is purely academic.

But if they have you that way cold, why are they negotiating with you?

On the surface there is no reason, but if you examine it more carefully you will see that your position is not as weak as it looks.

In the unhappy circumstance of a hijacking or kidnapping, your only chance of getting out from under *without giving in* is to find something to negotiate about.

The hijacker holding a plane-load of people hostage needs material things from those he is threatening. He needs fuel to get away, he needs food, water and, perhaps, medicines, while arrangements to meet his demands are made (you can spin that out to increase his dependence on your goodwill which has the effect of lowering the pressure on you too), and he needs good communications otherwise his threats slacken by an inability to reinforce them. Experience suggests that long negotiations between the authorities and the hijackers weakens the pressure from the latter and produces a stalemate, and the longer the stalemate the more the hijackers will reduce their demands (down to a final one – escape).

The hijackers can increase the pressure by carrying out their threats, or they can avoid the pressure of a stalemate by changing location. The first may provoke a violent ending to the hijack and the second weakens the pressure on the original target.

The delay in gaining their ends also increases the chances that they can be disarmed successfully by special anti-terrorist units. The hijackers get tired, jaded and mentally stressed as each hour passes. The assault troops are well-trained, rested and fresh and need only be brought into contact minutes before the assault.

In the case of a kidnapping, we are in an entirely different environment. You know where the hijacker and his hostages are – sitting out there on the tarmac with the world's TV filming every move – but you don't know where the kidnapper's lair is.

The kidnapper issues demands from a secret hideout, shuns physical or visual two-way contact with his target, relies on his own resources of food and water, and is able to cut out if things go wrong.

But the kidnapper's Achilles heel is the line of communication between him and the target for whatever it is that he is demanding. If it's money he wants, he has to get it delivered somewhere without being arrested in the process of collecting it. Negotiations on the means of delivery, the denominations of the currency, the dropping zone and the involvement of the authorities all take time.

The longer the time these negotiations take, the greater the chance of the kidnapper releasing his hostages.

The more difficult problem occurs when it is something political that the kidnapper is after – release of colleagues in prison, dismissal of a government official, distribution of relief to the poor, publication of a message by the media, ending of some programme that helps a racial or religious minority and so on.

For reasons of state, many governments refuse point blank to negotiate under the duress of a kidnapping for political demands on the grounds that this will lead to repetition by other ruthless and determined groups.

For tactical reasons the authorities might pretend to be negotiating with the kidnappers when in reality they are using whatever information they can glean in the negotiations to catch them. Or, they could be negotiating in earnest but a slip by the kidnappers could give the authorities another option.

So, in general, if threats are used against you in a negotiation it does not follow necessarily that you are trapped cold. If you have some room for manoeuvre you have a choice, *however limited*. Identifying that room, and expanding on it, is a task you have to face if you prefer not to comply with their demands.

Otherwise you are stuck with the 'lesser evil' they offer you as an alternative to their Russian Front.

In negotiating, each party has a veto – you don't have to agree to whatever is on offer – though this may have consequences for you. The plant could go on strike, they may try to get their way by force, you might have to do without supplies or you might be taken to court and so on.

It is legitimate in a negotiation to draw the attention of the other person to the consequences of his persistence with a deadlocked position, though there are ways in which this can be stated without provoking the charge that you are threatening them. Timing is the essence of making clear the consequences of deadlock without necessarily creating resentment.

In commerce you have the option to take your business elsewhere. The implicit 'threat' to do so is present in every negotiation and is widely accepted as being legitimate. By legitimate I mean that it is regarded as being within the norms of everyday negotiating.

The acceptability of the implicit sanction of not doing business if you fail to agree is a matter of degree.

The buyer (or seller) uttering the 'killer' sentence, 'you'll have to do better than that', implies that if you don't (can't) you won't get his business. That *might* be acceptable as a negotiating tactic if it is confined only to a relatively small transaction out of your annual turnover with him.

If you say that not only will he not get your business in the case in dispute, but he will not get *any* business from you at all, the sanction threat begins to move towards being unacceptable and you run the risk that your threat may dig him deeper into his position precisely because he resents your blackmail and cannot be seen to give in to those tactics.

If you use the threat of possibly large-scale damage to his business in pursuit of a relatively minor matter, he is likely to perceive your intentions as being hostile to him and his interests and his reaction could produce an equally negative response.

His quandary is (and ought to be) that if he appears to give in to a large-scale threat over a relatively small matter, how does he protect himself in future?

If you threaten that you will stop him doing business with everybody else in town, the territory, the country, the continent, even the world, your threat is pure blackmail, assuming that it is credible. And if it isn't credible you cannot possibly retain his respect.

As large-scale threats are less credible in pursuit of small objectives than they are when in pursuit of large-scale objectives, there is a natural limitation on using them in this way, without provoking legal intervention, public hostility or outright disbelief that you intend to do what you threaten.

If a man in a bar says 'pass me the ashtray or I'll kill you' it is unlikely that you would take him seriously (you would certainly doubt his sanity or sobriety or both!). Most people would pass the ashtray without such a heavy threat, but a lot of people wouldn't if they were treated that way. (In some bars that could be fatal.)

The United States does not use (hasn't so far, anyway) the threat of nuclear *attack* when in dispute with a smaller non-nuclear power. They reserve the nuclear option for retaliation if they are attacked by another nuclear power.

If you compared in 1973 the absolute capacities of the United States and North Vietnamese militaries to inflict damage on each other, there is no doubt that the US arsenal of nuclear weapons made it by far the most formidable of the two.

However, using nuclear weapons is not the same as having them. The North Vietnamese could, therefore, safely disregard the US nuclear arsenal in their calculations of the balance of forces.

The magnitude of the threat ought then to be relative to the issue at stake. This is the more so, the earlier in the negotiation that the threat is made: when a threat is a *last* resort, it has more legitimacy, i.e. it is more acceptable as a negotiating norm, than when it is the *first* resort.

To open up earlier in the negotiation with a threat is likely to raise the other party's eyebrows if not their hackles! It provokes more resistance than it overcomes.

Actually implementing a threat may also impose costs on the party doing the threatening – for a start you would have to do without their services, and they yours, at least in the short run. This is also your opportunity because it is rare to find the dependence only running one way.

Most of the time, just as we are vulnerable to a threatened action from the other person, he is vulnerable to some form of threatened counter-action from us. No wonder then that most threats do not provoke immediate compliance – they provoke retaliatory counter-threats instead.

One of the most devastating counters to a threat is to imply that it does not concern you all that much if the threat is implemented. The other person has to contemplate whether you are bluffing and what the cost is going to be to himself of implementing the threat.

If, however, you are the only supplier of a particular product which the other party must have (say, a drug company negotiating with a hospital), there is a strong moral pressure present (often backed up by a legal deterrence) for you not to exploit that position by making 'unreasonable' demands.

Market economies normally have legislation to limit monopoly powers, though the limitations vary for different types of monopolies and may be applied with more or less vigour. For instance, labour monopolies tend to be less regulated than corporate monopolies.

A threat raises the costs of disagreement – assuming that the threat will be implemented if we disagree and that it is not just a bluff. If you are dependent upon the other person, you are vulnerable to a threat from him.

A DISCOUNT, OR ELSE!

A hotel chain selling a branded vodka in its bars decided to widen its profit margin on sales by increasing the discount it got from the supplier.

The negotiators deadlocked when the vodka people insisted that the chain was already on a top discount and anything more 'would make it unprofitable to supply them at all'.

The hotel chain was adamant in its demands as it had been offered by another company a 'hotel brand' vodka at a higher discount.

The last statement of the vodka people was taken as a threat to withhold supplies. In fact, the so-called 'threat' became the main issue at the next meeting, but the other side heatedly denied they had threatened anything at all – they were 'just drawing the attention of the hotel chain to the financial realities'.

The hotel negotiators insisted on a larger discount and added that if they did not get one they 'would stop buying the branded vodka altogether'.

The vodka people took this as a threat – 'blackmail' they called it – and the negotiatons broke down.

The hotel chain changed its vodka suppliers and customers were offered the in-house brand when they asked for the other company's (well advertised) vodka. This did not always go down well with those customers who asked for the vodka by name.

It might have been possible for the hotel people to get a better financial deal if they had simply switched from a demand for a discount to a demand for extended credit. This (minority) view was expressed at the time but was overruled once the hotel chiefs got their tails up at the alleged threat not to supply them with vodka.

Casual remarks can be taken as threats, and can be thrown back as a challenge. If the negotiations break down the threat may have to be implemented.

Wolfgang's problem was his dependence on his colonel who had the power to decide where Wolfgang fought in Hitler's War.

Being dependent upon the other party increases the possibility of being Russian-Fronted. It follows that lessening your dependence improves your chances of being able to defy threats, ill-timed or otherwise.

Chain stores that place their orders with small suppliers can get a lot of negotiating leverage into their hands if they can come to represent the bulk of a small supplier's sales. They can do this by placing large orders – which the small firm may at first be grateful for – or offering credit to buy machinery and such like.

They can (and often do) squeeze down the price of the goods they buy from totally dependent sources by threatening to cut them out as a supply source. They also take longer credit and insist on higher quality. At the very least they can determine the supplier's policies in areas where normally you would not expect to find them operating, e.g. hiring standards, trade union membership, even ethnic balance.

They also tighten the squeeze on dependent suppliers by locking them into exclusive purchase agreements, thus preventing them expanding out from under their dependence by acquiring other customers.

The threat to cut them out need not be made incessantly, because every time the smaller company looks at its markets (or lack of them) it gets the message. So the latent threat to cut them out – through, perhaps, the occasional demonstration of the disciplining of a 'troublemaker' – is enough to get the desired result. Many a large business has grown by swallowing up smaller suppliers that either needed cash for expansion or got into debt to their 'customer'.

Breweries often pick up hotels and bars because their owners fall into debt to them; retail stores acquire clothing manufacturers because they become so dependent on their customer that they cannot survive at the prices imposed on them for their clothes; petroleum companies take over garage outlets, and franchise operations acquire faltering businesses or the real estate left after debts are paid off.

You can save yourself a lot of grief at the negotiating table if you refrain from getting too dependent on one source and thus increasing the costs to you of disagreement with the other person on what he regards as being a substantial matter.

All threats boil down to some version of the Russian Front, forcing you to choose between unpleasant alternatives. If you believe they have the power to damage you and that they will do so if you don't comply or are not deterred, you will be Russian-Fronted.

However, unlike Wolfgang, you might have a choice.

COMMENTS ON SELF-ASSESSMENT TEST 23

1 a) You are threatening the wrong people. Accounts are more concerned with holding onto your money than they are that somebody else in the firm is not receiving your goods. An empty Donkey threat.

   b) Accounts are experts at ignoring the bleatings of Sheep. The headaches you give them are another excuse to delay payment.

   c) Yes. Foxes pressurize the people with the most to lose – and know that they will put internal pressure on accounts for you to avoid the inconvenience of non-delivery.

2 a) Likely to lead to a negotiation as long as, Fox-like, you stall payment.

   b) Might work if they decide not to fight because your machining costs are trivial, but you have reduced the pressure on them if they do fight. More a Sheep's move than a Fox.

   c) Only a move for a Donkey.

   d) Changes a quality grievance into a mere late payment. A Sheep's cop out move.

3 a) Likely to lead to a negotiation, as long as, Fox-like, you stall payment and supply the evidence for the quality failure and the legitimacy of your machining costs.

   b) Unlikely to succeed and risks total breakdown. How a Donkey would react.

   c) The weakest move almost certainly chosen by a Sheep.

SELF-ASSESSMENT TEST 24

1 You have been buying a component for your room divider systems, that you manufacture and install to order, from a large aluminium extruder for a number of years. Their new marketing manager rang you this morning with the news that they have decided to cease extruding your line because they are unable to make a profit on it at current prices. Do you:
   (a) Suggest that you re-negotiate the current contract price?
   (b) Ask for details of their costings and profit requirements?
   (c) Check for availability and prices with other extruders?
   (d) Tell them you are well aware of what ploy they are up to?

2 You are told by a customer, who buys simple forged components from you, that they have decided to make them in-house when current orders are delivered. Do you:
   (a) Offer to discuss your prices?
   (b) Warn her that in-house manufacturing of these components would be more expensive when tooling, casting's dies, training and quality controls are costed?
   (c) Suggest that you discuss the problem?
   (d) Say, 'Fine', and wish them all the best?

3 The aluminium extruding company's marketing manager is back on the phone, saying that your most recent purchase order will have to be unfulfilled because it looks as if there will be a strike at the plant and all existing stocks of aluminium ingots are being diverted this month for the manufacture and delivery of components to their long-term priority customers. Over your protests – as you need a delivery – he tells you that their priority customers pay a premium per ton over what you pay, despite the recent price increase you agreed. Do you:
   (a) Ask what size of premium the priority cutomers are paying and offer to match it?
   (b) Ask what size of premium the priority customers are paying and offer to beat it?
   (c) Check the contract to see if *force majeure* includes strikes?
   (d) Urgently take your business elsewhere?

311

CHAPTER 24

Hard Gals and Guys

or how hard bargainers make it hard to bargain

Commerical buying is rife with hard gals and guys.

Some businesses reason that the usual adversarial bash-ups with sales people endanger their own products, if their suppliers screw up in any way with whatever they send over for whatever pittance they have had to accept, merely to get a signature on a purchase order.

Other businesses take a different view and are proud to practise what some people call 'hard bargaining', though what relationship their behaviour has to any form of bargaining is not clear to me.

One gal I know, Gloria Nearsight, is one of the sharpest exponents around of the school of so-called 'hard' bargaining. May you be so lucky as not to meet her on a professional basis (she's a pussy cat socially, but you would never guess!).

She claims her behaviour extols the virtues of competition. Now I am no slouch when it comes to appreciating the virtues of competition, as I believe it is the primary driver of our living standards, but of her claims to connect her negotiating behaviours with it, I have severe reservations.

Hard bargaining with sellers, Gloria believes, is good for us all – irrespective of the discomfort it causes those who seek protection from the power of the competitive market (which, she incessantly reminds hapless sellers, protects the consumers not the producers).

Gloria urges the use of the competitive forces of the market to maximum effect. Her role, in the quietness and privacy of her office, is to conduct her negotiations as a conduit of the market into the seller's prices. Feeling that she is serving our interests, she works on the assumption that all sellers pad their prices and that stripping out the padding makes for a more efficient economy.

Suppliers, Gloria points out, whine about their right to make a profit and if you buy this whinging you only invite the seller to relax on their mark-ups. She is adamant, also, that it is not any of her business if the seller makes a loss. (Perhaps, you can see why she is often described as being 'Nearsight by name and nearsighted by nature'?)

BUYING CHEAP CAN COST YOU MORE!

A General Manager was showing a guest through a plant they had just opened and stopped at a bench to pick up a very small spring. She showed it to her guest and said: 'See this. It used to cost us 15 pence but I have managed to get its price increased to 45 pence and hope to get it up to 60 pence in six months.'

Her guest was somewhat astonished at this news and asked for an explanation. 'We used to buy this and every-thing else the old way – we wouldn't feed our buyers for a week and then on Friday we would open the cages and set them loose on the sales people and only stop their bleeding when they had cut their prices to the bone.'

'So?' exclaimed her guest.

'Well, we were certainly buying cheap,' explained the

GM, 'but all that was doing was shifting costs from our procurement budget to our production budget. It made the Purchasing Manager look good but wasn't so hot for our profitability. Every time a 15 pence spring broke it costs us a thousand man-hours of highly expensive skilled labour to disassemble the missile, rework it, de-gaus it and re-calibrate it. We realized that it would be cheaper to pay more to get a proper spring in the first place.'

She went on to explain that the new buying philosophy had reduced the firm's suppliers from 800 to 350 (and was still going down). The results could be seen in lower production costs, net of what she had spent on retraining her buyers that not all *el cheapos* are really as cheap as they look on a purchase order.

If the seller can get away with selling his products higher to one buyer then he can afford to sell them lower to other buyers. Gloria sees no reason whatsoever why she should not take advantage of her less determined rivals, who pay higher prices for the same product.

A large volume order might provoke a seller to set the price at 'marginal cost', because it suits his company to keep a production line running. If this is the case, why should Gloria not exploit the opportunity offered to her? The seller may be buying business (in response to Gloria's 'sell-cheap-get-famous' ploy), or because they are under pressure from creditors.

A bankrupt supplier, however, is an expensive problem for Gloria if she is caught by a below-cost deal from the seller and her supplies are stuck and under ransom at the receiver's warehouse. Gloria defiantly disdains to recognize this as a real risk on the grounds that sellers can avoid bankruptcy by spotting it coming!

Gloria expects sellers to submit prices above what they are prepared to accept. Their entry price is higher than their exit price, as it should be. What does she do about this? She aggressively attacks the seller's prices.

A tit-for-tat struggle ensues between sellers padding their prices and slackening the customer's specifications and Gloria stripping out padding and tightening her specifications. So far, so familiar, as adversarial sellers and buyers will recognize, but Gloria adds a new twist to get those prices down – she forces the sellers to compete with themselves.

It works like this. Gloria accepts none of the bids she receives for a supply contract but waits quietly in her office for the inevitably over-keen sellers to enquire about what she thought of their bids.

Any that do enquire don't get through to her but she calls them back after a decent wait. The message is the same to all of them: 'your price is too high'. Naturally, the seller asks about the gap between their 'high' price and the supposed lower bid from somebody else, but Gloria does not disclose any information about the 'gap' (there may not, in fact, be one at all!), for she does not want to get drawn into a negotiation with the seller. Neither does she reveal which firms are competing for her business, which is usually the second question they ask. She only repeats that the 'gap' is considerable and: 'sorry, the names of competitors [surprise, surprise] are commercially confidential'.

TRADING BEATS HARD BARGAINING

Between a five-star hotel and a Conference Centre there is about five acres of semi-derelict land, part of it leased by the hotel from the local council, who are owners of the Conference Centre, for open air car parking.

The local council wanted to build an office block on the land to the north of the car park. The problem was that some years previously, in marking out the land to be leased as the car park, the council's surveyor had placed his red and white marker sticks on top of a sloping bank that ran along the proposed boundary, because he could easily see the markers up there. This extended the land leased to the hotel by 3×120 metres, though, of course it was useless for parking cars.

Well, the surveyor's lethargy became highly contentious when the building plans for the offices were drafted. The sloping bank crossed the building line, making it legally impossible to build while the strip was leased to the hotel.

I asked another consultant (over a glass or two of wine) how my client might persuade the hotel to give up the strip unnecessarily assigned to them?

The hotel had said they wanted £500,000 for the strip because they knew we needed this strip for our £20 million office building.

He suggested that as the council was also in charge of the licensing of the drink and catering trade in the city, it should hold regular inspections of the hotel's kitchens and bars; it should monitor street troubles; it should send in officials from trading standards; it should check the licenses of every parked car, as well as conduct vehicle checks for pollution and non-payment of road tax; and that it should make itself 'a general nuisance until they saw sense'. This behaviour obviously, would not do.

The hotel, however, also wanted planning permission to extend their banqueting facilities, build a leisure centre and add 90 bedrooms.

The rest was easy. 'Drop the demand for silly money for the strip and donate the land back to the council,' they were told, 'and we would support the hotel in its quest for planning permissions.'

Some suppliers, predictably, drop out quickly and, as predictably, the prices drop from those still contending for the business, sometimes considerably. The sellers compete with each other, without knowing who is in or out of contention. To stay in the game they have to sharpen their pencils!

Most sellers, she finds, tend to re-bid at lower prices. Gloria intimates that their price is still too high and, again as adamantly, refuses to comment on how high, or against whom they are bidding. The sellers are no wiser having reduced their prices, perhaps through more than one round of this game. Some of them, she says proudly, will come back again and again with lower bids, only to be told that they are 'closer'!

Gloria is in a strong position. She uses the seller's imagination about the existence of other suppliers, not only to receive lower quotations, but also details of just how low someone is *prepared to sell* the product she requires.

Note, that if she does accept somebody's low price quotation, the game is not over, for she now turns to the other parts of the contract (terms, conditions, performance standards, etc) and applies her aggressive 'negotiating' technique on them.

She derides those who consider her 'bargaining' tactics as unfair, it being a fact that while every seller has a right to obtain the maximum possible price, so every buyer has a right to try to obtain the lowest.

The seller, Gloria insists, can always walk away and seek better profit margins elsewhere. In a freely competitive market, nothing compels him to sell, any more than anything compels her to buy. Whether the competition is real or imaginary is not relevant as long as the selected supplier *thinks* it is real and acts accordingly, with Gloria doing everything she can to let his imagination about competition run riot across his price list.

Gloria also has suggestions to manage sellers by intimidation. If she is in dispute over an invoice, she sends the seller a 'paid-in-full' cheque for an amount less than the invoice price which ends the dispute when it is banked, because the seller needs the money.

LOVE ME, LOAD MY DOG

I saw a man at O'Hare airport, Chicago, shouting like a barrack room sergeant at a new recruit, and complaining vividly, complete with gesticulations of a kind that would have made Mussolini envious, at the damage done to a dog crate by somebody loading or unloading the plane. The dog was slumped in one corner (presumably having heard his master in full throttle more than once) and, to put it mildly, the crate stank (suggesting, perhaps, that it had been dropped when the loaders carrying it had fainted!).

The airport official, a quiet lady in uniform, stood there listening to the tirade but otherwise appeared unperturbed by it, and kept calling calmly on her personal radio for the supervisor.

When the supervisor arrived, she told the loaders to move the crate from the area, at which the irate man blew his top even more. Nothing, apparently, was to be moved until his lawyer got there and the airline boss arrived and paid compensation ('the damn dog cost me six thousand bucks and the crate is evidence that you've tried to kill it').

Having not much to do, I (and about a hundred others) watched the scene with interest. The man had a point but his manner seemed a trifle absurd to me – even counter-productive – and I thought he should be concentrating on his proposed remedy (compensation) rather than competing for an Oscar for dramatic acting.

You will not, however, negotiate in the US of A for long

before you come across a version of the dog owner at O'Hare. You will also learn not to take the dog owner type too seriously, or too personally. To the uninitiated, the dog owner's behaviour is pure intimidation. It is the verbal equivalent of the massive damages claim put in by his lawyers to scare the timid into a quick settlement. Courts do it too. They set you up for ninety-nine years in jail and then let you plea-bargain it down to six months suspended!

If she wants to entrap a seller into reducing their price she encourages them to begin preliminary work on the basis of an anticipated order. Then she backs off, with plausible excuses about policy changes, budget crises and anything else she can credibly make up. This has some similarities to the Mother Hubbard, except that the costs to the seller of the preliminary work are real while the potential order is not. Sellers, apparently, sooner or later get round to suggesting a cut in price if the order goes through.

A notch or two up the unethical practices column, Gloria told me that she once had a machine tool delivered to one of her company's plants and then made up some excuses for rejecting it. The seller, wishing to avoid calling to take it back, offered a much better price and some concessions on spares, to which a reluctant Gloria allowed him to persuade her.

When I expressed surprise at this deception she told me that her boss once told a supplier that the material he had delivered a week earlier had already been cut up in the machine shop before the job had been cancelled by a customer and, because of litigation, he couldn't pay as promised. The supplier went berserk at this news and threatened litigation too. Her boss said: 'Sure, sue me, but it still won't get you your money for a year or more!'

The supplier rang back a couple of hours later and agreed a

price for immediate payment worth 60 per cent off in cash. The rub was, according to Gloria, the materials were still sitting in 'goods inward' in pristine condition!

Where does all this outright intimidatory behaviour get you? Usually into permanent bouts of warfare with the sellers with which you do business. You reap as you sow.

For instance, 'Slik' Sid, a now retired salesman, old enough to be Gloria's grandfather (but, perhaps, maybe not smart enough to give her a run for her money) told me of some of the intimidatory tricks he learned in a lifetime of selling to people much less gullible than Gloria was ever likely to be.

LOW MARKS FOR HIGH MARKS

Years ago, I think I was caught out by a Slik Sid when I bought a German washing machine, which was more expensive than its British branded competitor. Our existing machine was driving the household wild from regularly breaking down, usually inconveniently before or during a big wash.

I found a shop in the *Yellow Pages* that sold the German machines and was quoted a price about 30 per cent cheaper than its rivals, though still a third dearer than the British brand. I placed my order and awaited delivery, assuring Patricia that the 'seventh cavalry' was on its way.

The shop owner rang back a couple of days later with the bad news that when he placed his order with his German supplier, he was told that the price had gone up 'due to the exchange rate fluctuating'. Apologetically, he wanted to know what to do.

As the new price still left a 10 per cent differential under his rivals I told him, reluctantly of course, 'to go ahead'. The thought of delaying the relief of the laundry department, and of my revisiting the four shops who were sales agents for the brand in Edinburgh, put me off arguing but I still do not know if his increased price was genuine or phoney. I never dealt with him again and have not recommended him to friends in the market for washing machines, so he paid some small price if it was a ploy and again if it wasn't.

He worked for a while for a photocopier manufacturer. By accident he had learned from a customer, whose copier his people had collected for a repair job, that when he called them to report that the equipment had cost a lot more than he had thought, the customer told him to get the copier back as soon as possible 'whatever the price'.

Slik Sid over the years worked this dodge into hundreds of repair jobs, adding thousands of dollars to his company's profits, because on most occasions these 'add-ons' were totally imaginary and, therefore, pure profit. Few buyers, apparently, kicked up a fuss and those that did simply got their machines back from a sullen Sid.

Any time a service is time-critical it is a time to make unilateral changes in some key term of a deal, particularly when it is too late for the buyer to find a substitute supplier. This was when Sid would offer to negotiate a solution to the problem caused by the changes. In the extreme, Sid would simply stop work on the customer's project and suggest that they negotiated a new price based on the 'unfortunate and unforeseen circumstances' that had arisen.

Building firms, even reputable ones, pull the dodge that they need a little more money 'to finish the job'. I dealt with one such example recently, in which a cost overrun on the refurbishment of a theatre was mounting at £12,000 a week. The builder appeared to be convinced that because it was a high profile project subsidized by the National Lottery and the Arts Council, that any cost overrun would eventually be paid for out of a higher subsidy.

Yet, this was the second emergency funding crisis the project had got itself into in the three years of the project. The last time, a line had been drawn under the then cost and a budget had been supplied by the builder that they assured the project team would lead to the successful completion of the project. This, albeit higher total cost for the whole project (by about £1.2 million) was described verbally as a 'firm final price' by the builder.

Now they were back with a requirement for another £150,000 to complete the project and hand it over to the theatre managers, 'without prejudice to the outstanding variation claims from Day One of the project'!

Hard bargainers only make bargaining hard work.

COMMENTS ON SELF-ASSESSMENT TEST 24

1 a) Sheepishly hasty, even if you need deliveries to complete current orders. You've fallen for the 'Gotcha' ploy!

   b) Owls need information before they act and how they respond will indicate how genuine is their problem. Meanwhile, compare with details already collected in (c) (because, to be frank, this is something an Owl would have been doing on a regular basis).

   c) If this information is not to hand you are a Fox not an Owl, because though the Fox knows what to do in a crisis, the Owl anticipates the crises and prepares for them before they have to negotiate.

   d) Very clever of you to spot their ploy to raise prices by creating a delivery crisis but if you are that smart why are you so unprepared? More a Sheep than a Fox, and certainly not an Owl.

2 a) Now that is an invitation, isn't it? You should feel Sheepish because you may well have been tricked into a panic price cut. Another case of the 'Gotcha'!

  b) Sounds like a case of sour grapes, doesn't it? Not very Fox-like; more like a Donkey's response!

  c) Much better. Owls need information before they react to possible ploys. Comments, such as in (b), are more appropriate while discussing the reasons for taking the forging in-house.

  d) Say 'Fine' and wish them all the best? Too Sheepish for words to let the business go just like that – yet this could be the long shot of a very clever Fox if you intend by it to call their bluff. Honestly, which are you?

3 a) Not unless you must have that delivery. Unprotected Sheep are always vulnerable to the 'Gotcha' – (though because you agreed to change prices in 2 and 3, it is an example of the 'Gotcha, with Oak Leaved Clusters'!

  b) Not unless you absolutely must have a delivery. Unprotected Sheep are always vulnerable to the Gotcha – (and in your case, it's the 'Gotcha with Oak Leaved Clusters and bar'!

  c) What a waste of time, but then Donkeys have plenty of that.

  d) Clearly should have been done at the first sign of the 'Gotcha' in question 1. A Fox scrambling for a recovery!

SELF-ASSESSMENT TEST 25

1 You have been given an interview with a leading local Arab agent and have spent several hours socializing and drinking coffee. No business has been discussed and you are anxious to get the discussions of your proposals under way. Do you:
   (a) Raise the subject in a lull in the conversation?
   (b) Wait until your host raises the matter?

2 You are in Tokyo negotiating for a long-term contract with a Japanese producer of conduit and the negotiations have stalled for several days. It feels like you are going round in circles. Do you:
   (a) Wait for them to make the first move?
   (b) Make a small concession to shove the boat out?
   (c) Change the subject entirely?
   (d) Adjourn?

3 You have been granted a sales interview with President of a US corporation who might be interested in your product. The conversation after five minutes is still concentrated on small talk. What does this tell you:
   (a) That you are getting on fine with him?
   (b) That you should raise the subject of your visit?
   (c) That you should wait for him to open the business discussion?

CHAPTER 25

In praise of self-interest

or how addresssing other people's interests gets them interested

Trade or stay poor – that is the bottom line for every country that aspires to take advantage of the global economic system.

It doesn't matter whether you are exporting or importing, piling up raw materials, processing bits and pieces, assembling parts, packaging entire plants, supplying electronic signals that convey intangibles like information or knowledge, or selling on what others have sold to you. Nor does it matter if you are a capitalist or a communist (or anything in-between), a saint or a sinner, a Buddhist, Christian, a Muslim, a Hindu, a Confucian, a Jew, an atheist or a devotee of voodoo, and it certainly doesn't matter whether you are rich or poor, deserving a break or due a come-uppance.

If you don't trade profitably you won't trade for long and if you don't trade at all you will have sealed your fate as surely as if you had gone in for sky diving – without a parachute.

There is just no way that the goods and services that you take for granted can be got without the act of trading. And there is no way that the goods and services that the poor countries quite rightly aspire to can be got on a long-term basis unless they trade for them too.

Those societies that attempt to produce and distribute goods and services without trade must always compromise their no-trade principles or face the steady ruin of their people.

What is not permitted occurs illicitly. People will trade whatever the risks. Those traders whom dictators or ideologues (often the same people!) condemn as 'bandits', 'social parasites' and 'profiteers' are usually regarded, quite rightly, as 'heroes' by the vast majority they serve. Traders provide the people with the one thing that the dictators hypocritically reserve for themselves – choice of what they want to consume.

So-called black market traders are a product of any government that suppresses the freedom of trade. Hunt them down and you commit an injustice to add to your economic illiteracy.

Trade has a long history. Primitive trade has taken many forms, some of it implicit in obscure (to us) complex social obligations, but most of it is explicit, in the bargaining exchanges we are more familiar with today. Several earlier forms of trade survived in 'archaic' societies well into the 20th century, in parts of Africa, the uplands of New Guinea and parts of South America. Trade, in short, pre-dates the emergence of what we call capitalism (a word invented in the 19th century – but **not** by Karl Marx!).

The mere existence of trading contracts (and of any other form of contract) was absolutely conditional on the ability of the parties to the contract to make and keep their promises about the future. Otherwise, once out of sight of each other, one or both of the partners might defect on their promises. Regimes of fear were necessary to force those who made trading promises to comply with their obligations.

HARD SECURITY

I met an aged Arab trader in the Gulf recently who told me how his grandfather, when a ten year old boy, was sent by his father to stay with the Emir. This was as a pledge to keep the family's promises to successfully complete a

327

trading voyage under the patronage and protection, and for the profit, of the Emir. There were no excuses and no concept of *force majeur* for failure. Fortunately, the great-grandfather of the aged Arab completed the voyage safely and returned with the Emir's share of the cargo. This preserved the integrity of the family's reputation and spared his grandfather's throat being cut (a fate he indicated awaited the young boy if for any reason the voyage had not been completed).

Indeed, the history of buying and selling through the early millennia was almost certainly a brutal business. Early societies were soaked in the blood of those traders who broke their promises (or for whom it was convenient for the more powerful party to assert that they had done so).

In some parts of the world today, and in some lines of illegal business everywhere, it still is a bloody affair. Thankfully, for most readers, legal sanctions have replaced the gory revenge that was the mandatory fate of people who broke their promises among our ancestors. However, despite the bloody history of these earlier societies, they nevertheless laid the necessary foundation for today's trading system.

In the 1770s, about the time that George Washington and his friends were stirring themselves to fight for the right to trade without English interference, a Scotsman, Adam Smith, had recognized the importance of trading to civilized society. He made this a major theme of his magnum opus *The Wealth of Nations* (1776) which took him 12 years to write – largely, it seems by dictating the text while warming his rear quarters by a coal fire and drinking claret. It became a best seller, and it is still in print in several languages (though only a few – too few! – get round to finish reading it).

Smith asserted that there is a propensity for people to negotiate. This propensity is not found in animals because they know nothing of contracts and their concomitant promises.

Nobody, for example, has ever seen two dogs negotiate over a bone and nobody ever saw an animal signify to another that it was willing to give 'this for that'. Animals distribute the bounties of Nature, primarily food, mates and territory, among themselves by violence and the threat of violence.

Barbarian societies behave similarly to animals when consuming the bounties of nature and the fruits of human labour. Exponents of the 'Ghenghis Khan school of wealth accumulation' take what they want and leave their victims to shift for themselves.

But while it is certainly possible to violently redistribute the bounties of Nature and the fruits of human labour, it is not possible by violence to sustain the *creation* of human wealth nor to protect Nature from becoming a desert.

The behaviour of two dogs, therefore, is significant. If humans can arrange their affairs differently from dogs by practising traditional negotiation they can create and distribute quantities of the fruits of labour and the bounties of Nature beyond the wildest dreams of only a few centuries ago.

People are (or *can* be) different from animals in their behaviour. Civilized people need the cooperation and assistance of millions of others. Yet a whole lifetime is scarce sufficient to gain the friendship of but a few persons and while friendship has many rewards and joys it is not a sufficient way to acquire all, or even most, of what we want.

'A friend in need is a friend indeed' and friends, therefore, are important (on occasion they can be life-saving). You do not, however, have enough friends to provide over prolonged periods your daily necessities of life.

Hundreds of thousands, perhaps millions, of people in our global village are necessary to produce the multitude of things we all want. If you know only a few people and, of them, even fewer are close to being your friends, how can you rely solely on them and they upon you to produce but a fraction of what you want?

Trillions of negotiations occur every hour of every day and involve people you never meet nor know. These negotiations occur whatever your love or dislike of other people. Of one thing you can be certain: unless you reciprocate with the necessary efforts required for you to access the products of their labour, you will do without them.

Such is the power of the global market, that whoever you are you rely on the anonymous cooperation of others for the most basic of your necessities and the most trivial of your luxuries. And they depend on you playing your part too.

This leads to the absolute necessity of negotiating according to the *interests* of the other party.

If you disregard their interests you must rely on their charity but you will be more likely to prevail if it is for their own advantage to do for you what you require of them.

Whoever offers to you a bargain of any kind says in one form or another: 'give me that which I want, and you shall have this which you want'. It is in this manner that you obtain the far greater part of those things of which you stand in need.

It is not from the benevolence of others that you should expect your dinner but from their regard to their own interest. That is why it is better to address yourself not to their humanity, but to their interests. Never talk to them of your necessities, but of their advantages in supplying you with what you require.

If everybody relied on everybody else acting like those few friends on whom you can depend *on occasion*, we would as a species rapidly reduce our living standards.

If you were to rely on unknowable strangers responding to your pleas to supply you with everything you want under no more than their supposed sense of charity at your plight, you

330

might wait a long time. (Anyway, where and how did these strangers get what you want?)

In the meantime, I suggest that you make more traditional trading arrangements for tonight's dinner!

Anybody who produces anything that somebody else might want can participate in trade, perhaps through long chains of intermediaries who know nothing about anybody two or three links along the chain in either direction. Thereby people can satisfy their desires without knowing you.

It does not matter to others what kind of person you are: what race, nationality, or religion with which you are blessed, what your politics are, what your age, your sex, your personal orientations, or your likes and dislikes. This is because if you trade you become connected with those others who trade with you and with the people who trade with them in a world economic process that has raised living standards to levels undreamt of by Adam Smith and his contemporaries.

Now, if you want to trade you have to negotiate, or accept what the other person offers or demands. By negotiating you can improve on what you are first offered (always challenge the first offer!) and, by having read this far into *Everything is Negotiable!*, you know some of the things you must do – and some you must avoid doing – when they challenge your own offers.

But let's go back to that deceptively casual notion of Adam Smith about addressing the other person's interests and not appealing to their goodwill, if we expect them to supply us with what we need on a continuous basis.

Buried into this 220-year-old notion of Smith's is a very powerful negotiating technique. It is so powerful, in fact, that some people who recently became aware of it, actually believed that they had discovered a completely new negotiating method!

Let's call it **interest-based bargaining**.

To see what is involved in interest-based bargaining, I shall run through some simple ideas.

Issues are what is on the agenda of a negotiation, expressed (normally) in positions. A wage increase is an issue, by how much (or little) you want it to be increased your position. Price is an issue and the amount is a position. Got it?

It is not possible to negotiate without positions, except at the most general level of 'yes' or 'no' – but even your 'yes or no' must be in reference to some position, otherwise to *what* are you saying 'yes or no'?

Positions are *what* we want, interests are *why* we want them.

The two are inseparable. It would be wrong to assume that considering the interests of the parties removes the need for deciding on positions because interests and positions are *not* mutually exclusive – they are intertwined. To believe otherwise is a profoundly silly error.

Let us take the vexed question of a proposal to build a new airport runway, an event usually accompanied by intense opposition from residents who have an interest in the quiet enjoyment of their properties. This interest is counterpoised to the interests of the wider community in having safe, reliable and frequent air-travel facilities, which include somewhere for the aircraft to take off and land. Interests can clash, as can your aspirations for your positions on an issue. I offer '12' and you insist on '17'.

Uncovering a party's interests helps you to understand what they are about; identifying your own interests likewise helps you to decide on your positions on the negotiable issues.

The issues are commonly addressed by stances (build/not build; buy/not buy; yes/no, etc). Less commonly, they are explored by reference to your interests. If the stances on the issues and the consequent alternative positions that are possible on any one issue are in conflict, this creates the need for negotiation. If nobody took a stance on an issue there would be no dispute to resolve.

What is non-controversial is not negotiated. Peace is the acceptance by all of the status quo and disputes (from differences of view through to violence) arise when at least one person wants to change the status quo and at least one other person does not.

The positional gap, in theory, can be bridged without recourse to the kind of positional posturing commonly found in negotiating ('No way could we consider a dilution of our shareholding!'; 'Either you release our supplies, or we will come and take them!') though conflicts over positions are a fact of negotiating life, as are violations of the laws of football (which require, albeit sadly fallible, referees to adjudicate).

If the emotional and, sometimes, overblown rhetoric of some types of positional negotiation upsets you – and it has this effect on some inexperienced or over-sensitive people – you will either learn to take it in your stride or you will strive to avoid nego-
. tiation.

Experience teaches you to ignore posturing behaviours and concentrate on the management of movement from conflicting positions towards an agreement.

Parties adopt particular positions on an issue for many reasons. Some have a strategy of intimidating you in to surrender. Others do so because they believe that they need 'negotiating room' in the expectation that they will require movement to cut a deal.

If negotiators are stuck in a conflict of interests it makes sense to shift your attention to the possible positions that could be taken by both sides on some issues, such as noise limits on aircraft engines, airport normal flying times, pollution controls, traffic management, landscaping and exact runway alignments, amounts of compensation to residents for listed disamenities, and so on.

If people are stuck in a positional stand-off (little progress is made on any of the issues and no movement is signalled in any of their positions), it makes sense to switch to consideration of the parties' interests. It does not have to be a case of always

333

and only considering interests to the exclusion of positions, or vice versa.

The negotiable issues form the agenda and in negotiating these issues you aim to deliver your interests. Whether you focus on interests or issues at particular stages in the negotiation is a tactical question not a principle.

SOMETIMES WE MUST RISE ABOVE PRINCIPLE!

Long-running disputes between religious and secular communities in Israel are an example of negotiators needing to switch from considering the conflict of interests of each side to negotiating on specific and immediate issues.

How do you reconcile secular and religious differences that affect every aspect of the lifestyles and culture of their respective communities and when they are so driven with conflicts of interest that they slip into violent confrontations?

Negotiation on issues is about the here and now and negotiation on interests takes a while longer. As neither side will forego their principles attention must switch to what can be done about issues.

You might be able to negotiate for how many hours a public road can be free of cars where it is close to communities that hold the Sabbath sacred. In a world of daily traffic jams, cars can absent themselves for a short while without it becoming a principle of civil liberty. Demanding that one side or the other foregoes their interests and beliefs is a ruinous route to disorder.

In Israel, appealing to interests may be less productive than concentrating on the details of a compromise on issues and positions. You cannot negotiate principles (if

we could they would not be principles!) but you can negotiate their application. Or as Dr Mates, a Yugoslav
diplomat, expressed it to me in 1967: 'sometimes we must
rise above principle!'

The reverse applies if you are stuck on an issue: can you
make progress by turning to the 'bigger picture' and to the
interests of the parties? The airport runway dispute illustrates
why the answer is 'Yes'.

You should not become frozen into interests, or issues, only.
A dose of pragmatism is the antidote to restrictive negotiating
practice. You should adapt your negotiating method to suit the
circumstances and not try to impose only one method in all circumstances.

COMMENTS ON SELF-ASSESSMENT TEST 25

1 a) Do not introduce a business subject with an Arab under
   any circumstance. Wait for the subject to be raised by
   him. Avoid appearing to be in a hurry to talk business
   and certainly avoid appearing to be irritated by lack of
   progress in this area (unless you insist on showing them
   how like a Donkey you can be).
   b) Yes! Another example of just how different Owls are from
   Donkeys.

2 a) With the Japanese you could Sheepishly wait a long time.
   b) Free gift concessions don't push the boat out. They
   encourage them to sit tight and wait for your next free
   gift. A very Sheep-like response.
   c) Yes. Owls know how to get them to understand their
   message.
   d) Weak. It shows your Donkey-like impatience.

3 a) If you are still stuck in small talk after a minute, either he is your long lost relative or your deal is dying, if not dead already. He is probably wondering how to get you out of his office before you waste any more of his time. Silly Donkey!

b) Yes. You'd better get on with it if you wish to retain your reputation as a Fox. Clearly, the buzzer under his desk he is pressing is not working and you have been spared the attentions of his security gorillas. Tell him what you want, NOW.

c) If you wait much longer, he will throw you out himself. Go for (b) NOW! Or remain a Donkey.

SELF-ASSESSMENT TEST 26

1 You are stopped by a policeman in Ogoland and he demands that you pay him 50 quonks (about £20) not to book
you for speeding. You were almost stationary at the time
and could not have been speeding at all. Do you tell him:
   (a) Not before you see your consul?
   (b) Does he take bribes?
   (c) Certainly, if he has change for a 100-quonk note?

2 An Indian importer owes you £100,000 and you demand
payment before any more shipments take place. He tells you
he is going through a short-term cash flow crisis and needs
more time to pay and that he cannot pay if he does not
get more of your products. Do you:
   (a) Tell him he cannot get more deliveries unless he pays what
       he owes?
   (b) Tell him that if he does not pay you will sue him?
   (c) Decide to visit him in India and see for yourself what his
       financial situation is really like?
   (d) Tell him if he pays you £20,000 on account you will make
       another delivery?

3 You are a contractor in East Africa and the project is running
behind schedule. The Minister in charge constantly interferes
with the project, changes his mind on details, holds up papers
needed to clear supplies through customs, and makes untrue
and slanderous public statements about your company's
efforts. As a last straw, he issues a public warning that he will
cancel the contract and arrest your staff for 'malingering',
'corruption', and most ludicrous of all, 'spying'! The local TV
station asks you for a comment. Do you:
   (a) Tell them what you think of the Minister's mental age?
   (b) Deny the charges and give your side of the story?
   (c) Say 'no comment'?

CHAPTER 26

The long distance negotiator

or a salute to those who go out and get the business

This final chapter is by way of a short salutation to the men and women who go out at all times of the year and negotiate to get the business that their country depends upon. Without exports we could not pay for our imports, and without imports we would be both poorer and at the mercy of over-protected domestic producers who know (and they all do!) how to take advantage of the lack of international competition.

Undertaking business abroad is no easy task and it takes a special breed of executive who is willing to fly off (often at too short notice) to a distant land and negotiate on behalf of their company, many employees of which care little about what is being done in their name and know even less about what is involved in doing it.

Faraway places, like green fields, can look very attractive at a distance. Go through the hassle of getting there and of functioning in what is, after all, for you a strange environment, and you begin to appreciate the kind of job which keeps you close to your hearth.

This is not to say that international business negotiators are all tired, worn-out and boring. I met a fresh-faced lass only last month who was simply oozing with enthusiasm for her new job as an international representative for a designer clothes company. She was on one of those round robin trips that take in a handful of European capitals in five days, and she was positively keyed-up to go out and get the job done. I admired her enthusiasm though I could not share it, as I was returning from a particularly gruelling sixteen-hour a day week with a client in Sweden.

There is no doubt that the international negotiator is one of the great unsung heroes of modern times. As world trade increases, the role of the international negotiator is growing commensurate with the job in hand. Goods do not sell themselves – would that they could! – and it takes hard work in many different environments to get the business to keep the goods flowing from one country to the next.

CASH OR KIND

Exchange regulations and controls can be extremely tight in certain countries because the government desires to use the country's foreign currency earnings with the greatest care and attention to political priorities. The penalties for breaches of these regulations can be severe – imprisonment for offenders, confiscation of property (and not just the bag full of dollars you were caught with) and heavy fines are among them.

Many have been tempted to engage in illegal dodges to get round the problem.

For example, in some countries you can arrange to have payment made to you not in the form of cash but in real goods which you then sell-on to recover your money. If you are unable to get paid in dollars but can acquire good quality cocoa against payment in local ogis you can ship out the cocoa to Europe and sell it for hard currency. The fact that you have to pay CIF may mean you taking a loss on the original amount owed to you – but in a choice

339

between a loss and a total loss you don't really have a choice.

To obviate the cost of shipping real goods out you can try some high-value item which you can take with you, though here you run the risk of being stopped at customs and searched. Diamonds, gold, artefacts and such-like are too obvious for even the dimmest customs official to miss (and by no means assume that customs officials in other countries are any less smart than they are in your own).

I know of a negotiator who has avoided currency regulations for years by the simple expedient of using local currency to buy rare stamps which he sticks in his wallet and sells in London. Two things favour his choice of payment: he knows a rare stamp when he sees one and, though he has been searched at customs several times, nobody has yet noticed his postage stamps!

In international business many are called and few are chosen but still hundreds and thousands of new faces join the ranks each year and try their best to extend their company's business or hold on to what it has already. Those that fall by the wayside are the necessary casualties in a continuous striving for business deals the world over; those that persevere deserve their material rewards, for they certainly do not acquire them easily.

International negotiating requires travel and travel soaks up energies as sure as any sport, only the strain is prolonged over longer periods.

At any airport you will see scores of negotiators embarking or disembarking, or more likely waiting between flights, each carrying with them the hopes and the future of their company. What these men and women do when they get to where they are going can determine whether there is a company to come back to, or one worth making long-terms plans for.

You can tell the negotiators from the tourists. Negotiators

travel more often to more places and consequently they are more at home in the complex tangle of an airport. They move around with an air of certain purpose about them rather than fidget their way from the indicator board to the gates.

The smarter negotiators seldom have too much luggage with them (tourists always have too much of everything, except patience) and they are organized for their flight. If they are in company they form a merry band, swapping stories of their last deal and their hopes for the next. In this sense, they are like sales staff the world over who regale each other with tales and jokes, mutual 'atrocity' stories of this or that dealer they all know; when, that is, they are not slashing into the reputations of their colleagues in other functions who don't understand anything about how tough it is out in the field.

There is a camaraderie among international business negotiators, partly expressing their competence and their pride in their work, and partly their inner tensions about the next deal that they must tackle. True, some of them (all of them at one time or another!) talk-up the deals they have negotiated – a little exaggeration here or there is as surely par for the course among negotiators as it is among those who would catch fish by rod and line. Mostly these little peccadilloes are harmless invasions of personal integrity and are mostly caused by the need to appear worthy of one's trade in a world where it is not always sensible to go into the details of a private commercial deal.

SUMO WRESTLING AND NEGOTIATING

The Japanese can spend what appears to Westerners to be an unprecedented amount of time in preliminaries before discussing their business. These preliminaries have, however, an essential role to play and cannot be skipped through, if you want to get the best deal that is available.

An international banker, with many years' experience of negotiating with the Japanese on joint US-Japanese ventures, explains it as follows:

Negotiating with the Japanese goes through several phases, of which the first is probably the most crucial (for the other phases, in the main, follow internationally recognized norms).

The opening phase is like two Sumo wrestlers facing each other before the start of their contest. They make highly ritualized and absolutely expected genuflections, and go through a detailed ritual involving salt being thrown in each corner and much bowing and other demonstrations of respect.

Then they engage each other's attention and prepare themselves. They examine each other and pace their breathing, gradually increasing the tempo until they are both sure that they are ready. Then, and only then, do they lunge forward.

Neither will move towards the other until they are absolutely sure that they are in balance with each other, both physically and mentally.

When you next sit in an airport lounge – for, be sure, if you travel at all by air you will sit in some lounges for some time, perhaps for longer than you planned – look around you at your fellow travellers. Having separated out the tourists, check over the others. Most of these will be travelling on business. If you count them you will be surprised just how many men and women fly out for this reason only.

You will spot the first-timer, nervously checking and re-checking his or her ticket, ever-willing for someone to talk to them so they can confirm their status and appear more confident than they feel. The old-timer will probably be pretending to be totally relaxed, even dozing to prove it, though his ears will be well attuned to departure announcements through his deepest of cat naps. Their faces will show the years, in some cases better than others, but the lines will be worn with the pride of experience. So will the condition of their bags – working bags, a trifle battered but everywhere serviceable in every condition they might encounter – no smart Sunday supplement luggage sets for them!

Between the new and the retiring come the vast mass of business negotiators, in all shapes and sizes, in all temperaments and moods, waiting for the 'off' like a marine-packed landing craft on D-Day. Those who want to talk and socialize will – it is from this band that you get all the advice on where to stay and what to do about foreign exchange rip-offs – and those who want to travel in solitude and contemplation will try to do so, either by physically slinking crabwise away from the hearty souls looking for a foursome for a bridge game from London to Bahrain (or just somebody with whom to drink their duty-free), or they will immerse themselves in a large paperback.

I know one guy in search of being left alone who prominently displays about him a couple of issues of *Watchtower*, a Jehovah's Witnesses newspaper, to ward off potential talkers!

The best of the breed of international business negotiators have several things in common. Observe them at work, imitate them, improve upon what you learn, and you will join their ranks. Here are my ten rules for negotiating for business anywhere:

- **First,** you must get used to the idea of being a foreigner. There is no substitute for the acquisition of a little national humility. You don't have to go overboard the other way and renounce your birthright ('go native' it used to be called in the Empire). But you must accept your place as a foreigner in the order of things, and this means above all accepting that the world neither owes your country a living nor does it necessarily owe it a good turn. What you get from them will depend upon how much they think they need what you are offering in exchange, and if they can get a better deal elsewhere they should and will take it.

HOW NOT TO TACKLE
A SUSPECTED RIP-OFF

I was minding my own business at Gothenburg airport when I was approached by a businessman who asked if I was travelling Business Class and if I was would I join him for a drink (I said yes to both questions). He wanted to talk about something that was exciting him greatly and when he heard I was a consultant negotiator his tale poured forth.

Briefly, his story was that he had been selling children's clothes to a Swedish chain store for three years. On this visit he had arrived early and had taken time out to casually wander through one of the branches of this chain, and, naturally, he had gravitated to the children's department and looked out for his company's products.

What do you think he found? Yes! His clothes were there and were prominently displayed. This pleased him immensely and in his pride he informed the staff that he owned the firm that made what they were selling. They were most impressed and told him that there was a steady demand for his clothes, given their excellent quality.

He was in turn very pleased at this news and after a while he left. One thing, however, stuck in his mind and that was the price tag on one of his lines. It wasn't until he left that he realized that the Swedish Kroner price represented in sterling a mark-up of several hundred per cent on his selling price to the store.

Such was his concern that he went back to the shop and noted down all the prices of every one of his products. He worked out the mark-up and found it was consistent throughout – the chain store, whch had always pleaded poverty and tight competition as reasons for squeezing his prices, was, he said, 'ripping me off'.

He was upset about this, even though the price he had got for his product was profitable to his business. He raised this immediately with them in the negotiations later that morning and told them he felt they had been cheating him. They were obviously offended at this charge but after much discussion they agreed to raise their purchase prices. They claimed this would squeeze their profits because of their very high labour costs and taxes on their stores.

He was now even more worried because he felt he had over-reacted and gone in too strong and perhaps damaged their good relationship. I suggested it would have been better if he had raised the question of their retail pricing policy quite neutrally and let the implications of that lead them to either a credible defence of their mark-up or to a revision of their purchase price. By charging in he had risked causing offence when none was necessary and whatever he had gained in the immediate trip might be followed by a falling off in orders as they eased out an obviously disgruntled supplier. By paying him more they partly confirmed his feeling of being cheated, whether this was the case or not.

- **Second,** you must get yourself organized for international business travel. Those who want to be the most successful negotiators fly first or business class, stay in good quality hotels, take with them only that which they need, do not regard a long flight as an excuse for a boozy party and are sensible about the very real problems of jet-lag (they only go to bed in other time zones when it is time to do so there, not when they feel like it on arrival).

- **Third,** you must learn something about the manners and customs of the people with whom you want to do business. You should not assume that anything that is quite acceptable in your culture is necessarily acceptable in all other cultures. One way to improve your acceptability as an international negotiator is to learn something of the language of the people with whom you deal.

This advice also applies to those countries where the people speak a language akin to your own. For example, Australians and most North Americans speak recognizable English, but you would be foolish to leave it at that when you go to these countries to negotiate. The English-speaking peoples are separated by their common language, and you would be well advised to gen up on the local slang, dialect, and manners if you want to do business with your 'cousins'.

If you have any doubts on this score think about the differences in approach within the tiny British Isles between the English and the Scots, and then consider how different the Australians etc. have become from both English and Scots over the years of separation.

When dealing with non-English-speaking peoples the advice is the same, only more so. Japanese manners and courtesies are entirely different from those of the Mid-West of the United States. Fortunately, once you observe them, you can adjust without too much discomfort to your sense of what is right or wrong – though Japanese bathtime might be a tiny surprise the first time!

- **Fourth,** you must adjust the pace of your negotiating to that of the people with whom you are keen to do business (they might have to do the same if they visit you in your country). It is no good trying to do anything much in a hurry, and it is absolutely hopeless to expect to be able to ginger them up just because Father Time is knocking on *your* schedules.

In most parts of the world you will have to slow down (in the US of A you will probably have to speed up), and it does not matter whether the delays are caused by bureaucratic procedures or by the way they make decisions (Japan and the Middle East). Have patience, take longer, and don't give yourself unrealistic schedules.

- **Fifth,** you must develop those skills of negotiating that are the same the world over. Beginning with preparation (or knowing your own business better than your rivals), you must know how to listen, react to what you hear, make conditional propositions ('If, then perhaps'), re-package creatively and bargain using conditional, and only conditional, offers ('If, then').

- **Sixth,** you must always remember that in a negotiation with anybody anywhere you always have the option of saying 'no' to a deal that is in any way suspect, whether your suspicions concern the contract they want you to sign, the terms they want you to agree to, or the business ethics they want you to abandon.

You do not need to sign anything that does not meet your best and long-term interests, but if you do sign something you ought not to have then you will have to live with it (or without it).

This is all the more true when you have been working hard for a long time to get some kind of deal. You must adopt the attitude that 'bygones are bygones' and previous investment in time and energy can never be recouped, and certainly you must never try to do so by agreeing to something that is not strictly what you can live with.

Hence, if Ogoland negotiators want you to take goods in place of cash, or Germans want you to accept penalty clauses for delivery commitments, or Chinese negotiators want you to cut your prices on a 'sell cheap, get famous' promise, or Australians want your goods on a consignment only basis, or Americans want exclusive US of A rights, or Arabs want 15 per cent commission, or Ogolanders want side-payments in a numbered Swiss account, or whatever (and there will be many 'whatevers'!), you should always remember that, though you have the authority to say 'yes', you also have the responsibility for what you say 'yes' to. So perhaps you should say 'no' a little more often?

BAKSHEESH, BACKHANDERS AND DASH

You will not spend much time in certain parts of the world before you come up against petty bribery – if you hang around long enough and have the right contacts, you will also become aware of *big* corruption, but that's another story (and I don't want my book banned for discussing it!).

In West Africa they call petty corruption 'dash'.

If you want *anything* done by an official you ought to know about *dash*, because if in your innocence you don't, you will wait ages for even the most routine of trans-actions.

Aeroplane reservations in Ghana (and Nigeria, etc.) mean nothing unless the guy at the front desk has been paid his dash – a few cedis or whatever – out of which he pays the guy in the back office for the use of the rubber stamp, or signature, or even a sight of the passenger list.

Likewise with hotel rooms, appointments to see the boss, the civil servant, the tax accountant, or to use the fax.

This is common practice wherever you have to use the services of people who by virtue of their positions can extract a few dollars here for a few favours there.

In Egypt, the ministries are riddled with locally created

monopolies. Maps are not published openly but are kept in locked drawers to be extracted for a 'little something', statistical tables are treated likewise, i.e. sold page-by-page like ancient Scrolls, and official forms and licences can be little gold mines to the clerk who is in charge of them.

In India, the fastest – indeed, sometimes the only – way to move paper through the bureaucratic labyrinth (courts, tax offices, even railway stations) is by paying a *baksheesh* (tip or 'bribe'):

> Baksheesh! Baksheesh!
> Sixteen Annas, One Rupee
> One Rupee, One Baksheesh!

How you approach this petty corruption is a personal matter, but don't moralize about it, unless you *never* give tips to taxi drivers, waiters and the kids who find your golfball!

• **Seventh**, you must cultivate the habit (until it requires no effort whatsoever) of never getting involved in discussions or comments upon any country's politics, religion, way of life, ethics of doing business, racial mix, legal processes, constitutional arrangements, methods of selecting their leaders, public or private morality, prevalence of tips, bribery and corruption, modes of dress or undress, laws regarding your personal preferences in sex, booze, drugs, porno videos, press freedom and citizens' rights.

If you wish to combine a business career with reforms of other countries you should reconsider your personal prospects. The internal affairs of other countries are none of your damn business and in many parts of the world they do not take kindly, or treat lightly, interfering visitors who forget what their visas say they are there for.

Your wonderful views on democracy, feminism, the free market, income distribution, social welfare, local wars, racial strife, the treatment of offenders and such-like should be left at home, and if in your case that is not possible then you should stay at home too!

- **Eighth**, you must treat everybody with whom you deal with the greatest of personal respect, no matter how you feel about the way the negotiation is being handled. This applies to personnel on your own side as well as on the other side (even if you feel some of your people seem to be working for them too!). Respect for the individual in business life is always a rare treat if you are on the receiving end of it, and, for that reason alone, it is well worth adopting as a policy for your own behaviour towards others.

No matter how new and strange to you any culture is in the world, and no matter how intricate are the social obligations of the people you deal with, you can be sure of being accepted anywhere, in spite of any courtesy gaffes you make out of your ignorance or forgetfulness, if you display constant evidence of your respect for your opposite number as a person. There are no parts or peoples of the world where you will find exceptions to this principle; everybody reacts more warmly to those whom they can see respect them than they do to those whom they suspect do not.

- **Ninth**, you must always endeavour to the best of your ability – and sometimes beyond that – to meet the terms of the contracts you negotiate and agree to. Each deal for you has to be a personal as well as a company commitment. Your role does not finish when the signatures are recorded. In many respects it continues through the lifetime of the deal.

You must take a personal interest in what happens thereafter and be ready to use your good and best offices to get things put right that manifestly are wrong. Good and enduring personal relations between negotiators will lead to long-term relationships between their companies and it is

350

from this that the mutual prosperity of trading partners grows.

Your best action is always to follow through on a deal – call the other person on the phone, or drop in to see him on your next visit, to check that everything that you agreed to is actually happening and that he is well-satisfied with the outcome. In other words, you do not sign the contract, grab the cash and run. Follow through and follow up if there are any problems. Your pride alone should incline you to do so, but your long-term best interests should make it mandatory.

- **Tenth**, in deciding how to conduct your business affairs abroad, particularly when operating in parts of the world where social licence is somewhat slacker than it is elsewhere, you must be guided by what you feel comfortable doing rather than by what you feel is right or wrong.

This is by no means a prescription for abandoning the distinction between right and wrong – quite the reverse! – nor is it a prescription for turning you into a hardened cynic. The facts of life are that many parts of the world with which your country trades do have different standards of personal conduct and these standards influence whether you get business, or even get around the country itself, and you will have to learn to live with this and adapt to it, or you will not do business there.

Deciding on what is right in the circumstances is no easy matter, and it is, therefore, a highly personal decision which you cannot pass on to somebody else. What you will be advised to do by people sitting on their safe and comfortable seats back home may be fine for an assembly of ostriches approaching a sandy beach but absolutely useless for you as you go down the ramp from your aircraft and approach the ranks of officialdom at customs and immigration (and the serried ranks of their colleagues along the corridors of the ministries you need to get past to complete your negotiations). It is you who is faced with the moral dilemmas

351

in Ogoland and you who must decide what to do about what you face there.

It is presumptuous of me to advise you on this matter, except perhaps to suggest that you talk to the older hands about it on a country-by-country basis. Listen to what they have to say, reflect on the fact that billions of dollars worth of business is being conducted every year in that environment, and decide on a case-by-case basis what you feel most comfortable about doing (remember the sixth rule about your right to say 'no').

For every set of ten rules there is always an **eleventh**. The eleventh commandment is usually to the effect that you must avoid getting caught while breaking any (or all) of the other ten.

My eleventh is somewhat different. It is to remember, when all else is said and done, that *everything is negotiable*. Practise that commandment and you will reap opportunities in the bleakest of circumstances, the most forbidding of environments and the unremitting of pressures. Moreover, the same principle will reward you endlessly when circumstances are favourable, when environments are welcoming and when pressures are relaxed or in your favour.

What more satisfying way is there to make a living than negotiating for it?

And finally, if you are passing through an airport, a hotel, a corridor, a corporate office, or whatever, and you see me sitting about without not too much to do (if I am up to my ears in a deal I will soon let you know!), why not amble across, introduce yourself, and swap experiences with me?

We can have a chat and a coffee, or, if we are both in funds or on expenses, we might stretch ourselves, and our clients' budgets, to a glass or two of the local nectar!

Ex bona fide negotiari

1 a) That's the fast way for a Donkey to get into trouble (of the 'more than it's worth' kind).
  b) Sometimes Foxes are just too clever by half!
  c) Excellent, even for an Owl – though you may not get any change.

2 a) A Donkey choice and it still might not get you your money (he now has an excuse not to pay).
  b) Another Donkey approach that puts your £100,000 at the mercy of the notoriously slow Indian legal system.
  c) Yes. Owls check out the situation where Donkeys rush in.
  d) Approach of the Fox, best tried after (c).

3 a) You obviously want to join all the other Donkeys in jail!
  b) Nobody, Sheep included, wins arguments with politicians, even ones as stupid as you think this one is.
  c) Correct. Owls know you need behind-the-scenes clout in these situations and the best way to get it is not to make it difficult for political friends to support you. Public rows entrench politicians in positions they cannot move from without losing face (and you, perhaps, losing something as closely attached to you!).

Appendix 1:
The Negotiator's Grid

Mark in the relevant column the catergorization of your choice of answer for each Self-assessment question as you go along (no cheating, please! – including from the Foxes).

Total the responses in each column to identify the balance of your answers over the possible selections.

Broadly, if more than half of your answers are designated in a single column then you are showing attitudes that would produce the qualities (or lack of them!) represented by that column's designated category.

More often, a negotiator's responses will be spread across the columns – there is a bit of an Owl, Fox, Sheep or Donkey in most of us.

The question is: what is the balance across the columns?

If more than half of your answers fall neatly into the Donkey and Sheep columns, then you have some work to do to change your predominant attitudes that, in turn, guide your negotiating choices and behaviour. Fortunately, training (and practice!) can help you achieve this.

If more than half of your answers fall neatly into the Fox and Owl columns, then you are well on your way to practising the behaviours that are driven by appropriate attitudes to negotiation. But do not relax the practice – indeed, how did you get on with the Negotiation Scenarios? Did your performance confirm your results in the self-assessment tests?

If your answers fall regularly across the columns – a not unusual result – the conclusions are somewhat more difficult to be general about without specific examination of the choices you made. Each set of choices indicates different reasoning and you should consider the choices you made in particular questions against my comments. Is there a pattern?

Note:
Again, do not fret about the outcome of these tests. They are not, nor are they meant to be, a scientific analysis of your negotiating proclivities. They are indicative only and their main function is to get you to think, and re-think, and think again, about why you made this or that choice.

Appendix 1: THE NEGOTIATOR'S GRID

Self-assessment test		DONKEY	SHEEP	FOX	OWL
SA1		True	True	False	False
SA2	1	c	b	–	a
	2	–	c	a	b
	3	a	c	–	b
	4	b	c	a	–
SA3	1	b	a	c(?)	c(?)
	2	c	a	b	–
	3	–	b	a	c
SA5	1	b	c	a	–
	2	c	a	b/d	–
	3	a/b/c	–	–	d
SA6	1	c	a	b	d
	2	–	b/c	–	a
	3	b	–	–	a
SA7	1	b	a/c	–	d
	2	–	a/c	b	d
	3	b	–	a?	a?
SA9	1	–	a/b	c	d
	2	a	b	c/d	e
	3	d	a/b	c	–
SA10	1	d	a/b	c	–
	2	–	b	a/c	d
	3	–	c	a/b	–
	4	a	b	c	–

Self-assessment test		DONKEY	SHEEP	FOX	OWL
SA11	1	a/e	d	b/c	–
	2	–	a/b	c	–
	3	c	d/e/f	a/b	–
SA12	1	b	c	–	a
	2	c	a/d	–	b
	3	–	a/c	b	–
SA14	1	c	–	a	b/d
	2	–	a/b	c	–
	3	b	–	a	–
SA15	1	c	a/b	–	–
	2	a/b/c	–	–	d
	3	–	a	b	–
SA16	1	a	–	c	b
	2	–	a/b	–	–
	3	b/c	–	–	a
	4	–	a/b	–	c
SA17	1	c	a	b	–
	2	d	b	a/c	–
	3	b	–	a	c
	4	–	c	b	a
SA18	1	b	–	a	c
	2	c	b	a	–
	3	n/a	n/a	n/a	–
SA20	1	a	c/d	b	–
	2	–	a/b	c	–

Self-assessment test		DONKEY	SHEEP	FOX	OWL
	3	b	a	c	–
SA21	1	–	a/c	b	–
	2	a	b/d	c	–
	3	c	–	a	b
SA22	1	–	c	a	b
	2	a	b	–	c
	3	n/a	n/a	n/a	n/a
SA23	1	a	b	c	–
	2	c	b/d	a	–
	3	b	c	a	–
SA24	1	–	a/d	c	b
	2	b	a	d	c
	3	c	a/b	d	–
SA25	1	a	–	–	b
	2	d	a/b	–	c
	3	a/c	–	b	–
SA26	1	a	–	b	c
	2	a/b	–	d	c
	3	a	b	–	c
Totals					

Appendix 2:
Practice Examination

This practice examination should take about two hours to complete. When you have completed your answers to the questions that follow the case scenario, please follow the instructions if you wish to be assessed and receive comment on your answers.

PART 1: SCENARIO EXAMINATION

Marcel is an electronic engineer, who has invented from his own resources and in his spare time, a revolutionary operating system for mini-computers. From a technical point of view, Marcel's operating system is way ahead of current systems that run the world's PCs. Nothing that the big computer corporations are producing is remotely comparable to Marcel's product.

But Marcel has insufficient capital to develop the prototype into a mass market product. He has tried several banks for funding but they are too risk-averse to support his project; having suffered substantial losses in the recent past from 'revolutionary' inventions.

Marcel is currently opening negotiations with a venture capital fund managed by Rich Investment Bank (Guernsey) Limited, who see the great potential for the new system if it can be developed and licensed to one or more of the major computer corporations.

Rich Bank are aware of the undoubted risks but are willing to advance the necessary funding (US$15 million) if they are satisfied with the contractual arrangements they negotiate with Marcel.

Basically, Rich Bank is seeking a majority shareholding in Marcel's company. They have also stated that their involvement is motivated by a desire to make a profitable return on their investment and that they do not intend to maintain their shareholding.

Marcel is considering how best to exploit his invention, possibly by licensing major computer manufacturers, or even joint ventures with PC manufacturers in the Far East or in Scotland and the United States.

Marcel is concerned about Rich Bank taking a majority stake in his company but feels compelled to consider this prospect as he is desperate for funding – every month's delay could produce a rival operating system to be announced. He is convinced that if he gets to market first and his system becomes an industry standard then he could earn millions of dollars in profit.

Marcel has asked you to assist him in the negotiations to find a way to secure the funding he requires and to protect his legitimate interests if he accepts Rich Bank's conditions. Marcel's questions to you are:

1 'Where am I vulnerable if I accept Rich Bank's proposals for a majority share of my company's equity?'
2 'What are my longer-term interests?'
3 'What proposal could I put to Rich Bank to reconcile mine and Rich Bank's interests on our shareholdings?'
4 'What should I include in a licensing agreement with a computer manufacturer?
5 'What could I do to strengthen my negotiating position with Rich Bank?'

PART 2: ESSAY QUESTIONS (ATTEMPT ANY TWO)

1 What is the appropriate method for dealing with difficult negotiators?
2 Why are the distinctions between interests, issues and positions important and why must they be kept linked?
3 Why do negotiators resort to tactical ploys?
4 Illustrate how a contingency proposal can meet the concerns of each party about the future course of a business after it is sold.
5 What role could the cultural context have on the conduct of a negotiation?

For assessment and comment on your answers, please either post them to the address below or email me at gavin@negotiate.demon.co.uk:

Gavin Kennedy
Negotiate Limited
99 Caiyside
Edinburgh
EH10 7MR
United Kingdom

Appendix 3:
The HELPMAIL service

With the purchase of this 3rd edition, you are entitled to send to my HELPMAIL service one of your negotiating problems and, provided you pay for the postage (mine included!) your first use of the Negotiate HELPMAIL service is absolutely FREE of charge!

But please, do not try to use the HELPMAIL service via the telephone – that's why we call it HELPMAIL – because over-eager beavers would soon clog up my phone lines and prevent me conducting Negotiate's business in a professional manner. Otherwise, I am happy to hear from you and to try to help you with your business negotiation problems.

The more relevant the detail that you include in your HELP-MAIL the more effective my response, but please do not send original letters and documents (photocopies are more than adequate). My comments will be confined to the negotiation aspects of the problem only. I do not offer legal, financial nor technical advice, for which you should consult the relevant licensed or bonded professionals, nor do I advise on domestic or political disputes. All information is treated absolutely con-fidentially and no data will be disclosed to third parties (but problems of an illegal nature will be declined and the materials shredded).

Please send a self-addressed envelope plus an International

362

Postal Coupon for the same amount of postage as it cost you to write to me. The address for the **HELPMAIL** service, which must be written **exactly** as shown (otherwise for legal reasons, I cannot respond) is:

HELPMAIL
99 Caiyside
Edinburgh, EH10 7HR
United Kingdom

Disclaimer: *The HELPMAIL service is confined to general background advice for training purposes only, and is given solely on the understanding (which is deemed to be accepted by all who address their letters as shown above) that neither the author nor Negotiate Ltd will be liable for any outcomes that may arise from that advice or from its execution by the recipient.*

Index

OTHER TITLES FROM
RANDOM HOUSE

ALL ARROW BOOKS ARE AVAILABLE THROUGH MAIL
ORDER OR FROM YOUR LOCAL BOOKSHOP AND NEWS-
AGENT.

PLEASE SEND CHEQUE, EUROCHEQUE, POSTAL ORDER
(STERLING ONLY), ACCESS, VISA, MASTERCARD, DINERS
CARD, SWITCH OR AMEX.

☐☐☐☐☐☐☐☐☐☐☐☐☐☐☐☐☐

EXPIRY DATE .... SIGNATURE ....
PLEASE ALLOW 75 PENCE PER BOOK FOR POST AND
PACKING U.K.

OVERSEAS CUSTOMERS PLEASE ALLOW £1.00 PER COPY
FOR POST AND PACKING.

ALL ORDERS TO:

ARROW BOOKS, BOOKS BY POST, TBS LIMITED, THE
BOOK SERVICE, COLCHESTER ROAD, FRATING GREEN,
COLCHESTER, ESSEX CO7 7DW.

TELEPHONE: (01206) 256 000
FAX: (01206) 255 914

NAME ....

ADDRESS ....

....

Please allow 28 days for delivery. Please tick box if you do not wish
to receive any additional information ☐

Prices and availability subject to change without notice.